ALSO BY ANDREA DI ROBILANT

Autumn in Venice

Chasing the Rose

Irresistible North

Lucia: A Venetian Life in the Age of Napoleon

A Venetian Affair

THIS EARTHLY GLOBE

THIS
EARTHLY
GLOBE

A VENETIAN GEOGRAPHER
AND THE QUEST
TO MAP THE WORLD

ANDREA DI ROBILANT

ALFRED A. KNOPF | NEW YORK | 2024

THIS IS A BORZOI BOOK
PUBLISHED BY ALFRED A. KNOPF

Published in the United States by Alfred A. Knopf,
a division of Penguin Random House LLC, New York, and distributed in Canada
by Penguin Random House Canada Limited, Toronto.

www.aaknopf.com

Knopf, Borzoi Books, and the colophon
are registered trademarks of Penguin Random House LLC.

Library of Congress Cataloging-in-Publication Data
Names: Di Robilant, Andrea, [date] author.
Title: This earthly globe : a Venetian geographer and the
quest to map the world / Andrea di Robilant.
Description: First edition. | New York : Alfred A. Knopf, 2024. |
Includes bibliographical references and index.
Identifiers: LCCN 2023038270 (print) | LCCN 2023038271 (ebook) |
ISBN 9780307597076 (hardcover) | ISBN 9780593801703 (eBook)
Subjects: LCSH: Ramusio, Giovanni Battista, 1485–1557. | Geographers—Italy—Biography.
Classification: LCC G69.R236 D5 2024 (print) | LCC G69.R236 (ebook) |
DDC 910.92 [B]—dc23/eng/20231023
LC record available at https://lccn.loc.gov/2023038270
LC ebook record available at https://lccn.loc.gov/2023038271

Jacket image: *Map of Brasil* (detail) from *Delle Navigationi et Viaggi*, 1565,
by Giovanni Battista Ramusio. Photograph © Christie's Images / Bridgeman Images
Jacket design by Jenny Carrow

Manufactured in the United States of America
First Edition

For Tommaso and Sebastiano

CONTENTS

PROLOGUE   3

CHAPTER ONE The Education of a Geographer   9

CHAPTER TWO Pigafetta's Diary   33

CHAPTER THREE Cadamosto   47

CHAPTER FOUR An African Masterpiece   61

CHAPTER FIVE Meeting Prester John   78

CHAPTER SIX Indian Journeys   96

CHAPTER SEVEN Navagero's Embassy   110

CHAPTER EIGHT In the Land of Biru   150

CHAPTER NINE Sailing to Hochelaga   158

CHAPTER TEN The Return of Marco Polo   165

CHAPTER ELEVEN Stealing Time from Time   207

POSTSCRIPT   229

Bibliographical Note   233

Index   245

THIS EARTHLY GLOBE

PROLOGUE

IN THE AUTUMN OF 1550, A THICK VOLUME CONTAINING A
WEALTH OF NEW GEOGRAPHICAL INFORMATION AND STAR-
tling woodcut maps of Africa, India and Indonesia was published
in Venice by the house of Giunti under the title *Navigationi et Viaggi*
(Journeys and Navigations). The person who had assembled and
edited this remarkable collection of travel narratives, journals, private
letters and classified government reports remained anonymous.

Two more volumes appeared, in 1556 and 1559. They included,
respectively, the most up-to-date information on what the Europeans
referred to as the New World and on Asia. The combined publication of the three volumes—over two million words—constituted
an unparalleled release of geographical data into the public domain.
It was, to use an expression of our time, the biggest Wikileak of the
Renaissance.

The man behind this herculean effort of transparency was Giovambattista Ramusio, a highly regarded but little-known public servant who spent a lifetime in government quietly working behind
the scenes. His contemporaries invariably described him as a gentle
and generous man, very learned and wise yet modest to the point
of self-effacement. To this day he remains an elusive figure. Ran-
nusio, Ramusius, Rhamnusius, Rhamusius: even the spelling of his
surname was not fixed.

Although he lived through the golden age of Venetian portrai-
ture, no painting of him has come down to us. Paolo Veronese, the
great Renaissance artist, included him in a large group portrait that
showed him in conversation with a senator; but the canvas, which
hung in the great hall of the Maggior Consiglio, in the Ducal Palace,
was destroyed by a fire in 1577.

His publisher, Tommaso Giunti, who knew him well, would probably have explained the absence of a formal portrait by invoking his friend's modesty and reserve. Ramusio, however, was a *cittadino originario,* not a patrician; he belonged to a caste that, although indispensable to run the sprawling government, was rarely celebrated in a public way. True, he moved with ease in certain patrician circles, but he knew his place; and he would never have allowed vanity to come in the way of his prudence.

Fortunately, a small contemporary etching of Ramusio has survived. In the Biblioteca Marciana, the very library which Ramusio took loving care of for many years, is a rare catalogue of bronze medallions depicting notable cultural and scientific figures of the Renaissance. The collection belonged to Giovanni Maria Mazzucchelli, an eighteenth-century literary figure from Brescia. The two-volume catalogue was published in 1761 under the title *Museum Mazzuchellianum.* It contains several hundred small portraits of famous and less famous people and is often used by scholars as an *ante litteram* image bank.

Ramusio's handsome profile (medal VI, table LXIV—*Io. Baptista Rhamnusius*) is among the most finely executed of the lot. The broad forehead and balding head and the long, elegant nose are drawn with great precision. He appears to be in his late fifties or early sixties and looks vigorous, alert, inquisitive; and also wise—a man of definite experience. The well-groomed beard, presumably graying, adds gravitas to his expression. There is nothing elusive about him here—quite the contrary.

Ramusio was a child of the Age of Discovery. He was seven years old when Christopher Columbus made his first journey across the Atlantic, eleven when John Cabot reached Newfoundland and twelve when Vasco da Gama rounded the Cape of Good Hope. In the decades that followed, Cortés landed in Mexico, Vespucci sailed down to Brazil, Balboa reached the Pacific, Magellan circumnavigated the globe, Pizarro invaded the Inca Empire and Cartier explored the Saint Lawrence River.

While the world was opening up to European navigators at an astonishing speed—often with results that were disastrous to the

Portrait of Giovambattista Ramusio, eighteenth-century
bronze etching published in the *Museum Mazzuchellianum* (1761)
by Pier Antonio Gaetani

people who inhabited the lands they visited—the field of geography
was lagging behind, stirring slowly back to life after a long slumber.
During the Middle Ages the outline of the known world had faded
into a disquieting vagueness. Portolan charts of the coastline along
commercial routes were relatively accurate, but the contours of the
world at large had blurred considerably since Roman times, generat-
ing mysterious landscapes made of myths and mariners' tales. Even
the most educated people had a very limited and fanciful notion of
what the world looked like.

A turning point came in the mid-fifteenth century, when a Greek
copy of Ptolemy's *Geography—A Guide to Drawing a World Map* was
dug up in a library in Byzantium. The manuscript reached the
Medici court in Florence, and was translated into Italian and printed
in Vicenza, on the Venetian mainland. The book circulated widely
and inspired a new generation of geographers and cartographers
who devoted themselves to the study of ancient maps.

According to Ptolemy, the great Alexandrian astronomer who
lived in the second century A.D., the world was formed by three
continents (Europe, Africa, Asia) loosely connected and surrounded
by water. This notion gained new and wide currency in the early
Renaissance. So much so that at the end of the fifteenth century,

Woodcut map of 1545 based on Ptolemy's *Geography*

before Columbus's historic voyage, Ptolemy's *Geography* was still the only existing atlas of the world. Even more remarkable is the fact that the Ptolemaic world continued to hold sway during the following decades, long after the major discoveries had been reported back to Europe.

The deference to the Ancients on the part of Renaissance humanists was partly responsible for this peculiar disconnect. Cartographers felt safer stretching and modifying Ptolemy's old maps to extraordinary degrees in order to accommodate new discoveries rather than boldly charting a different world.

Another reason Ptolemy's outdated vision lasted so long was the secrecy which surrounded the reports written by returning mariners. These highly classified manuscripts were so jealously guarded in Lisbon, Seville, Paris and London that while each naval power had a privileged view of the lands its explorers had visited, the overall picture remained obscure.

Ramusio realized that as long as the discoverers' reports were locked up in the secret archives of European courts, world atlases were bound to maintain their primitive form. Acting upon that intuition, he began to collect and study all the original travel narratives he could get his hands on. He took advantage of his position at the heart of the Venetian government to pursue his objective. He used his political skill and ingenuity, not to mention the help of conniving diplomats and spies across Europe, to ferret out the manuscripts he coveted. The mild, soft-spoken official was not above resorting to trickery or even larceny if he felt this was absolutely necessary for the success of his mission: to capture accurate knowledge.

It was soon evident to Ramusio that Ptolemy's world map was irreconcilable with the world described in contemporary narratives. Taken singly, each report offered a fascinating glimpse of distant, exotic lands. Together, they revealed a much larger world than anything previously imagined.

CHAPTER ONE

THE EDUCATION
OF A
GEOGRAPHER

I N THE SPRING OF 1505, AT THE AGE OF TWENTY, GIOVAM-
BATTISTA RAMUSIO PASSED A RIGOROUS EXAMINATION TO
enter the Venetian Chancery and landed a position as junior
clerk, with an initial salary of thirty ducats a year.

It was a momentous event not just for Giovambattista but for
the entire Ramusio family, which had migrated to the Republic a
generation earlier and was still finding its footing in the stratified
structure of Venetian society.

The Chancery, located in the Doge's Palace, was the central
administrative body of the state. It was run by an elite corps of officials drawn from the ranks of the *cittadini originari,* an intermedi-
ate caste of citizens who were not allowed to rule—that was the
exclusive right of the nobility—but were relied upon to manage the
sprawling Venetian bureaucracy.

Giovambattista's new job was the first step toward a prestigious
career in government and an affirmation of his family's loyalty to
the Republic.

The Ramusios were originally from Rimini, a fiefdom on the Adriatic coast in what was then the northernmost region of the Papal

States. Giovambattista's father, Paolo Ramusio, emigrated to the Venetian Republic at the age of sixteen to pursue his education. He studied law at the University of Padua, which served as the Republic's main campus at a time when there was no university in Venice proper. His younger, wilder brother, Girolamo, soon joined him.

Paolo was a brilliant, ambitious student. He obtained his Venetian citizenship and entered the ranks of the magistracy. Girolamo studied medicine and philosophy and wrote clever erotic verse in Latin. When his lover, a prominent Paduan lady, was murdered in mysterious circumstances, he was caught up in the scandal and fled to Syria. He settled in Damascus, studied Arabic and translated parts of Avicenna's *Canon of Medicine;* he later moved to Beirut, where, according to a family chronicle, he died around 1484, apparently from indigestion after eating too many apricots.

Paolo, meanwhile, married Tomyris Macachiò, a Venetian who, although not noble herself, was related to several patrician families. Her unusual first name reflected the fashion, in humanistic circles, of naming children after figures of antiquity. Tomyris was the strong-willed queen of the Scythes who defeated Cyrus, King of Persia; according to one narrative, she had his head cut off and wrapped in a human skin filled with the blood of dead soldiers. A rather gruesome woman to some; but Boccaccio, the early Renaissance poet, glorified Queen Tomyris in his popular book *Famous Women*.

Paolo and Tomyris had two boys and four girls. Giovambattista, the eldest of the children, was born in 1485 in Treviso, forty miles north of Padua, where his father was a provincial magistrate. During the following years Paolo received government assignments in different provincial towns of the Republic. While he moved from post to post, the family stayed in Padua. Tomyris raised the children in a comfortable house in via del Patriarcato. Despite his long absences, Paolo made sure his firstborn received a solid humanistic education, which meant Greek and Latin but also mathematics, physics and natural sciences.

At university, Giovambattista did not study law, like his father, but stuck to humanities in order to prepare for the entry examination at the Chancery. Junior clerks, known as *secretarii,* were expected to have a thorough knowledge of history, to write superior prose and to be excellent public speakers. And Venetian authorities felt that those who aspired to such a career were better served by a solid education in literature, history and the classics rather than in the dry intricacies of the law. In Padua, Ramusio studied with some of the great scholars of his time—Latin with Giovanni Calfurnio, Greek with Leonico Tomeo, history with Marco Antonio Sabellico.

Paolo also introduced his son to the star-studded circle of humanists gravitating around Aldus Manutius, a publisher who ran a flourishing press in Venice that specialized in Greek and Latin classics. In time, Aldus would have a decisive influence on Giovambattista, teaching him how to edit old manuscripts and publish fine-quality books.

Paolo used his connections to get his son onto a fast track at the Chancery, and very quickly Alvise Mocenigo, an influential senator and a strong supporter of Aldus's publishing house, took Giovambattista on as his personal aide.

Young Ramusio had barely settled into his new position when his new boss was picked to lead a tricky diplomatic mission to the court of Louis XII, the King of France. And so, in early October, Giovambattista bid farewell to his family and joined Mocenigo on the monthlong journey to Blois, the royal residence in the Loire valley.

It was a golden opportunity for a junior clerk to immerse himself in the complexities of European politics and witness firsthand an experienced diplomat like Mocenigo try to defuse a threatening set of circumstances.

FALCONS FOR THE KING

Venice's expansion in northern Italy had alienated its powerful neighbors. To the north, Emperor Maximilian of Austria eyed with increasing appetite the rich plains of the Po valley and was planning an invasion. To the west, Louis XII had already conquered the

Duchy of Milan and was looking to consolidate his dominions in Italy. To the south, the fiery new pope, Julius II, angered by Venice's encroachments along the border with the Papal States, was itching to teach the Republic a lesson.

Venice had a long tradition of playing foreign powers against one another to hold on to its provinces on the mainland. But this balancing act was becoming harder to maintain as French and Austrian ambitions in Italy firmed up. And if France and Austria moved together with the backing of the Pope, Venice would find itself surrounded by enemies. The consequences would be catastrophic.

The Venetians saw Louis XII as the key player—neither Emperor Maximilian nor the Pope was likely to move against Venice without the support of France. Mocenigo's brief was to gain the French monarch's goodwill while keeping alive the rivalry between France and Austria.

It turned out Louis XII was in no rush to meet the Venetian delegation when it arrived in Blois in early November. Mocenigo found a friendlier ear in Philippe de Commynes, a veteran diplomat brought out of retirement to help formulate France's Italian policy. Humanist, memoirist, lover of Italian culture and a keen expert in Italian politics, de Commynes had many friends in Venice, where he had served as French ambassador a decade earlier. He enjoyed dropping by Mocenigo's quarters to banter and reminisce.

De Commynes's influence at court was not what it had been. Still, he was able to mollify Louis XII, who finally received the Venetian ambassador. An awkward moment occurred when Mocenigo began to read his prepared speech in Latin: the king stopped him in his tracks and ordered him to read in his own language, explaining that he was curious "to hear someone speak in Italian."

Was it a friendly remark or a chilling allusion to the king's plans for expansion in Italy?

After a moment of confusion, Mocenigo recovered his poise; but as he wrote in his report, a certain apprehension lingered.

The Venetian envoy was left to wait for the next summons. But a sudden, unexpected rapprochement between France and Spain shook the court and forced Mocenigo to take a back seat. Only two years before, Louis XII and King Ferdinand of Spain had gone to war over the Kingdom of Naples. But after the recent death of his wife, Queen Isabella, Ferdinand was now proposing to strengthen the ties between the two erstwhile enemies by taking a wife of French royal blood. Louis XII, realizing he could gain leverage over Austria, offered Ferdinand the hand of his niece Germaine de Foix.

Mocenigo saw the advantage of this plan: it foreshadowed a distancing of France from Austria, and therefore a possible weakening of the anti-Venetian front. Eager to have another interview with Louis XII, he urged de Commynes to speed things up. "Give him falcons" was de Commynes's friendly advice—the king loved falconry and owned more than three hundred specimens, including the rare white falcon from Greenland. But Louis XII, bedridden with acute chest pains and high fevers, was in no mood for falcons. His condition worsened and, by the end of the year, vigils were held across France. "It is said here that he will not live long," a worried Mocenigo reported back to Venice.

Louis XII was given last rites. His death was likely to encourage the aggressive impulses of Emperor Maximilian, who made no mystery of his desire to move swiftly against Venice and "rob it of its gold." But after a gloomy winter the king recovered and by the early spring of 1506 he was out of danger.

During his convalescence, Louis XII softened toward the Venetians. In April, Mocenigo and his young aide Ramusio were invited to follow the king to Tours, another place of residence of the House of Orleans. The court settled there until midsummer.

Louis XII was a popular king, often referred to as the "Father of the People." He had brought an end to the internal wars that had wracked the country during the reign of his predecessors and had presided over a long period of economic growth. But while all was relatively well at home, he was consumed by his ambitions abroad. Now that relations with Spain were on a surer footing, Louis XII let loose his impatience with Emperor Maximilian's greedy designs on the rich territories of northern Italy.

At the end of the summer, having fully recovered, the king returned to Blois to plot his next move. Ramusio had by this point gained familiarity with the court and had established solid contacts; he spoke fluent French and could better grasp the subtleties of government policies. But as tension between France and Austria increased, news reached him that his father, Paolo, had died in Padua. Overcome with grief, he asked to go home to be with his mother and his sisters. Given the volatile political situation, his request was denied.

In the early autumn of 1506, Emperor Maximilian moved troops into northern Italy. In December, Louis XII left Blois and traveled south with his army aiming to cross the Alps and take back the port city of Genoa, where the French governor had been toppled during a local insurrection. A wary Mocenigo reported to his fellow senators that "the king is going to war with 18,000 men." Once in Italy, he could well be tempted "to inflict damage on us" as well.

The Venetian Senate instructed Mocenigo and Ramusio to stay with the French army.

In the spring of 1507 Louis XII reached Grenoble at the head of his men, crossed the Alps, descended into Piedmont, marched through Asti and continued south to Alessandria, where the royal cortège established headquarters.

There Mocenigo took leave of the king and hurried on to Venice to provide a full report on the French advance into northern Italy. Ramusio stayed behind and followed the French army south to Genoa, where the uprising was quickly quashed. The king entered the city, installed a new French governor and by the end of the month was back in Alessandria, where Ramusio found Antonio Condulmer, the new Venetian ambassador to France, waiting to present his credentials.

It seemed that Louis XII did not intend to attack Venice—for the time being. But now the French and the Austrians both had large armies stationed in northern Italy.

Ramusio briefed Condulmer on the events in Genoa and hurried home at last.

ALDUS'S SHOP

At twenty-two, Ramusio was now the head of the family. His father left him all his properties: four houses in the coastal city of Rimini, in the Romagna, and three plots of land in the surrounding countryside; the house in Padua where the family lived; and two recently acquired properties at Paviola and Cittadella, on the Venetian mainland.*

From the start, he took an active interest in the management of the land, and over the years he was to build a sizable, well-run estate. He transformed the old farm near Cittadella into a comfortable country house, the Villa Ramusia, where he kept a well-tended garden, orchards and vegetable patches, and where he liked to experiment with new crops and plants.

All of that was in the future. Meanwhile, he resumed his clerkship at the Chancery and found a suitable arrangement with his mother: she continued to live in the big house in Padua and raise Cornelia, Livia and Faustina (Girolamo and Eugenia had died in infancy), while he took up lodgings in Venice and frequently commuted back to Padua to be with the family.

Whenever his job and his family duties allowed him, Ramusio visited Aldus Manutius. The print shop at San Paternian was a den of thriving activity. As many as thirty employees—inkers, type-

---

* The family properties had increased after the death of Pope Alexander VI—the corrupt Rodrigo Borgia, father of Lucretia—in 1503. The Venetian Republic, wishing to expand its territories on the mainland—a process of conquest and annexation that had been going on for a century—decided the time was right to lure Rimini and other cities south of its border away from the Papal States. Ramusio's father, Paolo, was chosen to lead the negotiations because of his old links with Rimini and its leading family, the Malatestas. Paolo skillfully led the deal through: Pandolfo Malatesta handed Rimini over to the Republic and moved to Venice with his family. Paolo received for his legal services the two large properties not far from Padua, at Paviola and Cittadella.

setters, etchers, proofreaders, translators and editors—worked tire-
lessly under Aldus's orders, surrounded by clatter and confusion.

A plaque at the entrance of the print shop made clear idlers were
not welcome:

> *Whoever you are Aldus earnestly begs you to state your business*
> *in the fewest possible words and be gone, unless, like Hercules*
> *to worthy Atlas, you wish to lend a helping hand. There will always*
> *be enough work for you and all those who come this way.*

Ramusio, drawn to the intoxicating atmosphere of the place, was
eager to lend "a helping hand." A first-rate classicist himself, he was
hardworking and reliable. Aldus took him under his wing and gave
him increasing responsibilities around the shop.

Shortly before the trip to France, Aldus had learned that a precious
cache of letters written by Pliny the Younger to Emperor Trajan
during a tour of duty in Bithynia had surfaced in the library of the
Abbaye de Saint-Victor in Paris. It was a sensational find: the 375
letters—known as the *Codex Parisinus*—were extremely old, possibly sixth-century copies.

Aldus had urged Mocenigo and Ramusio to do all they could to
get their hands on the letters during their stay in France. Whether
they obtained them from the resident abbot or whether they secretly
smuggled them out of the Abbaye de Saint-Victor with the help
of some conniving friar is unclear. But somehow they managed to
bring the booty safely to Venice.

The calligraphy on the ancient parchment was so tiny that the letters were barely legible. Still, Aldus was thrilled to have them in his
hands. He threw himself into the grueling editing process, "truly
happy to be the first to publish these letters."

The publication of the *Codex Parisinus* was an example of Aldus's
extraordinary reach in his quest for precious manuscripts and
of his determination to publish them according to his own high
standards—a lesson that was not lost on young Ramusio.

The colophon of the Aldine Press: a dolphin and an anchor entwined

Aldus, who is now regarded as the greatest editor of his time, came late to publishing, after living the roving life of the scholar-for-hire until he was forty. Born around 1450 in Bassiano, a mountain village in central Italy, he studied classics in Rome and made a living teaching the young sons of wealthy patrons. Later, he traveled north, settling first in Ferrara and then in nearby Carpi, a small seigneury in the Romagna ruled by the Pio family. He taught Latin and Greek to the young prince, Alberto. In recognition for his services, the Pios gave Aldus "fields and orchards" to which he remained attached for the rest of his life.

When Prince Alberto, Aldus's young charge, left Carpi to begin his university studies in Milan around 1490, Aldus, a middle-aged tutor looking for a job, migrated to Venice. He found employment with several important families and soon made a name for himself in humanistic circles by publishing a Latin grammar that sold well. But he encouraged his students to study Greek, for he believed that the language, long neglected in Italy, deserved the same literary status as Latin. In fact, he dreamed of starting a small quality press devoted to classic Greek literature.

Venice was fast becoming the Mecca of the book business. There were more than 150 printers operating in town. Roughly half the books sold in Europe were published in the city. But most editions were poorly edited and shoddily assembled. Aldus, on the other hand, wanted his books to be paradigms of scholarly and editorial excellence. He also wanted them to be user-friendly. In the early days of publishing, books tended to be large and cumbersome and difficult to read. Aldus envisioned agile, elegant, eminently practical devices that would transform the experience of reading. In a word, the quality paperback.

In 1495 he opened up shop by a side canal in the neighborhood of San Stin, facing a bakery. Pierfrancesco Barbarigo, the wealthy nephew of the Doge and the owner of paper mills, provided most of the initial capital in exchange for a 50 percent stake in the company. The other 50 percent went to Andrea Torresano, the printer who had published Aldus's Latin grammar; he had the publishing experience and owned the printing presses. In a separate agreement, Torresano gave Aldus one-fifth of his share, or 10 percent of the company, with full editorial responsibility.

A small press devoted to Greek literature was a risky venture, but Hellenism was becoming fashionable in literary circles. Plus, a stream of refugees had swelled the Greek community in Venice after the fall of Byzantium in 1453. Aldus and Torresano were betting the demand for books in Greek was there.

The most urgent task was to design and produce a Greek typeface because the characters available in Venice did not come close to the quality standards Aldus was aiming for. He enlisted Francesco Griffo, a talented engraver from Bologna, who set to work drawing and cutting the letters of the Greek alphabet. On the editorial side, Aldus hired Marco Musuro, a respected Greek scholar who taught at the university in Padua and whom Lorenzo de' Medici, no less, had recruited a few years before.

Aldus drew up a list of Greek authors he wanted to publish— the core curriculum of a solid Hellenistic education. The complete works of Aristotle were the centerpiece of his editorial undertaking, and a massive one at that. But how many aspiring Hellenists would be able to read Aristotle in Greek? Or Sophocles? Or Thucydides?

First, Aldus's readers needed to learn the language well enough to read it.

The only Greek grammar that existed in Italy at the time was an out-of-print volume by Constantin Lascaris, a Byzantine humanist who had fled Constantinople after the fall of the city. He had now retired to Messina, in eastern Sicily, where he ran a prestigious Greek academy at the monastery of San Salvatore al Faro.

Enter Pietro Bembo, the brilliant twenty-two-year-old son of Bernardo Bembo, a leading Venetian statesman and renowned collector of ancient manuscripts. In 1492 young Bembo traveled to Sicily on his father's allowance to perfect his Greek with the great Lascaris. After two years of intense study, he brought back to Aldus a copy of Lascaris's old Greek grammar on which the master himself had made more than 150 handwritten additions and corrections.

It was a publishing coup. The new grammar, elegantly printed with the characters cut by Griffo and with an accompanying Latin translation, was the first book to come off the presses. It sold very well and the publishing house was up and running.

Aldus started printing the works of Aristotle while he put out in quick succession books by Theocritus, Thucydides, Herodotus, Xenophon, Sophocles, Euripides and Aristophanes. Some volumes sold as many as two to three thousand copies—impressive numbers considering the pool of potential readers was relatively small and good books were expensive, costing the equivalent of as much as two to three hundred dollars in today's currency.

As the new century began, Aldus and his partners sensed that they had saturated the market for Greek authors, so they expanded their range to include Latin classics: Virgil, Ovid, Horace, Cicero and other major authors. At the urging of Bembo, a champion of Italian vernacular, Aldus also published Dante and Petrarch to give their work the literary standing of the classics.

Aldus was a hands-on editor, a perfectionist who worked ceaselessly to weed out mistakes, errors of translation and typos before he sent books out to his clients. He cared as much about the material aspect of the book as he did about the reliability of the text, and he was constantly thinking of ways to improve his product.

He introduced the *octavo*, a pocket-sized book. He developed new, more readable letter types. He was the first to use cursive, in imitation of the *stile cancelleresco*, the stylish handwriting for which the Venetian Chancery was famous. His editions were elegant, polished and free of pompous commentary in the margins—just the original text in its simplest, purest, most correct form.

By the time Ramusio returned from France in 1507, the publishing house had undergone significant changes. Aldus, by then in his late fifties, had married Maria Torresano, a daughter of his business partner. To economize, the print shop had been moved from the original site in San Stin to the ground-floor building where Torresano lived with his family, in the neighborhood of San Paternian. Aldus and his young bride had settled on the top floor.

Bembo, long one of Aldus's star writers and editors, had left town in a huff two years before. Consumed by his ambition to forge a modern Italian language, he had written an experimental novel, *Gli Asolani,* on the topic of love: six friends—three young men and three young women—meditate on the vagaries of the heart during a three-day-long wedding party in Asolo, a hill town in the Venetian countryside.

In the midst of writing the novel he had fallen in love with Lucretia Borgia, daughter of the infamous Pope Alexander VI and new young wife of the Duke of Este, ruler of Ferrara. The two began a passionate and very dangerous affair; at the very least, their entanglement risked sparking a diplomatic crisis between Venice and Ferrara.

During their secret relationship, Lucretia, a book lover, became closely involved in the writing of Bembo's novel, reading and commenting on every page and urging him—an endless reviser—to finish the job and get it out to the public. Aldus probably thought *Gli Asolani* a frivolous departure from the classics, but he agreed to publish it at Bembo's expense. They chose a small format that could easily be carried about (*libellus portatilis*). The layout was clean and easy to read; the typeface, an elegant cursive.

Against Aldus's advice, Bembo insisted on dedicating the book to Lucretia. It was a long, loving dedication: pure folly, bound to provoke the wrath of the Duke of Ferrara. The Council of Ten, Venice's ruling body, sent the police to stop the presses—the last thing the Venetian government wanted was a confrontation with the House of Este over an illicit love story. Bembo relented, and once the dedication had been removed the printing resumed.

The book was a hit and went into several printings. But Bembo, pressured by his father to enter public service and give up his literary career, turned his back on his family and his city and migrated south to Urbino, in those years the most scintillating Renaissance court.

The loss of Bembo was offset by the arrival of no less an erudite than Erasmus of Rotterdam. While studying at the university in Bologna, the Dutch philosopher had written to Aldus to say that he had edited two plays by Euripides—*Hecuba* and *Iphigenia*—and hoped he would publish them. "I should think my lucubrations more secure of immortality if they were printed in your type," he added flatteringly.

Aldus opened his home and his shop to Erasmus, who shared a room with Girolamo Aleandro, a brilliant young editor; the Dutchman took his meals in the house and did his fair share of editing. "Aldus," he later noted, "was astonished by the amount of work I could get done despite the terrible racket the workmen made at the presses."

Erasmus got his reward: Aldus published the two plays by Euripides but also, more important, Erasmus's own *Adagia,* a collection of sayings and aphorisms gleaned from the classics. The other in-house editors—all humanists of the first rank—helped him find material and turn his initial idea for a small book into a major publishing project. "I [had] brought with me to Venice only some very confusing and indigestible material," he later admitted with unusual candor.

Erasmus left Aldus's shop to take a job as tutor to Alexander Stewart, the illegitimate son of James IV, the King of Scotland. Aldus never saw him again. A few years later, the philosopher wrote an ungrateful account of his stay in Venice, in which he described the Torresano/Manutius household as a wretched place where "damp roots burned in the fireplace instead of wood" and boarders were served "soup made of old cheese crusts, rotten tripe and watered down wine that tasted like acid."

AGNADELLO

The prolonged effort to keep European powers from coalescing into a formidable anti-Venetian alliance finally collapsed in the winter and spring of 1508. Louis XII, as we have seen, was in northern Italy with his troops. He was now joined by King Ferdinand of Spain, his new ally. Emperor Maximilian, meanwhile, announced he was crossing Venetian territory with a military contingent in order to go to Rome to be crowned by the Pope. The wary Venetians replied that they would escort him across their country, but he would not be allowed to march through with his army. Furious at this rebuff, Maximilian invaded Cadore, the northernmost Venetian province, with five thousand men. Once the province was under imperial control, however, three thousand troops were sent back to their barracks in Austria. The Venetians easily took back Cadore and massacred the small Austrian contingent that had remained. Then they fatally overplayed their hand by taking two imperial cities, Trieste and Gorizia, pushing Maximilian into the arms of his rival, Louis XII.

In December 1508 Venice's adversaries met in Cambrai, a small town now in the north of France that in the sixteenth century was part of the Holy Roman Empire ruled by Maximilian. France, Austria and Spain, joined by England, Hungary and a number of smaller states, formed an alliance known as the League of Cambrai. The purpose was to destroy the Venetian Republic and carve up its rich territories. Or as Maximilian put it, still seething after the debacle in Cadore, "to stamp out, as a commonplace fire, the insatiable greed of the Venetians and their thirst for dominion."

The spoils were apportioned in advance. Brescia, Bergamo,

Crema and Cremona would go to France. Austria was to have Padua, Vicenza, Verona, Rovereto and Treviso, plus the regions of Friuli and Istria. England, Scotland, Hungary and the city-states of Florence, Urbino and Ferrara, would all get their share for joining the alliance. Even Pope Julius II, after being promised the city of Rimini and parts of Romagna, swept aside any lingering reservations about joining the League. He also issued a papal edict excommunicating the Venetian Republic.

Venice's fabled diplomacy had failed spectacularly. The Republic, with no friends to turn to, faced the mightiest alliance ever assembled against it. Two *condottieri* of great experience, Nicolò Orsini da Pitigliano and Bartolomeo d'Alviano, were hired to command the Venetian army. Andrea Gritti, an able and ambitious senator, was elected *provveditore,* the civilian authority that was to make sure the Senate's guidelines were carried out in the field.

On April 14, 1509, the League declared war. The Venetians took position on the western border of the Republic, along the river Adda. There followed several skirmishes as the French advance guard made its first forays into Venetian territory. Bartolomeo d'Alviano, a brilliant but impulsive general, argued the Venetians should cross the Adda and take the French by surprise before they were joined by the bulk of the army, which was marching east under Louis XII's command. But d'Alviano was overruled by the more cautious Pitigliano, the commanding officer, who reminded his deputy that they were under clear orders from the Senate not to provoke the French into a pitched battle at the outset. On May 14 the French advance guard crossed the Adda again, and this time d'Alviano suddenly found himself face-to-face with the enemy. Judging that he had no choice but to engage, he deployed his troops on a hill above the vineyards around the village of Agnadello and sent Pitigliano an urgent request for reinforcements. Under pouring rain, d'Alviano held back the French for several hours, but the Venetian reinforcements never came and eventually Louis XII arrived on the scene with the main army. Faced with an overwhelming force, the Venetians were quickly surrounded. Although most of the cavalry managed to escape the stranglehold, the infantry was massacred in a gruesome bloodbath. In one day, more than four thousand Venetian soldiers were killed. D'Alviano, badly wounded, was captured and taken to France as a hostage.

At ten p.m. the following day, a cluster of senators was still gathered around maps of northern Italy when a messenger arrived at the Doge's Palace bearing the *"funestissima notizia,"* the most grievous news, of Agnadello. The magnitude of the disaster had some senators literally "in tears." The initial attempt to keep the news a secret proved hopeless. Within minutes it spread through the city. During the night throngs of frightened Venetians gathered in front of the Doge's Palace clamoring for more information and inveighing against Pitigliano and d'Alviano.

Despite the late hour, the full Senate scrambled to come up with a defensive strategy. There was no point in trying to defend Venice's mainland possessions in the face of such a powerful coalition. A dispatch was sent out to Pitigliano ordering him to retreat all the way back to the shores of the lagoon. Meanwhile, the Council of Ten was invested with extraordinary powers to prepare the defense of the city. The Venetians had entered the war with a self-confidence that bordered on hubris; after Agnadello, the very survival of the Republic was suddenly in jeopardy.

The rapid succession of events that took place over the following days and weeks only made the threat clearer. One by one the cities of the Venetian mainland were taken by the allies, often with little or no fighting. The French took Brescia, Bergamo, Crema and Cremona in the west. The Austrians swept down from the north and gained control of Verona, Vicenza and Padua.

In only a month Venice lost all the mainland dominions it had conquered during the previous century. The only question remaining was whether Venice itself would survive or, to paraphrase Maximilian, would be stamped out for good.

The Venetians hunkered down in the lagoon, as they had always done in the face of grave danger. Over at San Paternian, Aldus scrambled to print one last book, Horace's *Odes;* then he sent everyone home and closed down the print shop. He left Venice and headed south to his small land holdings in the Romagna.

In spite of the Pope's bull of excommunication, the authorities did not cancel the celebration of the Corpus Domini (Corpus Christi), one of the Church's holiest occasions, judging it was important, at this critical time, to seek God's mercy and pray for survival. But Venice did not put its hopes in prayers alone. The government set up a commission to requisition and stock up food and grains. Makeshift mills were set up on barges moored along the Grand Canal. Patrol boats were sent out into the lagoon to prevent spies and enemy intruders from reaching the city.

As Venice made preparations to endure a prolonged siege, its diplomacy was busy trying to extricate the Republic from its dismal predicament. The most immediate objective was to lure Pope Julius II away from the League. Venice offered to return several cities to the Papal States while suggesting that Julius had done himself no favor by allying himself with foreign powers in Italy. At the same time emissaries were sent off to appease Emperor Maximilian with an offer to hand back territory in eastern Friuli. The beleaguered Republic even began to make overtures to its traditional enemy, the Ottoman Empire, pressing the point that if the League of Cambrai was allowed to crush Venice, it would not be long before it declared war against Constantinople.

Meanwhile, the Council of Ten made secret preparations to recapture key cities on the mainland. Venice, which had long ceased to be an exclusively maritime power, could no longer survive as a viable state without its territories in northern Italy. Padua was the gateway to those territories, and if Venice was to live, it would have to recapture that city first. Secret informants revealed the weaknesses of the Austrian defenses in Padua. A small shallow-water fleet was quickly assembled, and on July 16 the boats sailed across the lagoon and up the Brenta Canal carrying heavily armed soldiers and horses. At dawn the next day three men camouflaged as farmers drove their grain-laden carts up to the southern gate of the city. The Austrian guards lowered the drawbridge and the first two carts entered the city while the third stopped halfway through the gate. Whereupon a well-armed band of Venetian horsemen burst onto the scene, charged across the drawbridge and took the city after a short, bloody battle with the Austrian garrison. Andrea Gritti took command of the city while Venetian rule was reimposed on the small towns and villages of the Paduan countryside.

The recapture of Padua was a turning point in the war and a huge morale booster for the Venetians. But the Austrians were not about to give up such an important city. In less than a fortnight Emperor Maximilian assembled an army of forty thousand men and headed south to retake it. French and Spanish contingents soon joined, as well as smaller foreign forces. But food shortages and general disorganization slowed the allies' progress, and the Venetians had time to prepare for the siege by mobilizing troops and building up defenses. Old Doge Loredan himself said he would gladly go off to defend Padua if he thought he could be useful. He sent his sons instead, at the head of a two-hundred-strong contingent of volunteer noblemen, each with his own well-armed retinue.

The siege began in mid-September. For two weeks the allies' heavy artillery pounded the city walls, opening wide breaches. But each assault was turned back and by the end of the month, facing mounting casualties and with no sign of capitulation, Emperor Maximilian lifted the siege and took the bulk of his army back home, leaving only a small contingent to defend the other cities still under Austrian control. The Venetians crushed the Austrian garrison at Vicenza while other towns in the Veneto—Bassano, Feltre, Belluno, Este, Montagnana, Monselice—declared themselves for Venice.

The Republic had gained a temporary advantage but it still faced a coalition of enemies with vastly superior forces; it could not hope to be victorious if the League remained in place. Seizing the favorable moment, Doge Loredan sent to Rome a delegation to make peace with the Pope. Julius II, still furious that Venice had managed to recapture Padua and most of the Veneto, snubbed the Venetian emissaries. But the mercurial old pontiff now understood that by encouraging the major European powers to invade northern Italy in order to teach Venice a lesson, he had created a bigger problem than the one he had set out to resolve. By the end of 1509 he begrudgingly admitted to the Venetians his displeasure "at seeing your state in ruins while the number of barbarians [in Italy] continues to grow."

Still, Julius II was not about to make peace without extracting humiliating concessions from Venice. He demanded substantial compensation for military expenses and the abolition of Venetian tariffs on his subjects in the region of Romagna. Venice was also to relinquish the traditional right to appoint bishops and clergy in its territory. The Senate felt it had no choice but to accept these conditions—to a point. Even as it instructed its emissaries to sign on, the government secretly approved a resolution declaring the agreement null on the grounds that it had been forced upon Venice. It did, however, agree to a public act of contrition to pacify the Pope and obtain an annulment of the bull of excommunication. On February 24 the Venetian envoys, clad in scarlet robes, walked up in solemn procession to the papal throne placed for the occasion in front of the main portal of Saint Peter's. They knelt down and kissed the Pope's feet and respectfully made their request. The Pope kept them on their knees for nearly an hour as a lengthy list of grievances was read out to them. After twelve cardinals meted out a symbolic scourge, the Venetians were at last granted a papal absolution, and again they kissed his feet in gratitude.

The worst was over. Julius II abandoned the League, and Spain soon followed. Although the war against France and Austria continued, life in Venice returned to relative normality. So much so that the Carnival of 1510 would long be remembered for the explosion of gayness and revelry.

FIELDS AND ORCHARDS

The print shop at San Paternian reopened in 1512. After his three-year-long sojourn in Romagna, Aldus felt regenerated and full of new projects. The first book off the presses, symbolic of a new beginning, was a revised edition of Lascaris's Greek grammar, by now the house staple. Then he turned his attention to a long-delayed project: an edition of the odes of Pindar.

He assigned the project to Andrea Navagero, a distant cousin of Ramusio's and a rising star in Aldus's circle. Navagero was only two years older than Ramusio but was already an experienced editor and often acted as an older brother to him around the print shop. He had a natural gift for Greek verse, and in a house dedicated to Greek letters he had thrived quite naturally. He was also warm and gregarious: everyone loved Navagero, a bighearted poet with a passion for Pindar. Aldus thought him one of the finest Hellenists of the new generation: "You have a sharp mind and a sure judgment," he told him. "And so much talent, brilliance, inventiveness, both in prose and poetry, that you are truly up there with the great authors of antiquity—you and Pietro Bembo, that other glorious erudite of our time."

And what of Bembo? After his self-imposed exile to Urbino, where he had continued to work on his seminal book on the foundations of a modern Italian language, he had landed a plum job in Rome as assistant to the new Medici pope, Leo X, a friend to writers and artists. Bembo still kept his distance from his native city but remained in touch with Aldus's world. Ramusio in particular kept him abreast of the publishing activity; he also ran errands for him and sent him the books he requested. But even as their friendship grew, Ramusio maintained a certain deference toward Bembo, who was fifteen years his senior and belonged to an old and respected patrician family.

Ramusio, meanwhile, was finding time outside his day job to help Aldus out as an all-around "pinch editor." The publication of the letters of Quintilianus, a classical stylist who was much admired by humanists, is a good example of his role in the publishing house. Aldus originally assigned the project to Navagero, who was forced to interrupt the work to join Venetian forces fighting the Austrians in the north under the command of Bartolomeo d'Alviano, the commander who had been taken prisoner at Agnadello and had later been released by the French. The printers, always on a tight schedule, were soon clamoring to have the final draft. So Aldus called in Ramusio to take over the job.

Aldus, whose references were always drawn from antiquity, liked to compare Ramusio to Achates, the devoted friend that Aeneas (in this case Navagero) could always count on. Old and overworked, Aldus himself increasingly depended on Ramusio. "You always come to my aid in my difficult hours," he told his young friend after he had completed the Quintilianus. "If there is one person to whom I should dedicate all the books I print it is you, my dearest Ramusio"—touching words that sound like a loving farewell.

On a cold winter morning in 1515 a large crowd gathered at the Church of San Paternian to mourn the passing of the great editor.

The coffin lay on a riser inside the old Romanesque church, surrounded by neat little book towers made with Aldus's editions of his favorite Greek and Latin authors: a symbolic tribute to his success in reviving and spreading the great literature of the past.

The funeral brought together the community that had flowered around the Aldine Press in twenty years of activity. There were scholars and common readers as well as editors, printers, engravers, binders, suppliers and business associates. Raphael Regius, who held the chair for humanities at the prestigious Scuola di San Marco, pronounced the oration.

Ramusio, a mandatory of Aldus's will, had taken time off from work to help out with funeral arrangements and attend to the last wishes of the deceased.

A dispute arose about the burial site. Aldus had indicated that he wished to be interred not in Venice but on the plot of land— "the fields and orchards"—he owned near the town of Carpi, in Romagna. And he wanted Maria, his young wife, and their three children to move there. His wishes had come as a surprise to many of his friends, not to mention the Venetian authorities. Venice, after all, was where Aldus had flourished as a book publisher. And even though he was not a Venetian by birth, Venice had come to see him as one of its own.

After the ceremony the coffin was moved to a storage room, where it lay for several days while a decision was made. What happened next remains a mystery. There is no tomb in Aldus's name in Venice or Carpi or anywhere else. All we know is that Maria and the children stayed in Venice. And apparently so did Aldus's remains. He was probably buried where his funeral took place, San Paternian, a neighborhood church familiar to every Venetian on account of the unusual pentagonal shape of its bell tower. But we will never be certain: San Paternian was closed down during the Napoleonic occupation and demolished later in the nineteenth century. Thus no tomb, no remains, no trace of any kind: as if Aldus, in death, had been swiftly subsumed into the eternal myth of Venice.

STRABO'S WORLD

During the decade Ramusio spent as a clerk at the Chancery, his growing interest in the wider world and his knack for languages earned him the reputation of being the "geographer" among his fellow workers—a reputation that he continued to build in the early stages of his career. He learned French and Spanish in order to read the travel journals and reports that reached Venice (he was now the Doge's official interpreter in those two languages), and he developed a network of correspondents and private channels of communication.

Shortly after Aldus passed away, Ramusio, now thirty years old, was promoted to the position of secretary of the Senate; his salary more than doubled, from thirty to seventy ducats a year—a sum which allowed him to take care of the family with greater ease.

His new job at the Senate gave him direct access to the secret dispatches of Venice's far-flung ambassadors. He did not hesitate to use the Republic's diplomatic network to satisfy his own curiosity, pressing his colleagues abroad to send him information about the countries they visited. One apparently exasperated envoy wrote back: "Yes, I will also send you the maps of Muscovy and Tartary and all those other places." This after the poor man had already sent Ramusio lengthy descriptions of Hungary, Poland and Transylvania!

His ties to the publishing house inevitably loosened. After Aldus's death, management was taken over by the partner, Torresano, and his two sons; Aldus's own son, Paolo, was still a boy and would take charge years later after being properly groomed. During the first year of this new arrangement, only a few books came out— mostly editions that had already been in the works during Aldus's last months.

Among these posthumous titles, one stands out: Strabo's *Geography*.

A Greek writer and geographer who lived in early Christian times, Strabo had used his own travel notes as well as written accounts and stories he had heard over the years to write his encyclopedic book on the world as it was known in his time.

Geography, published in the original Greek, was an unusual choice for Aldus. In fact, the project was sponsored by Alberto Pio, Prince of Carpi, who had gone from being a devoted student of Aldus's in his youth to one of his major patrons. Pio was now an influential player in European diplomacy with a keen interest in geography. He probably covered the printing costs, including the fee of the editor, Benedetto Tirreno, a Greek scholar who worked for Aldus.

As a mandatory of Aldus's wishes, Ramusio is likely to have followed the preparation of the book closely. But he was beginning to feel that when it came to geography, it was no longer enough to search for answers in the great books of the past. The mass of new information available—information that, to be sure, needed to be carefully analyzed and confirmed—indicated the Ancients did not have a superior knowledge about what the world looked like. Ramusio probably saw the publication of Strabo's *Geography* not so much as an end in itself but as a point of departure for a new geog-

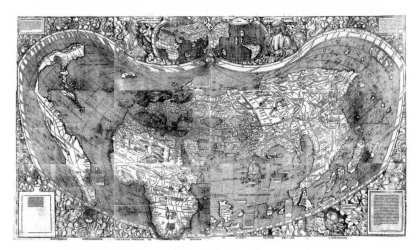

Martin Waldseemüller's wall map of the world (1507)

raphy that would take into account the extraordinary discoveries of his time.

For the world in the early 1500s was still largely a mystery. No one knew its size or precise shape; how much sea there was and how much land; where it was habitable and where it was not. The most influential maps drawn in those years—the Waldseemüller Map of 1507 and the Schöner Map of 1515—still offered a very primitive, distorted, essentially Ptolemaic view of the world.

The travel reports of modern navigators and explorers were like loose pieces of a grand puzzle. Still missing was a reliable framework in which to fit them.

CHAPTER TWO

PIGAFETTA'S
DIARY

ON SEPTEMBER 6, 1522, THE *VICTORIA,* A LEAKY, WEATHER-BEATEN NINETY-TON CARAVEL, REACHED THE harbor of Sanlúcar de Barrameda, in southern Andalusia, with a ghostly crew of eighteen—the sole survivors of the five-ship flotilla that had left three years before, under the command of Ferdinand Magellan, to find a strait at the antipodes and open a western route to the Spice Islands.

The captain of the ship, Juan Sebastián Elcano, immediately reported to Emperor Charles V that they had found the strait at 54 degrees south of the equator. Roughly a hundred leagues long, it debouched on a vast ocean which they had crossed in three months and twenty days, reaching an archipelago "abundant in gold" where their captain general had died. Afterward they had sailed "from island to island" for eight months until they had found the Moluccan Islands, rich in "cloves, cinnamon and pearls," and had finally made their way back to Spain with a cargo of spices.

The entire report was less than eight hundred words.

The next day the *Victoria* was hauled up the Guadalquivir River at high tide. It reached the inland port of Seville on September 8, docking by the Church of Santa María de la Victoria. A cluster of haggard men in tatters went ashore the following morning and filed into the church, each holding a tall candle, to pray at the shrine of the Virgin Mary.

It was hardly a triumphant homecoming for the ragged band of men who had survived the first recorded sea voyage around the world.

Ramusio, now a respected senior official at the Senate (with a salary of ninety-four ducats), received the news from Spain in early November 1522, two months after the *Victoria*'s return. Gasparo Contarini, the well-informed Venetian ambassador to the Spanish court of Charles V, accurately reported that the expedition had found a strait at 54 degrees below the equator, "which is about a hundred leagues long." Sailing westward, "they reached the islands where all the spices grow, and made their way back from Levant, thus going all the way around."

Attached to Contarini's short note was a copy of the secret report Elcano had written to the Emperor on the day the *Victoria* had reached Spain. Contarini vouched for its authenticity: the source was the Grand Chancellor himself, Mercurino Gattinara, the powerful Piedmontese adviser to Charles V.

Although still fragmentary, the news was sensational. The notion that the world was shaped like a sphere had been around since antiquity—the earliest known globe was built by the Stoic philosopher Crates of Mallus in the second century B.C. The idea had faded in Christian Europe during the Middle Ages but regained currency during the Age of Discovery. Martin Behaim, a German navigator and astronomer, produced the first modern globe—the *Erdapfel,* or Earth Apple—in Nuremberg in 1492 (proportionally smaller than the actual globe and without the Americas). Columbus himself sailed west that very year hoping to reach China on the assumption that the world was round, though he imagined it more in the shape of a pear.

It was still only an assumption in 1519, albeit an increasingly solid one, when Magellan and his five ships sailed from Seville to find a western route to the Spice Islands. But the cargo of cloves and cinnamon that found its way back to Spain in the hull of the *Victoria* was

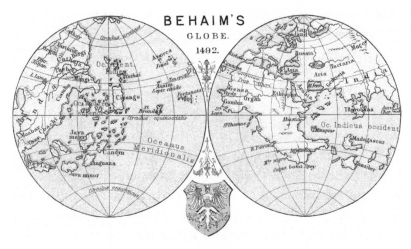

Planisphere of Martin Behaim's globe (1492)

empirical proof that the world was indeed *una balla,* to use Ramusio's expression. Furthermore, it appeared the ball was navigable all around and inhabitable in all its parts. It was not divided into separate entities, as the Ancients had believed, but one and whole. And much larger than expected, given how long it had taken to cross the Pacific. The age-old Ptolemaic view of the world, already undermined by the great discoveries of the previous three decades, was no longer sustainable. Magellan and his men had created an entirely new frame of reference.

Among the survivors who had straggled off the *Victoria,* scrawny and dazed but otherwise in good health, was Antonio Pigafetta, a thirty-year-old gentleman from Vicenza, on the Venetian mainland, who had joined the expedition "out of curiosity and a sense of adventure."

It is hard to imagine a more unlikely crew member. Pigafetta was born into a family of the small nobility with ties to the Knights of Rhodes. His mother, Lucia, died when he was about eighteen years old, and he grew up with his father, his stepmother and his young siblings in a late-Gothic palazzo in the heart of Vicenza. Although well educated, he was no scholar, did not show any particular talent and seemed destined for an unexceptional life in the provinces.

The turning point came in 1518. The Bishop of Vicenza, Francesco Chiericati, one of the leading intellectuals in the city, was summoned to Rome as an aide to Pope Leo X and took Antonio, then a bachelor in his mid-twenties, as his personal secretary. Six months later, Chiericati was sent to Spain as papal nuncio, and again his young protégé went with him. In Barcelona, Chiericati kept a vibrant intellectual salon where the conversation revolved around the Spanish and Portuguese discoveries that were shaping new notions of the world. Young Pigafetta listened intently and read about the journeys of Alvise da Mosto, Christopher Columbus, Vasco da Gama and Amerigo Vespucci. He became, as he wrote, "engrossed in all these stupendous stories."

When Pigafetta heard about Magellan's planned expedition, he became eager to join it. With the Emperor's permission and Chiericati's letters of recommendation, he sailed to Málaga and traveled overland to Seville. At the Casa de Contratación, the central agency that supervised the organization and funding of naval expeditions, he was hired as an aide (*criado*) to Magellan and as a man-at-arms (*sobresaliente*), with a combined stipend of one thousand *maravedí* a month, four thousand of which he received in advance.

Magellan, a driven, ambitious Portuguese navigator, had pushed hard for this westward expedition after seeing, in the Treasury of King Manuel I, a map by Martin Behaim that showed "a hidden strait" at the bottom of the American landmass. There was no empirical proof that such a strait existed. Yet Magellan made himself believe that the strait existed, and he became determined to find it.

However, he was out of favor at the Portuguese court: King Manuel denied his request for career advancement and higher pay and rejected his proposed expedition. So Magellan crossed over to Spain in 1517 and offered his services to the young king, Charles I, soon to become Emperor Charles V. As a further inducement, Magellan argued—wrongly, it turned out—that the voyage would not only open the way to a shorter route to the Orient but also demonstrate that the Spice Islands belonged to Spain's sphere of influence rather than Portugal's.*

Charles V gave his blessing to the enterprise despite the hostility of his court toward "the Portuguese fugitive." On August 10, 1519, after months of careful preparation, Magellan sailed out of the busy harbor of Seville with five caravels—the lead ship *Trinidad,* the *Santiago,* the *Concepción,* the *San Antonio* and the *Victoria*—loaded with cloth, glass beads, mirrors and other trading goods.

Pigafetta had no experience at sea, but he soon found a useful occupation, writing a diary to document the journey. He was a competent writer with a good eye for detail; he applied himself with diligence, and from the start he dreamed of making a name for himself "that would live on in posterity."

And he did, for his diary is the single most important source on the first known circumnavigation of the globe by a European navigator.

PACIFICUS

According to Pigafetta, Magellan and his fleet took the long, slow route to South America to avoid the Portuguese ships sent out to intercept him. They sailed down the coast of West Africa all the way to Sierra Leone before crossing the Atlantic, reaching the Brazilian coast in late November, more than three and a half months after leaving Seville.

After a pleasant two-week break among the indigenous people in the area of Rio de Janeiro, the convoy resumed its southbound journey. Magellan, who hoped to find the strait before the arctic

---

* By decree of a papal bull (1493) that formally endorsed the Treaty of Tordesillas, all territories discovered east of a line of demarcation drawn across the Atlantic from north to south belonged to Portugal, and all territories west of that line belonged to Spain. Magellan claimed that by sailing west he could prove that the Spice Islands belonged to Spain, not Portugal. But of course he was not aware of the immensity of the Pacific Ocean, which put the Spice Islands within the Portuguese sphere—just barely.

winter set in, thought he found it when they reached the estuary of Río de la Plata. But after a reconnaissance upriver, they finally turned around and pushed south along the coast of Patagonia even as the weather worsened and the ships were battered by storms and freezing weather.

The Captain General decided to winter in the bay of San Julián, where he soon faced a mutiny of his Spanish captains—they had been hostile and uncooperative from the beginning. Magellan quashed the revolt and showed no mercy to his enemies: one captain killed, another put to death and quartered, a third left ashore to die in the cold.

It was now October and temperatures were getting warmer in the arctic spring. The *Santiago* was sent out on a scouting mission but crashed against the rocky shore. The men were saved but the ship was lost. Magellan nevertheless resumed his quest, navigating to latitudes never reached by European sailors before. At last they found an opening at 54 degrees south and slowly made their way through treacherous waters and tortuous passageways. They sailed past Tierra del Fuego into a bleak landscape of high mountains and glaciers; then, on November 28, 1520, after following a long, narrow canal carved into the rock, they reached the open sea.

Meanwhile, Magellan lost another ship: after seizing command of the *San Antonio,* Esteban Gómez, a sworn enemy of the Captain General, had deliberately fallen behind during the crossing of the strait until—out of sight—he had turned the ship around and sailed back to Spain.

The three remaining ships now ventured into a vast and mysterious sea, so calm that Magellan named it *Pacificus.* They sailed uninterruptedly on a westward course for three months and twenty days with no sign of land, missing Tahiti and the Marshall Islands. The men lived on a diet of rats, worm-ravaged biscuits and putrid water; toward the end of the crossing they were left to chew the toughened leather of the chafing gear. Nineteen men died of starvation, scurvy and disease before they reached the island of Guam, where natives came on board and took away everything they could lay their hands on. "Isla de los Ladrones"—the Island of Thieves—Magellan called it, before pulling up the sails and moving on.

It was only when they reached the southern Philippines that the Captain General was able to take his men ashore, tend to the weak and the ill on the beach, and get provisions from friendly tribes.

Since leaving Seville, Magellan had shown himself to be an exceptional commander. But now back in the known world, in territory Europeans had already reached from the east, he showed another face, meddling unwisely in local politics and becoming obsessed by his drive to convert the natives to Christianity, even burning down a village that did not want to embrace the new religion.

On the island of Mactan—the same island where Magellan had destroyed the village—one chief in particular, Ci Lapu Lapu, refused to submit to the authority and religion of the King of Spain. Magellan made the ill-fated decision of responding with force. He reached the island with three longboats, and under cover of darkness made a landing with forty-eight men. An army of about fifteen hundred men was waiting for them and immediately started pushing them back to the sea. A poisoned arrow hit Magellan in the right leg. He remained on the ground covering the retreat of his men. Soon the natives were upon him. One leg was hacked with a sword, his chest was pierced with a lance. Seven men were lost, and as the rest scrambled into the longboats to safety, the natives dragged Magellan's body away—it was never recovered.

After the heavy loss of life on the island of Mactan, not to mention the nineteen deaths that occurred during the crossing of the Pacific, there were not enough crew left to man three ships and the *Concepción* had to be sunk. The two remaining ones—*Trinidad* and *Victoria*—began to wander erratically in the Celebes Sea. Without Magellan's firm leadership, discipline slackened; acts of piracy became the norm. In early November 1521, eight months after the Captain General's death, the two caravels finally reached the Moluccan archipelago and slowly toured the various islands, establishing commercial alliances. Loaded with a hefty cargo of spices—cloves mostly, but also nutmeg, pepper, ginger and sandalwood—the

Trinidad and the *Victoria* were now ready for the long voyage home across the Indian Ocean and around the Cape of Good Hope. But the *Trinidad* sprung a serious leak and had to stay behind—it eventually made its way back across the Pacific to the Spanish possessions in America.

Victoria, captained by Juan Sebastián Elcano, one of the mutineers at San Julián whose life Magellan had spared, sailed home, carefully staying away from Portuguese ports in the Indian Ocean. During the journey, fifteen more men died of starvation, dehydration and illness, as did ten of thirteen Indonesian natives forced on board in the Spice Islands. On May 22, 1522, the battered ship rounded the cape and sailed north to the Cabo Verde archipelago. This was Portuguese territory, but the men were so hungry and weak that Elcano decided to risk being arrested in order to make provisions for the last stretch home. He told the Portuguese they had been sailing the Atlantic route to the Americas when their foremast had broken and they had drifted south of the equator. The ruse worked at first and they were able to load a shipment of rice. But word got out that they were carrying cloves and other spices, the Portuguese became suspicious, and Elcano slipped away leaving thirteen men behind.

The remaining crew, frail and exhausted from working the pumps day and night to keep the ship afloat, sailed on past the Canary Islands until they were finally in view of the Spanish coast.

As soon as Charles V received word of the *Victoria*'s return, he summoned Elcano and "two of his saner and more reasonable men" to Valladolid, the capital in the north. Elcano took Pigafetta with him, together with Francisco Albo, a Greek who had risen through the ranks to become the pilot of the *Victoria*.

At the end of a brief audience, Pigafetta gave a copy of his diary to Charles V. He hoped the Emperor would be magnanimous enough to offer him an annual stipend in recognition of his achievement, or at the very least give him permission to publish his diary. Instead, the manuscript was put under lock and key and that copy was never seen again. Charles had no interest in publicizing the new route to the Spice Islands for the benefit of others, and no desire to glorify Magellan, a Portuguese.

During the next few days the three men were interrogated by the king's personal secretary, Maximilian Transylvanus. Peter Martyr, court historian and close adviser to the young monarch, supervised the debriefing. And from the start, Pigafetta witnessed the making of a smear campaign bent on destroying Magellan's reputation and erasing him from history.

In the eyes of Martyr, Magellan had betrayed his king in Portugal, killed Spanish commanders and discovered the strait by sheer fluke; his own death on the island of Mactan, he claimed, was the inevitable result of "his greedy quest for spices." All these accusations eventually found their way into *De Orbe Novo,* Martyr's monumental history about the making of what he referred to as the New World.

Pigafetta remained loyal to Magellan. His admiration for the Captain General bordered on veneration. "No one else had the audacity and the brains necessary to sail around the world," he wrote. "No one could read charts and navigate like him, or withstand the pangs of deprivation." True, the battle at Mactan had been brought on by his own crusading zeal, but even as Magellan lay wounded to death, Pigafetta noted, he protected his men during their retreat from the enemy.

These views found no place in Martyr's official counternarrative— from which Elcano, not Magellan, emerged as the hero. Charles V granted the captain of the *Victoria* a rich annual pension and an augmentation of his coat of arms, which now featured two crossed rolls of cinnamon and three nutmegs against a field of twelve cloves, and the motto: *Primus circumdedisti me*—You were the first to sail around me.

Pigafetta was not so lucky, but he got what he was owed in back pay: 37,924 *maravedí,* minus the 4,000 *maravedí* advance he had received when he had signed up. His share of the sale of spices came to 7,040 *maravedí*. All told, the expedition earned him the equivalent of about $20,000 in today's currency.

"I went away with as much as I could get," he sighed, and left Spain to sell his story elsewhere.

The news that reached Ramusio from Spain, while exhilarating, carried ominous implications for the Republic that spoke to him more as a senior civil servant than as a geographer in the making: the opening of a western route to the Spice Islands by Spain would threaten to cut Venice out entirely from that lucrative market, dealing yet another blow to its declining commercial empire.

ISABELLA

After leaving the Spanish court in Valladolid, his pockets lined with *maravedí,* Pigafetta had crossed over into Portugal, where he had no more luck with King João than he'd had with Charles V. In Lisbon, Magellan was still viewed as a traitor. Next, Pigafetta traveled to France. King Francis I was away at war, so he presented exotic gifts and excerpts from his diary to Louise of Savoy, the king's mother and powerful regent. But the French were more interested in containing the Spaniards in the New Indies than in a Pacific route to the Spice Islands. The court showed no interest in either purchasing or publishing his account.

He was heading home to Vicenza with a dwindling reserve of cash and a manuscript no one was interested in publishing when he was relieved to hear from his long-lost mentor Chiericati, who was now Bishop of Teramo and was in Nürburg as papal envoy to the Diet; Chiericati urged his old protégé to pay a visit to Isabella d'Este, the mother of the Duke of Mantua.

Isabella was admired for her intelligence and her taste as a collector and patron of the arts. Her famous *studiolo*—study room—was filled with precious books, paintings and beautiful objets d'art. She had a special interest in travelogues and maps—an interest she had inherited from her father, Ercole d'Este, when she was growing up in Ferrara and which she had cultivated after her marriage to Francesco Gonzaga, Marquis of Mantua.

In a letter of introduction to Isabella, Chiericati described Pigafetta rather patronizingly as "a young man from Vicenza whom I sent from Spain to India." He had now returned "rich in knowledge about the world, with a diary you will find divine." It is easy to imagine Pigafetta's excitement—Isabella was a celebrity in Renaissance Europe.

And she, in turn, was fascinated by his story. She urged him to turn the diary into a proper narrative and promised she would help him get the book published in Venice, where she had good connections in the publishing world (she had, in fact, been one of Aldus's best clients). A strong-willed woman who liked to have things her own way, Isabella instructed Mantua's ambassador in Venice and her de facto agent in that city to start interviewing printers.

Ramusio, who had ties to Isabella going back to Aldus's days, probably helped smooth the process of publication by pressing the authorities to speed up the granting of the obligatory *privilegio* (copyright). He was also eager to lure Pigafetta himself to Venice and to have him speak to the Council on his voyage. A private lunch with the Doge was added to the program.

Pigafetta arrived in early November, a little over a year after the return of the *Victoria*. "The Knight Errant from Vicenza has finally come," a snide Venetian chronicler quipped. But in truth his visit created great excitement. Everyone wanted to hear the full story of the circumnavigation of the globe. The officials convened in the council hall and listened "with rapt attention" to Pigafetta's vivid account.

Galvanized by his successful visit to Venice, Pigafetta retired to Vicenza to prepare the manuscript for publication as per Isabella's instructions. He had just settled down to work when he was summoned to Rome by the newly elected pope, Clement VII, who was eager to get his own full report on Magellan's expedition. It was not a summons Pigafetta could ignore. He took leave from Isabella and headed south with his manuscript, more confident than ever that he now had a valuable literary property in his hands.

Before reaching Rome, however, he took the time to stop in the little town of Monterosi, near Viterbo, to pay homage to Philippe de Villiers de l'Isle-Adam, Grand Master of the Order of the Knights of Rhodes.

The year before, Villiers de l'Isle-Adam had been forced to abandon Rhodes after a long and bloody siege laid by the troops of Suleiman the Magnificent. He and his knights and four thousand Christian refugees had sailed to Crete, then on to Messina, in Sicily, finally settling in Monterosi, thirty miles north of Rome, where the Pope had granted them temporary shelter while a permanent seat for the Order was found—they were eventually relocated to the island of Malta.

Antonio Pigafetta's family had a long-standing affiliation with the Order of Rhodes. The Grand Master was understandably enthused by Antonio's story, and he knighted him on the spot in recognition of his valorous accomplishment. He no doubt dangled before him the prospect of some future remuneration in exchange for a copy of his manuscript. But the Pope was waiting and so Pigafetta pushed on.

In Rome, Clement VII listened to Pigafetta's story, then put him immediately to work: it now appeared the Pope himself was interested in publishing the book. Fearful of losing the favor of Isabella d'Este, his earliest patron, Pigafetta nevertheless hoped she would understand his predicament. "I am now at [the Pope's] service and he treats me like a domestic," he complained to her vicariously. Although the situation was beyond his control, he sheepishly assured her that "the first copy will be for you."

Pigafetta misread the Pope's intentions. Clement VII was interested in taking a look at the diary but did not want to make the full story of the voyage public. Quite apart from his own misgivings, he had no desire to antagonize Charles V or King João III, who had clearly chosen to keep the story under wraps and to deny Magellan his rightful place in history.

Once the final manuscript had been studied at the Vatican, Pigafetta was let go. He headed home again, hoping to win his way back into Isabella's good graces. "I have the book in my hands," he wrote. "My will is to serve you until my death. I plead you to tell me what I must do. I would leave anyone, including the Pope, to serve you. If it were up to me, I would already be your servant."

Although her patience was wearing thin, Isabella was still committed to financing the publication of Pigafetta's book. In the summer of 1524, the Council of Ten finally issued the *privilegio*. Isabella's agent in Venice selected a printer. Everything seemed on track. But as soon as the printer learned who was commissioning the book, he raised his price to a staggering advance of fifteen ducats to cover costs, plus half the sales profits. The Duke of Mantua, who was footing the bill largely to please his mother, was a very rich man; but he did not like to be taken for a fool. Negotiations dragged on into the autumn, until the duke finally walked away.

There may have been another reason for the duke's change of heart, beyond the printer's demands: a version of Magellan's expedition was already out in print. Maximilian Transylvanus, the man who had interviewed Elcano, Albo and Pigafetta in Valladolid shortly after their return, had written a narrative of the voyage in the form of a letter in Latin to his mentor, the Archbishop of Salzburg, Matthäus Lang von Wellenburg. *De Moluccis Insulis* was published in Cologne by Eucharius Hirtzhorn, in January 1523, only four months after the return of the *Victoria*—quickly even by today's standards. Interestingly, the emphasis was still on the discovery of a new route to the Spice Islands, rather than on the circumnavigation of the globe. *De Moluccis* circulated widely in Europe. In Paris, the printer Pierre Viart put out a pirated edition in July 1523; four months later, another edition, by printer Minutius Calvus, appeared in Rome.

Ramusio was disappointed that the opportunity to publish

Pigafetta's original manuscript in Venice was lost over money matters. He had learned Aldus's lesson on the importance of staying as close as possible to the original source material; all these spurious, incomplete editions were bound to muddy the waters.

Ramusio had no doubt about the lasting importance of Pigafetta's literary achievement. "The Ancients," he wrote, "would have erected a marble statue to celebrate the man who circled the great ball of the world and described it so well."

Pigafetta never got his marble statue, but he did land on his feet. As Isabella was no longer of much use to him, he switched the dedication from her to his new patron, Philippe de Villiers de l'Isle-Adam. In return, the Grand Master granted him a commandry in Umbria, which included the towns of Norcia, Todi and Arquata (this last one today situated in the Marche). The income was modest but sufficient for a decorous life. How much of that life he was actually able to enjoy remains unknown for, at this point, Pigafetta faded mysteriously from written history.

The manuscript dedicated to the Grand Master also disappeared.* But by then Ramusio knew enough about Pigafetta's narrative that he could break the mold set by the Ancients and begin to reconfigure the world on a scale never imagined in antiquity.

---

* A contemporary copy was discovered by the Milanese scholar Carlo Amoretti, in the archives of the Biblioteca Ambrosiana, only at the end of the eighteenth century; it was published around 1800. A more complete version was finally published in Venice in 1894 by Andrea da Mosto, descendant of Alvise da Mosto, the navigator who opened up the South Atlantic routes by discovering Cabo Verde while in the service of the Portuguese.

CHAPTER THREE

CADAMOSTO

THE OLD-TIMERS AT THE CHANCERY STILL REMEMBERED CADAMOSTO, A VENETIAN SEA MERCHANT WHO HAD sailed down the coast of West Africa in the 1450s and was the first European on record to reach the islands of Cabo Verde. He was away ten years; when he returned to Venice, still in his thirties, he married well, entered public service and died in office after a relatively lackluster career. Yet he left behind an account of his African journeys that secured his place in the history of world exploration.

As Ramusio turned his attention to Africa, it was only natural that he would begin by studying a manuscript written by one of Venice's own and easily available to him in the family library of Cadamosto's palazzo, just a short walk from the Chancery.

Besides, there wasn't much else available to Ramusio. The only source on the geography of western Africa was an ancient Greek manuscript that described the sea journey of Hanno the Navigator, a Carthaginian admiral of the sixth century B.C. who led a fleet of sixty ships beyond the Strait of Gibraltar and down the coast of present-day Morocco to colonize the region and control the Atlantic trade. Some historians have claimed Hanno reached Senegal, others that he even sailed as far south as Equatorial Africa.

After the Romans defeated Carthage in 146 B.C., Scipio sent

Polybius, the great Roman geographer, on a reconnaissance mission to look for those Carthaginian settlements on the coast of West Africa. Alas, the books Polybius wrote about that journey are lost.

In the absence of any reliable information, a certain idea of sub-Saharan Africa as a region peopled by monsters, where extreme temperature made human life impossible, took root in antiquity. Ptolemy himself assumed it was not possible to navigate down the coast of Africa beyond a certain point, believing the heat caused the seawater to evaporate until the ocean was reduced to a swamp. Variations of this view prevailed in medieval cosmography.

By the time Cadamosto ventured down the coast of West Africa in 1455 and 1456, Portuguese captains sponsored by Prince Henry of Portugal had already pushed their way south, possibly as far as the river Gambia. These early European forays began to modify the age-old image of sub-Saharan Africa from a lifeless inferno to a strange palimpsest formed by new data, old legends and geographical notions rooted in antiquity.

It was Cadamosto's vivid reporting, however, that brought the region into focus for Ramusio—a flash of light that illuminated the coast of West Africa.

Cadamosto was the eldest son of an old Venetian family that had fallen on hard times. (His full name was Alvise da Mosto; Cadamosto, the name by which he became known, is a contraction of Ca' da Mosto, for Casa da Mosto, the family palazzo on the Grand Canal.) He started out as an apprentice in the merchant house of Andrea Barbarigo, one of the richest traders in Venice, earning his stripes on the commercial routes to Alexandria and to Crete and eventually on the Atlantic route to Flanders. He was still in his early twenties when he opened his own business and joined a convoy of Venetian galleys headed to the North Sea.

When the convoy reached Cabo de São Vicente, on the southernmost tip of Portugal, the northerly winds blowing down the Atlantic were so strong that the ships were forced to take cover in a sheltered bay on the promontory of Sagres. It so happened that Prince Henry was headquartered only a few miles away in a fortified compound, Raposeira.

Years earlier, Henry, youngest brother of King Duarte, had left the court in Lisbon and had settled on this remote outpost in the southern province of Algarve to plan and execute Portuguese expansion in the southern Atlantic. Nestled at the top of a rocky cliff, with a sweeping view of the ocean, Raposeira had grown into a major center for maritime exploration, bustling with navigators, cartographers and astronomers from all over Europe. At first, Henry was interested in establishing trading posts down the coast of Africa to import gold and slaves. As Grand Master of the Order of Christ, which had replaced the Order of the Templars, he was also looking for ways to outflank and contain the Muslim world, which had spread as far south as the so-called Land of the Black People, a term that was used by geographers in Europe but translated the Arabic *Bilad al-Sudan*. It was only later, possibly after having read a manuscript of Marco Polo's travels in Asia, which his brother Pedro brought back to him from Venice in 1428, that Henry expanded his mission to include the circumnavigation of Africa—a goal that was eventually reached by Vasco da Gama in 1497, thirty-seven years after Henry's death.

When Prince Henry heard about the Venetians stranded down the coast, he sent his secretary, Antonio Gonzales, to welcome them. Venetian navigators were held in great esteem for their nautical skills. Gonzales brought with him some recently imported goods from Africa, including sugarcane from Madeira, to recruit some of the men with promises of great profits.

Only Cadamosto showed enough interest to follow Gonzales back to meet Prince Henry in Raposeira. Impressed by the setup and the available resources, he decided to give up his plans to go to Flanders and to take his chances on the new African route. As he later wrote, he was "young and willing to take on the most arduous task and eager to see the world."

Prince Henry offered Cadamosto the command of a caravel—the new, compact, very agile sailship designed by his nautical engineers for Atlantic exploration. At the end of March 1455, Cadamosto sailed southwest to the Portuguese-controlled islands of Madeira, on to the Canary Islands, then swung southeast to the coast of Africa, rounding the long, sharp-edged promontory of Cabo Branco (as the Portuguese then called it, now Ras Nouadhibou), and entering the Gulf of Arguin, at the southern end of what is now Western Sahara.

Cadamosto's seamen claimed that when the Portuguese ships led by Nuno Tristão, one of Prince Henry's favorite pilots, had first appeared at Cabo Branco twelve years before, with their billowing white sails embossed with the red Christian cross, the natives took them for "giant birds with white wings" that had flown in from another world. The first Portuguese to land that far south proved indeed to be vicious birds of prey, as they raided the fishing villages along the coast to capture native people and enslave them. But under Prince Henry's orders, peaceful arrangements were later brokered with local chiefs and a trading post was established on the island of Arguin, in the gulf beyond Cabo Branco. Henry hoped friendlier trade with the natives might also make it easier to convert them to Christianity.

Cadamosto went ashore and rode by camel to Hoden, a low-lying town six days inland which served as a terminal for caravans that traveled to and from Timbuktu and other major trading centers on the southern edge of the Sahara Desert, just north of the "Land of the Black People." An experienced merchant, he was fascinated by the commercial network that connected cities across the Sahara. The Portuguese were mostly interested in buying slaves and gold, but Cadamosto was surprised to discover that delicate fabrics made in Granada or copperware and silverware from Tunis had traveled that far south.

The region was populated by the Sanhaja (called the Azenaghi in some texts), a Berber tribe that belonged to the wider family of the Tuareg. "They were not black but tawny, average height and skinny," Cadamosto noted, and they lived mostly off dates and barley and camel milk. They were Muslim, and deeply committed to their faith—definitely not an easy target for a Christian proselytizing campaign.

Leaving the Gulf of Arguin behind him, Cadamosto sailed down the coast to the mouth of the river Senega. Another of Prince Henry's pilots, Dinis Dias, had touched land in the area ten years earlier. Henry's cartographers had concluded that the Senega was a tributary of the mighty Gihon, one of the four rivers in the book of Genesis that flowed from Earthly Paradise (the other three being the Tigris, the Euphrates and the Ganges; the Gihon was thought to be not so much a river as a vast fluvial network that included the Nile). Cadamosto deferred to the experts; but it was one of the rare instances in which he allowed remnants of medieval cosmography to cloud his otherwise very factual narrative.

Cadamosto assumed that the farther south he sailed, the more temperatures would rise, until they would become unbearable. And the "dry and barren" landscape he had seen since touching the African coast at Cabo Branco certainly seemed to suggest as much. So he was pleasantly surprised to see that on the other side of the Senega River the landscape was instead "green and fertile and covered with trees."

AT BUDOMEL'S

The natives seemed to manage the heat quite well and looked to be in fine shape, "very dark, and big and strong and well built." As they showed no particular hostility, he took his chances and sailed up the river on high tide. He moored the caravel in an inlet and let the locals know that he had sturdy horses with him, as well as woolen and silk fabrics, and was eager to trade. The King of Cayor, a province of the great Wolof Empire, lived nearby. He was a jovial, friendly type, and when he invited Cadamosto to stay as his guest, Cadamosto instructed his seamen to sail back out to sea and wait for him off the coast.

The king, whom Cadamosto calls "Budomel"—a contraction of *bour,* a generic Wolof title, and *domel,* the regal title in Cayor—lived in a large village composed of some fifty thatched huts laid out in concentric circles. Cadamosto was put up in the hut of one of the king's nephews, but he was allowed to roam about freely in the otherwise restricted royal compound in the center of the village.

He stayed for a month, taking his time to explore the region and observe how the people of Cayor lived. They got by with very little, mostly millet and beans. There were no organized plots, no enclosed orchards; they planted crops quite randomly, wherever there was a little space. Instead of hoeing and turning the soil, they scratched the surface no more than four fingers deep with tiny shovels, throwing the earth forward as they moved along. It was a pity, Cadamosto noted, as the soil was rich and could have yielded plenty more.

Market was held twice a week in a wide meadow outside the village. The display of goods was very modest: a few rolls of cotton, some floppy legumes, palm oil and palm wine, little piles of millet, some carved utensils, mats made of woven palm leaves. Still, Cadamosto enjoyed the bustle and liked mixing with the men and women. A small crowd of curious natives always followed him around as he checked the stalls. At first, some of them had sidled up to him and had rubbed his forearms with their spit to see if the whiteness went away.

In the village, the atmosphere was friendly. The natives walked around barefoot and mostly naked. The men, he thought, were generally quite laid-back and kind. The women, always bare-breasted, were "cheerful and fun and loved to sing and dance by the moonlight." Cadamosto took to dropping by Budomel's quarters at the end of the day for a cup of palm wine.

The conversation often turned to sex. The king had nine wives, and each one had her own handmaiden, and he slept with all of them—wives and servants. It was very exhausting, he told Cadamosto. Since Christians seemed to know all the tricks, Budomel wondered if his new friend had a remedy that could help him satisfy all his women. Cadamosto confessed he had nothing to offer— which was a pity, as the king "was willing to give a great many things in exchange."

In addition to sex, the two men talked about religion. Years back,

the Azenaghi had come from the other side of the river to pro-
pagate the religion of Islam. They had been fairly persuasive with
the people of Cayor, so Budomel had decided to embrace the faith.
The village now had a small mosque. "Ours is the true faith, yours
is the false one," Budomel joked with Cadamosto. The king was
intrigued by Christianity and readily admitted that God had been
more generous to Christians. But that was one more reason to be a
Muslim. "You had your paradise in this world, we'll have it in the
next," he chuckled.

Cadamosto felt that Budomel was secretly ready to convert to
Christianity but was not going to abandon Islam—and wisely so,
because a conversion on the part of the king might have led to political instability, perhaps even to his own overthrow.

After twenty-eight days as Budomel's guest, it was time to move
on. But the sea was rough and the caravel was anchored a couple
of miles from the shore. The local inhabitants had simple barks
that were not seaworthy. How was he to let his crew know that he
wanted to be picked up? Two strapping young men volunteered
to swim out to the boat in exchange for a large tin platter each. At
first Cadamosto discouraged them, as he thought they would never
make it. But the men insisted and swam out against powerful cur-
rents and crashing waves. Cadamosto was sure they would both dis-
appear. One of the swimmers soon gave up and returned to shore,
but the other one managed to battle his way to the rocking ship. "It
was a wonder to behold. Surely these men are the best swimmers in
the world."

Cadamosto got back on board with a few slaves he had purchased
from native traders during his stay in Cayor. He showed them the
ship's arsenal: swords, lances, pikes, crossbows and bombards, which,
he told them, could kill up to one hundred men at a time.

"These are the instruments of the Devil," one of the slaves
remarked.

They marveled at the complexity of the ship's rigging. "They
know nothing about compass and charts and navigation and believe
the two bow holes are real eyes that allow the ship to see where it

is going," Cadamosto reported. He then led them inside to his own quarters, which were illuminated by a candelabrum. Back at the village, Cadamosto had seen them suck the honey off honeycombs and throw away the wax. "So I asked my men to bring some beeswax and had a few candles made in front of them as they watched in disbelief."

The next day, as the crew set sail to continue the southbound voyage, two Portuguese caravels appeared on the horizon, the largest of which was captained by Antoniotto Usodimare, a Genoese navigator employed by Prince Henry. They too were headed south, so the three caravels sailed on together until they rounded the Cape Verde Peninsula (not to be confused with the Cabo Verde archipelago), a lush green cape at the southernmost part of the Wolof Empire, where Dakar, the capital of modern Senegal, stands today. The coastline was dotted with thatched fishing huts. In the gulf just beyond the cape they dropped anchor off an island full of bird nests. They gorged on eggs and spent the day fishing for bass and sea bream. (The island was later named Gorée; it became the major terminal for the slave trade on the western coast of Africa.)

They sailed south alongside a thick wall of tropical greenery. "The trees," Cadamosto later wrote, "grow all the way to the edge of the water, as if drinking the ocean—and it's a beautiful sight to behold."

The fierce Sereri tribes lived in the region. The kings of the Wolof Empire had never managed to subjugate them. And their animistic culture had resisted the influence of Islam. Nine years earlier, Nuno Tristão, the Portuguese pilot, had reached this coast and was killed by the natives. Prince Henry, deeply moved, had halted reconnaissance expeditions for nearly a decade.

Despite the grim precedent, Cadamosto was determined to make a landing and attempt a peaceful engagement. Sixty miles south of Cape Verde, the three caravels reached the mouth of the Saloum River and sent one of the interpreters—a former slave who had been taken to Portugal ten years before—to tell the natives that they came as friends and wanted to trade. The man was butchered while the rest of his companions watched helplessly from a distance. Cadamosto decided there was no point in lingering, "as they would have done the same to us, and maybe worse."

The three caravels headed farther south aiming for a region they had heard was rich in gold. They reached the mouth of a big river—it was the Gambia—and sailed upstream for two miles. They went in "wishing to reason with the natives and not use force." Some thirty tribesmen soon paddled toward the caravels in their barks and paused at a safe distance, looking mystified and wary. Then they went away.

The next morning the ships sailed another few miles upstream. Now they were surrounded by at least fifteen barks carrying as many as 150 natives—big, strong men wearing white cotton shirts and ready to shower them with their poisoned arrows. Cadamosto and the other two captains let loose their bombards and the natives watched helplessly as heavy stone projectiles wrecked their vessels and sent them flying into the river. The crossbowmen started taking the natives out one by one. The latter withdrew, regrouped and, paddling at great speed, came up from the rear and attacked the smallest and most vulnerable of the three caravels. A second barrage of cannonballs again dispersed the assailants. Taking advantage of the confusion, the captains chained the three caravels together.

Cadamosto made a new attempt to initiate peaceful talks, "our interpreters gesticulating and shouting on the deck." One of the barks eventually came close enough to engage in a rudimentary exchange. Little came of it. "We told them we came in peace and were only interested in trading goods," Cadamosto later wrote. "But they were convinced that Christians ate human flesh, and that the only reason we wanted to purchase slaves was to eat them.[*] They were not at all interested in our friendship; they wished to kill us

---

[*] Cannibalism did exist in Africa in Cadamosto's time but was quite rare. The fear of cannibalism, on the other hand, was very widespread, and Cadamosto's reporting reminds us that it ran both ways: Europeans often suspected native tribes of cannibalism, and vice versa.

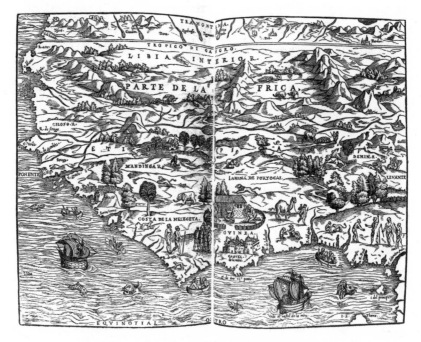

Early map of western Africa, published by Ramusio
in Book One of *Navigationi et Viaggi* (1550)

all and present our dead bodies to the King of Gambia, who lived three days away."

The breeze blowing upstream picked up, the sails filled, and the natives scattered. There was some talk among the three captains about the opportunity of continuing upriver for a hundred miles or so, in hope of making contact with the King of Gambia. But the crew were exhausted and done with fighting, and clamored to go home. And so the next day the ships lifted anchor and sailed back down the muddy river.

Night fell and as the caravels headed out to sea the men saw straight ahead, low on the horizon, a constellation they had never seen before: a cluster of stars "clear and shiny" in the shape of a cross reclining horizontally in the southern sky.

·   ·   ·

To Cadamosto and his men, the appearance of that constellation, which astronomers later named the Southern Cross, was a sign that they had truly ventured into a new part of the world.

ELEPHANT STEAK

Cadamosto spent the winter at Prince Henry's court in the Algarve studying the information he had brought back and helping cartographers draw up new maps and portolans of Africa's western coast. But he was eager to return to the Gambia region, "having seen little or nothing of it." The following spring he and Antoniotto were given license by the prince to rig up two caravels for a second journey down the coast. Henry was so enthused by the tales of the two Italian navigators that he personally invested in a third caravel.

This time the small fleet sailed to the Canary Islands, then tacked east-southeast toward Africa, aiming directly for Cabo Branco. The promontory was already in sight when a violent storm engulfed the three caravels. Battling furious southwest winds, the captains decided to head away from the coast in a west-northwest direction and wait the storm out. After three days in uncharted waters they suddenly saw land "where none of us expected to see it."

A string of volcanic islands rose before them in the middle of the Atlantic. Cadamosto and his companions actually only saw four of the ten islands that form the Cabo Verde archipelago, and they made a landing on two of them (Boa Vista and Santiago, the largest island). As the islands were uninhabited, they decided to move on, but not before spending two days resting, fishing and bringing in supplies of salt and fresh water. They salted and stocked sea turtles, which Cadamosto found "very tasty and tender like veal," and roasted wild pigeons they were able to catch with their bare hands "as they had never seen a human."

The storm, meanwhile, had subsided. They sailed to Africa and touched land south of the river Senega. As Cadamosto noted, "The terrain was now familiar." They rounded the lush Cape Verde Peninsula (again, not to be confused with the archipelago), and after steady sailing they reached the mouth of the Gambia and slowly, carefully navigated upstream. This time the wary natives followed the three ships at a distance. Cadamosto and his men called out to them, offering presents and expressing peaceful intentions. Every day the natives "took courage and came a little closer," until finally one of the barks accosted Cadamosto's caravel. A man came on board and began to touch the seamen and look around. "He was astonished by the color of our skin and by the clothes we wore; we stroked him gently and offered small gifts."

The native was able to communicate with the interpreter at a basic level. He led Cadamosto and his men some sixty miles upstream to a land ruled by a local chief called Battimansa. Cadamosto presented the chief with a colorful Moorish silk shirt; Battimansa was delighted with the gift and welcomed the newcomers to his small kingdom.

Word soon spread and a large number of men emerged from the jungle to see the strange ships. They climbed on board, looking to trade simple cotton fabrics, furs, wooden utensils and different types of fruit. "Every day we had new people on the boat," noted Cadamosto, who avoided tasting even so much as a date for fear of dysentery.

Gold was one of the main reasons for returning to Gambia. But the natives only brought small strands and nuggets to market—"much less than what we had hoped to find after hearing so many tales." The prospects of a flourishing trade along the Gambia River dimmed, but not Cadamosto's curiosity about the geography of the region. He took down copious notes on the river system, the tropical vegetation (he spent hours scratching his head over the strange proportions of the baobab tree, measuring and remeasuring its height and width). He saw his first hippo bathing in the muddy river ("they call this beast a horse-fish though it reminds me more of a large seal"), and his first elephants—a family of three had come to a watering hole but had fled at the sight of the caravels.

One day the natives killed a baby elephant with poisoned lances and arrows. Battimansa offered the dead animal to Cadamosto, who observed that, "though young, he was the equivalent of five or six of our bulls." He took a large chunk of elephant meat back to the boat and had a slice roasted and another one stewed to taste the difference. The meat was "tough and not very good," but he ate it anyway so he could say that he had eaten something "no one else back home has ever eaten."

After eleven days, the three caravels sailed downstream, and once back in the open sea headed south along the coast until they reached the wide mouth of the Geba River in what is today Guinea-Bissau. No European had ever traveled so far down the African coast. But the crew was tired. After a brief exploration of the Geba river system and the Bijagós archipelago, which faces the mouth of the river, the expedition headed home.

Cadamosto arrived at Sagres bearing exotic gifts for Prince Henry, including a slab of salted elephant meat and a large elephant hoof "three palms and one finger wide," which Battimansa had given to him as a goodbye present. Prince Henry sent the elephant hoof to his sister Isabella, Duchess of Burgundy.

Cadamosto stayed in Portugal for several more years. He advised Prince Henry, studied maps and travel reports, did a little business on the side investing in ships that plied the African route. He was still there in 1460 when Pedro da Sintra, a Portuguese pilot, traveled beyond Guinea-Bissau—the farthest point Cadamosto had reached—to Sierra Leone, so named because the perpetual tropical thunder in the mountains evoked the roar of the lion. Cadamosto interviewed da Sintra upon his return and compiled a short narrative of the journey, which he eventually took back with him to Venice. He left Portugal in 1463, three years after Prince Henry's death.

When he arrived in Venice like a long-lost Odysseus the following year, he was still only in his mid-thirties. He married Maria Elisabetta Venier, who came from another old family of Venice's oligarchy, and entered public service, slowly rising in the administration but never really shining. A merchant at heart, he continued his trading activities, doing business in Spain, Syria, Egypt and even England. In 1482, shortly after being appointed commissioner for grains and fodder, he was sent to the Polesine, south of Venice at the mouth of the Po River, to collect the income from lands the Venetian Republic had confiscated from the Duke of Ferrara. There he fell ill and died, at the age of fifty-two.

A printed edition of Cadamosto's writings on Africa appeared in Vicenza in 1507, but Ramusio went to work on the original manuscript he found in the da Mosto family archive. It is easy to see the appeal the narrative held for him. The writing was so refreshingly vivid and detailed that it had—and has preserved to this day—a mesmerizing quality about it. Cadamosto was neither a crusader nor a colonizer. He looked at these new territories with the eyes of an enterprising merchant interested in opening new markets. Curiosity nourished his writing. In this sense, the African natives were not inferior people to be conquered or converted or exterminated, but strangers with whom to engage for mutual benefit.

Cadamosto's manuscript was "truly worth reading for the light it sheds on those regions," Ramusio noted. But its greatest contribution, Ramusio added, was to show "how little the Ancients really knew" about that part of the world. "They thought it was burnt by the sun and uninhabitable, and it turned out to be very green and very pleasant and inhabited by a great number of people."

CHAPTER FOUR

AN AFRICAN MASTERPIECE

IN NOVEMBER 1518, RAMUSIO LEARNED FROM THE VENETIAN AMBASSADOR IN ROME, MARCO MINIO, THAT A NOTORIOUS Spanish pirate had come to town with an unusual gift for the Pope.

Seeking absolution for his many sins, Don Pedro Bobadilla had presented the pontiff with a Muslim man he had captured and enslaved, and who had turned out to be a person of great learning and distinction.

Papal indulgences were easily obtained for the right price under Leo X, and the odds are that the Pope forgave the pirate for his sins; besides, Don Pedro had strong ties to the Vatican—his brother Francisco was the powerful Bishop of Salamanca.

Leo X received the gift with genuine interest. The struggle between Islam and Christianity had reached a new level of tension after the Ottoman ruler, Selim I, crushed the Mamluks and doubled the size of his empire, taking over Syria, Palestine, Egypt and much of North Africa. The mysterious captive was a potential source of information on the Islamic world.

The Pope had him imprisoned at Castel Sant'Angelo, the fortress on the Tiber that also served as papal residence. "During his interrogation he said he had traveled to the court of the Turkish Lord to congratulate him on his victories in Syria and Egypt, and had been taken prisoner during his journey home," Ambassador Minio reported, adding that many interesting papers were found among his things. "The Pope has asked to have them translated."

Ramusio was a thorough and discerning reader of diplomatic dispatches—one of his tasks was to go through the daily diplomatic correspondence and read out the most significant parts on the Senate floor (his "clear and powerful voice" was much appreciated). Even so, he could hardly have imagined the impact the writings of that enslaved man would later have on his understanding of Africa. And on his own role in making those writings known to the world.

The man under lock at Castel Sant'Angelo was al-Hasan ibn Muhammad al-Wazzan, a learned jurist and diplomat in the service of the Sultan of Fez. He was born in a relatively prosperous Arab family in the mid-1480s in Granada, the most beautiful and romantic city in the Islamic world, and for all we know had a happy childhood in the shadow of the Alhambra.

Al-Wazzan was still a boy in 1492 when the Spanish army conquered Al-Andalus, the Muslim-ruled region of the Iberian peninsula. His family fled to North Africa with thousands of other refugees and settled in Fez, where his uncle was a high-placed official at the court of Sultan Muhammad al-Shaykh. Al-Wazzan joined a local madrassa and studied the Koran, as well as grammar, rhetoric and, later, the law, for which he showed a special aptitude. The family purchased some land and a vineyard near Fez, where it gathered during the summer months and where al-Wazzan frequently retreated to concentrate on his studies.

After a stint as a notary in a major hospital in Fez, he joined his uncle on several tours of duty. Soon he was carrying out his own trade and diplomatic missions for the new Sultan, Muhammad al-Burtughali, traveling east along the caravan routes as far as Tunis, Alexandria and Cairo, and south to the Empire of Mali, with the great cities of Gao and Timbuktu, and farther to the Land of the Black People along the middle Niger and all the way to Lake Chad.

In over a decade of travels in the northern half of Africa, al-Wazzan established contacts, made trade deals and built political alliances, always living in close contact with the local population. A careful observer and diligent note taker, he amassed a wealth of information on everything from the price of grains to particular weaving techniques to the quality of local wines in the places he visited.

In the summer of 1518, as he told his interrogators at Castel Sant'Angelo, he was sailing from Cairo back to Fez when his boat was captured by Bobadilla and his fellow pirates.

Al-Wazzan was locked up for a year. But he was frequently taken upstairs to the papal apartments, where the Pope and his entourage questioned him on the countries he had visited in Africa and on his impressions of the expanding Ottoman Empire. These meetings also offered them the opportunity to learn about Islam from a polished student of the Koran. One can only wonder how strange it must have felt for this scholar and diplomat to be discussing his religion with a group of men who, for all their intellectual curiosity, were bent on crushing Islam.

The Vatican Library was then housed at Castel Sant'Angelo. It had several manuscripts in Arabic, but they were rarely consulted. The Pope gave his prisoner library privileges and encouraged him to read them. According to the loan registers, al-Wazzan borrowed eight books during his time in prison—these were mostly Christian works translated into Arabic.

"God's servant, al Hasan Ibn Muhammad [al-Wazzan], has read this book," he wrote in pencil in the margin of one text. "May God preserve him from the iniquity in his soul and make this day better for him than the day before. Amen."

Pope Leo, no doubt impressed by the progress of al-Wazzan's Christian education, offered him freedom in exchange for conversion. Al-Wazzan accepted the bargain: a religious man, he turned out to be a practical one as well. "Whenever a man sees his advantage," he later wrote, "he will follow it."

Al-Wazzan imagined he would one day return to his old life in North Africa, and it is possible that he pretended to embrace Christianity while secretly remaining a Muslim. Various strains of Islam allowed a believer to dissemble his true faith in the face of coercion, a practice known as *taqiyya*. As a student of religion, he would certainly have been familiar with this option.

And so on January 6, 1520, the day of the Epiphany, Pope Leo himself baptized his former prisoner at the font in the papal chapel at Saint Peter's and gave him his new Christian name: John Leo Medici (Pope Leo X was a Medici).

Saint Peter's Basilica was still a construction site. But the candlelit ceremony under the marble vaults was impressive enough that its propagandistic element was not lost.

"His Holiness has made a convert of the Moorish envoy of the Sultan of Fez," Ambassador Minio duly reported to Ramusio. "Now that he has baptized him he plans to provide him with an income."

Pope Leo carefully selected three godfathers for his illustrious convert, all of them powerful cardinals and militant soldiers in the struggle against Islam: Lorenzo Pecci, the overseer of papal indulgences; Bernardino López de Carvajal, a fiery preacher who had celebrated the fall of Granada; and Egidio da Viterbo, who dreamed of a world united in the Christian faith.

Of the three godfathers, it was Egidio, a humanist and a promoter of the arts, who developed the closest bond with John Leo. A general of the Augustinian Order, he lived in a palace near the Church of Saint Augustine, in the Campo Marzio neighborhood, right behind present-day Piazza Navona. He took John Leo on as his private tutor in Arabic and it is likely that he provided lodging for his godson during the initial stages of his new life in Rome.

John Leo, who soon acquired the moniker Leo Africanus, attracted the attention of another wealthy patron of the arts: Alberto Pio, Prince of Carpi, whom we've already met, first as a young student of Aldus and later as a sponsor of the Aldine Press. Prince Alberto was now in Rome as ambassador of Francis I, the King of France.

Vatican records show that in early 1521 he checked out of the library an early Arabic version of Saint Paul's Epistles. He then hired John Leo to copy the manuscript.

The Pope died later that year. John Leo may have contemplated the idea of returning to Fez, yet he chose to stay. He was, after all, just settling into a new, intellectually stimulating life. He had powerful protectors, an income to live on and a burgeoning web of literary connections. Three of these, as it happened, were close friends of Ramusio's: Pietro Bembo, Pope Leo's former secretary; the poet Piero Valeriano, who, like Bembo and Ramusio, had worked for Aldus; and the historian Paolo Giovio.

According to one biographer, John Leo may have set up house in the neighborhood of Regola, farther down the river, near today's Campo de' Fiori, and even started a family.

His wanderlust soon put him on the road, though. He traveled south to Naples. He visited Viterbo, Cardinal Egidio's hometown, and may have gone as far north as Venice. But his most important sojourn outside Rome was in Bologna, the university town where Pietro Pomponazzi, a great Aristotelian philosopher, was still teaching and causing trouble, most notably by insisting that one could not prove the immortality of the soul. Alberto Pio was a patron of Pomponazzi—he had studied Aristotelian philosophy with him in Bologna—and he no doubt encouraged John Leo to seek the old man out. And Pomponazzi, who had a deep interest in geography, would have been thrilled by the opportunity to speak with John Leo about Africa. In Bologna John Leo also met Jacob Mantino, a physician and the most learned Jewish scholar in the city. The two ended up collaborating on an Arab-Hebrew-Latin dictionary.

John Leo was back in Rome in January 1524. His literary output was already notable. He had produced an Arab grammar and a treatise on Arab metrics, both in Latin, and a series of biographical sketches, *Some Illustrious Men Among the Arabs,* which was followed by *Some Illustrious Men Among the Jews,* also written in Latin.

Encouraged by his influential mentors, he began to work on the book that would secure his place in history: a description of Africa based on his many years of wide-ranging travel. He was by now sufficiently fluent in Italian that he chose to use the vernacular instead of Latin. Years later, as Ramusio went to print with the first edition of *Descrizione dell'Africa,* he wrote that John Leo had probably written the book in Arabic and then had translated it into Italian "as best he could," suggesting, ungenerously, that the prose was a little rough around the edges. John Leo's writing was in fact very accessible and fluid, and is still easy to read today. He had a remarkable command of the language, given the few years he had spent in Italy. And the traces of Spanish, Latin, Arab and, most of all, the rich Roman dialect he had picked up in his everyday conversations in Campo Marzio give a special flavor to his prose. It was not, in other words, the clumsy attempt of a foreigner trying to write in the local idiom. Although he may have been working, at least in part, from earlier notes in Arabic, he conceived *Descrizione dell'Africa* as a work in Italian for Italians. Describing the fruit orchards in Barbary, for example, he compared them to similar ones on the plains of Lombardy; the slate roofs in a village in Numidia reminded him of those he had seen in Fabriano, on his way to northern Italy; the minaret of the Kutubiyya Mosque in Marrakesh was as tall as the brick tower of the Asinelli in Bologna; the streets of Cairo during the yearly floods of the Nile brought to mind the canals in Venice.

Although nearly thirty years had passed since Vasco da Gama had rounded the Cape of Good Hope, John Leo's visual idea of Africa was still limited to a territory that went from Guinea, on the Atlantic coast, to the Nile and included today's Morocco and Western Sahara, Algeria, Tunisia, Libya, Egypt, Sudan, Chad, Niger, Mali, Mauritania and possibly Senegal—roughly speaking, the northern half of continental Africa.

That Africa, he divided into four parts: Barbary, in his eyes the noblest and richest region; Numidia, the land of date palms and shepherds; Libya, a vast and empty desert that stretched to the Nile; and to the south, the "Terra Negresca," the Land of the Black People, that went from the Gold Coast, along the river Niger, all the way to the Kingdom of Nubia.

His narrative—a mix of geography, history, natural sciences and colorful sketches—drifted effortlessly from west to east, which was the general direction of the journeys he had undertaken for the Sultan of Fez. His objective was to lay down an accurate verbal mapping of the Africa he knew. He duly indicated the distances between one town and the next, described the landscape, recorded the number of families that lived in each town and village he visited, listed the staples of the local economy, the type of artisans and tradesmen to be found there. He wrote down what people wore, what they ate, how they spent their time. The writing was never dull or arid.

In fact, John Leo was a natural travel writer who could draw the reader in with a single line. In the mountain village of Teglessa, he wrote, "the men are all traitors and killers, and the woods all around are full of wild boars." In Pietra Grossa, a small town built by the Romans, "lions come to the gates to eat the bones they find; everyone is so used to their presence that not even the children or the women are afraid." In Culeibat, a local tyrant who had caused the country's ruin was killed by his wife "when she caught him fornicating with one of his daughters."

He indulged in richer descriptions when he wrote about places he had been especially fond of, as in the case of Eitihad (or Aït Ayad in today's spelling), a charming Moroccan town on the southern slopes of the Atlas range, where he had stopped in 1515. Three hundred families lived there, he noted, mostly artisans and merchants; and there was a strong Jewish community. He'd stayed with a local priest in a small but beautiful temple. The sloping terrain brimmed with natural springs, and the rivulets joined to form a stream that kept the air cool and pleasant. Each house had a pretty garden with damascene roses and a generous vegetable plot. He remembered eating the most perfect grapes and the juiciest figs. Great walnut trees provided shade, and silvery olive groves shimmered in the background. Wheat grew plentiful in the fields below, and the women were "beautiful and pleasant, adorned with silver rings and bracelets."

A bucolic temperament colored his writing. He was drawn to the poetry of a man-made landscape: a fresh mountain stream rushing through a vegetable garden; a well-tended orchard of apple and pear trees against an olive grove; a terraced vineyard by an old stone house. He loved making lists of the vegetables (onions, eggplant, zucchini, peppers, melons and cucumbers) and fruits (dates, peaches, apricots, pomegranates, prunes and figs) that grew in each village. He quoted *The Treasure of Farmers,* a popular almanac that taught how to sow and plant properly, how to fertilize and prepare the earth. It was an Arabic translation of a very old Latin text. According to John Leo, many books originally written in Roman times no longer existed in Latin, but they survived in their Arab versions.

Leo lovingly described African women as they fetched water at the stream or gathered at the public baths at the end of the day, praising the fullness of their bodies, the richness of their clothes, the jangle of their silver jewels. In Eithiteb (Aït Attab in today's spelling) "the women have a light complexion and are plump and pleasant-looking; they wear many ornaments and their hair is very black and so are their eyes." The desert women, instead, wore "beautiful black chemises with wide sleeves, and over them a black or blue shawl which they wrap around themselves and secure to their shoulder with a silver buckle." They wore silver earrings, and many rings and ornaments around their anklebones.

John Leo was never a detached observer. He was moved by a landscape in the Atlas Mountains, the charm of a country village, the simple pleasure of a bowl of camel milk in the early morning in the desert. He described the feeling of *grande melanconia*—his words in Italian—that invariably took hold of him as he traveled across regions filled with ancient ruins of cities that once flourished and were now reduced to piles of rocks. He remembered weeping when he arrived in the coastal city of Anfa. Everyone had fled to Rabat after the first Portuguese raids at the end of the fourteenth century. "The houses, the shops, the temples were still standing but the vineyards and orchards had grown wild even though they were still heavy with fruit."

The idea that history shaped the geography of Africa pervaded his writings: Phoenicians, Carthaginians, Berbers, Romans, Goths, Arabs—all had left traces that were still visible to his discerning eye.

THE DOVES IN FEZ

The largest section of his book was devoted to Fez, the city where he had lived and worked for much of his life. "If I have indulged in such a long description," he explained, "it is out of convenience. For I find that the entire civilization of Barbary is largely contained in this worldly, pleasant and beautiful city."

He gave, indeed, a dazzling tour of that remarkable capital, offering generous descriptions of palaces and temples and government buildings, but also taking the reader inside typical private homes and even up the stairs, to terraced roofs with sweeping views, where most families kept a dole of doves "for the sheer pleasure of seeing them fly" in the sky over Fez. Like an enthusiastic guide enamored with his own city, he made stops at the public hospital where he had worked as a young accountant; at the hostel where foreigners stayed; at the largest dining hall, which he compared in size to one where he had dined at the Collegio degli Spagnoli in Bologna.

The street life, too, came alive as he showed the reader around colorful markets and the different quarters where cobblers, tailors, carpenters, barbers, tinkers, clothiers, goldsmiths and wine merchants plied their trade. Every street had a bookstore—there were thirty, he claimed—and every street corner a flower shop. He described the hammams scattered around the city and even gave opening hours!

John Leo must have been an elegant dresser, for he wrote with flair about the local fashion. Men of his station, he said, usually wore a short-sleeved habit over a comfortable undergarment made of foreign wool; and over the habit, a short loose gown, and then the typical North African cloak, or *burnous;* and finally a shawl, wrapped tightly under their beard. The traditional headgear was a simple woolen cap similar to those one saw in Italy, he noted, but without the ear covers. Older men wore their short gowns with wide sleeves, like the one he had seen worn by officials in Venice. Men of lower station did not wear a short gown under their *burnous;* poor people wore a simple garment "cut of coarse white wool."

He was equally detailed in telling his readers what the people in

Fez ate for breakfast (bread, fruit and a liquid porridge to which they added a slice of cured meat in the winter), lunch (bread and cured meat or cheese and olives) and dinner (bread and some melon or grapes, and in winter a plate of couscous, which he described as a type of pasta "in the shape of confetti").

The European reader, he warned, would find table manners in North Africa "vile and miserable." Food was served on the floor, and there were no tablecloths or napkins. "They eat their couscous with their hands, having no use for spoons or knives, and only help themselves with a piece of flat bread."

John Leo proudly described the school system—there were upward of two hundred madrassas in Fez. He introduced the reader to local ceremonies: weddings, circumcisions, funerals. And local festivities, including old Christian celebrations like Christmas, that had lived on after the rise of Islam (on Christmas Eve one ate a traditional soup made with seven vegetables).

Although tempted to overlook some of the seamier aspects of "the city where [I] was raised," he nevertheless felt compelled "to be truthful in every way." And so he launched into a fascinating tour of Fez's underbelly, "where men without facial hair dressed like women . . . and drunken criminals went whoring in wretched taverns." There were also deprecatory asides on unscrupulous soothsayers, shady cabalists and so-called holy men who were free to wander naked around the city.

Leaving Fez behind, John Leo traveled across the Atlas range. He described each mountain village along the way, remembering in particular "a little garden filled with damascene roses, violets, carnations and chamomile [where] the plash of a small fountain and a vine-covered pergola made a pleasant shade." It was, he wrote, "always so hard to leave."

Then it was on to the coast of Numidia, the land of date palms, and to the great city of Tunis, "where the people are fond of eating hashish, a substance that will make you laugh and rejoice and behave like a drunkard; it will triple your appetite and excite your libido in the extreme."

From Tunis it was on to Tripoli and from there into the "harsh and distressing" Libyan desert, where Leo used to encounter "shepherds as well as raging lions who devoured many sheep, and men as well." Tracks in the sand ran all the way south to the Land of the Black People, a vast territory that stretched from the Atlantic coast to the Sudan, following the Niger River. Caravans that traveled the desert routes stopped at the fortified oases controlled by Berber tribes. They transported fabrics, earthen and metal ware and horses, and brought back gold and slaves.

John Leo explained that, in his time, the Land of the Black People was divided into fifteen kingdoms. The largest of these was the Kingdom of Songhai, and the two most important cities were Gao and Timbuktu, which he visited on several occasions. The houses there were built of clay and had thatched roofs; those closest to the river Niger rested on pylons. He remembered seeing the occasional stone building—a temple, a royal palace—but these were built by European masons who had migrated south from Grenada.

East of Songhai was the Kingdom of Bornu, a center of the African slave trade. John Leo, who had himself been enslaved, blithely reported that one could easily get "15–20 slaves for a horse." East of Bornu was the Kingdom of Gaogà, which extended all the way to the Kingdom of Nubia, in southern Egypt.

These kingdoms in the Land of the Black People were all alike, John Leo claimed with a slightly superior tone, and he didn't want to bore the reader. Besides, he felt the natives were very primitive: "Men and women and children live and work together, tending to their flock—they hardly know how to grow wheat; at night they gather under one roof, ten to twelve, lying on beddings made of sheepskins. They don't travel; they don't wage war. They worship the Sun, and every morning they wake up and kneel and pray to the Sun God, and that is their faith."

From the Kingdom of Nubia Leo traveled down the Nile, completing the great African loop. In the last chapters of his book he offered vivid glimpses of life in Cairo and Alexandria; but I suspect Ramusio found these less interesting, as Venetians had known those two great cities well for three centuries.

"The author cannot recall more so he falls silent," John Leo wrote on March 10, 1526. He had written nearly 250,000 words, for a total of 950 pages.

THE SACK OF ROME

Although John Leo led a comfortable life in Rome, one suspects it was always his intention to return to Africa one day. We know very little about his last phase in Italy, but the traumatic events surrounding the Sack of Rome surely accelerated whatever timetable he might have had.

The struggle between France and Spain for control of Italy led to catastrophe. Pope Clement VII played the usual game of setting one foreign power against the other, until Emperor Charles V grew tired of his dillydallying. In early May 1527 Charles de Bourbon, a renegade French prince who had switched allegiance, marched south against Rome at the head of the imperial army: twenty thousand men, including eight hundred cavalry, five thousand Spanish soldiers and ten thousand Germans, the infamous Landsknecht.

De Bourbon set up camp at Monte Mario, the hill that looks down on the Vatican. On the morning of May 6, he ordered his men to force their way into the city at the Leonine Gate. But the Romans put up a fierce resistance, thinking (wrongly) that an anti-imperial force was on its way to help them. Suddenly a thick fog moved in where the battle was raging. Chaos ensued and the sheer numbers of the imperial army made the difference even as Charles de Bourbon was killed.

Pope Clement retreated to Castel Sant'Angelo, the round chocolate-colored fortress on the Tiber, with a defensive force of about a thousand men. The Spanish and German soldiers poured into the medieval Borgo near the Vatican and went on a vicious rampage, killing men, women and children indiscriminately and targeting priests. Once the Borgo was destroyed and the streets were piled high with dead bodies, crazed troops swarmed into Trastevere, where the merciless killing, the pillaging, the random destruction continued. The narrow streets were a stream of blood and mud. Then the imperial troops crossed the Tiber at Ponte Sisto; the Germans headed toward Campo de' Fiori, while the Spanish moved on to Piazza Navona.

The carnage lasted another five days. Then the fury abated like a spent force. The imperial soldiers settled in the city and turned to kidnapping and ransoming wealthy survivors. They stayed through the winter in a ghostly city now in the throes of famine and disease.

In that apocalyptic setting, a deal was finally brokered. The siege at Castel Sant'Angelo was lifted and on February 15 a bedraggled imperial army regrouped and headed south to Naples.

John Leo emerged miraculously alive from the ordeal. But death and desolation were all around him. It is easy to see why he would have chosen this time to slip away from Rome. We know nothing of his southward journey. But his ingenuity and his survival skills must have served him well, because it appears that he reached North Africa and settled there in his old age.

In 1532 John Leo's name appeared in a letter by his godfather Egidio da Viterbo, who was no doubt disappointed that his godson had returned to "the land of the Infidels" but who still remembered him fondly enough to suggest that a young Orientalist by the name of Johann Widmanstadt look John Leo up in Tunis, where he was thought to be living.

Widmanstadt sailed to Tunis, but a storm forced the ship to turn back, and so any remaining hope of tracking down John Leo dissolved.

His manuscript on his African travels, however, was not lost. In fact, at least two copies survived the Sack of Rome. Ramusio never revealed how he got his hands on one of the two manuscripts, only

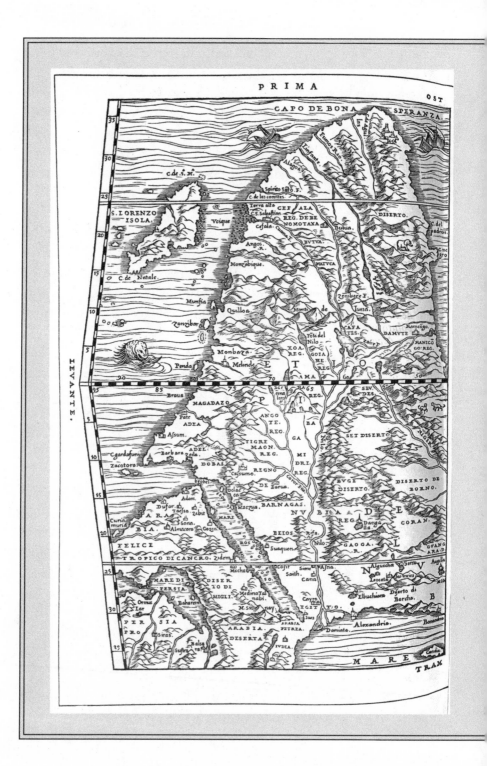

Full map of Africa by Giacomo Gastaldi for Ramusio,

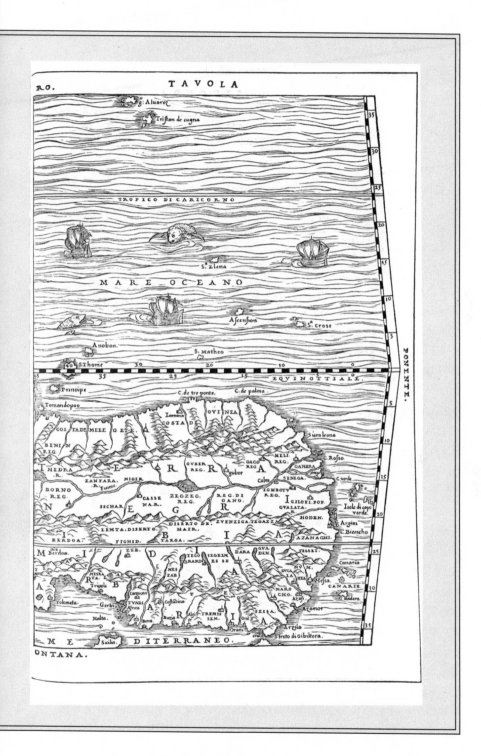

g: Aluarez

Tristan de cugna

TROPICO DI CARICORNO

S.ta Elena

MARE   OCEANO

Ascension

S. Crose

Anobon.

S. Matheo

S.t home   30.   20   10   0

35   35   25   15   EQUINOTTIALE.

Principe

C. de tre ponte.   C. de palma.

Fernandopoo

Lamina   OVINEA

COSTA DE

Siera leona

COSTA DE MELE G ETE.   MELI REG.   C. Rosso.

DININ REG.   GACO REG.   GAMBRA

I MEDRA   GUBER REG.   Aguber   SENEGA.   C. verde.

ZANFARA. R.   NIGIR   R. Tinne   Cabra   TOMBOTV REG.

BORNO REG.   CASSE NA R.   ZEGZEG. REG.   REG. DI GANO.   I GILOFI. POP.

ISCHAR   GVALATA.   Isole di cayo verde.

LEMTA. DISERTO.   MAIR.   DISERTO DE ZVENZIGA. TEGAZZA   HODEN.   Argim

BERDOA.   FIGHID.   TARGA.   AZANAGHI.   C. Biancho

M   Berdoa.   ZEB.   DARA   GVA DIN   TESSET.

RA L.   NES ZAB   DIEGO SEGELM ES SE   Canaria

Tripoli   B   DVCA   N.   CANARIE

Carnicon   MARO CHO.   T. Madera

Tolometa   TVNCE Africa   Costadura   Azomor

Gerbi   Buzia   ALAI TREMIE SEM.   TESSA   Argia

Malta.   Bona   Oran   Streto di Gibiltera.

M E   Sicilia   DITERRANEO.

PONENTE.

35 30 25 20 15 10 5 0 5 10 15 20 25 30 35

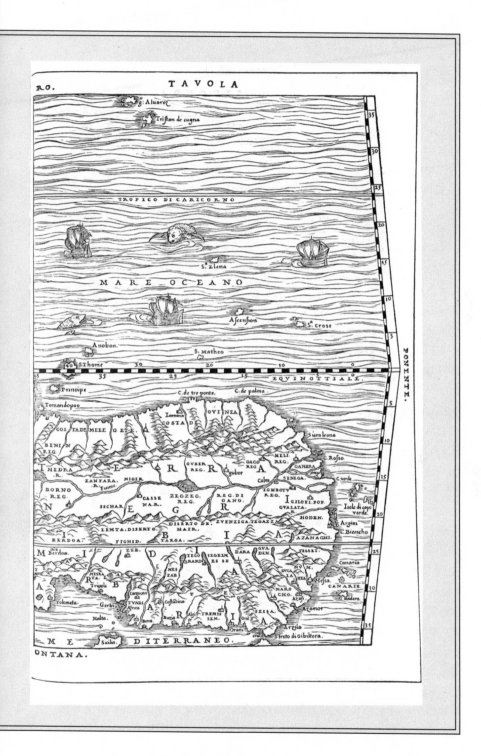

in Book One of *Navigationi et Viaggi* (1550)

saying, rather mysteriously, that it came to him "after a series of incidents it would take too long to describe."

Following the Sack of Rome, a number of intellectuals who belonged to John Leo's circle in Rome emigrated to Venice, all of them familiar with the African manuscript. Among them were the aforementioned historian Paolo Giovio, Leo's godfather Egidio da Viterbo, and the now former secretary of Pope Leo X, Pietro Bembo. They are the prime suspects behind the "series of incidents" that brought the manuscript to Venice and into Ramusio's hands.

Ramusio was quick to understand the historic value of John Leo's manuscript. "No other writer of our time," he noted, "has provided us with information about this part of Affrica [*sic*] with such abundance and clarity." This is what he was after for the collection he was now beginning to assemble: vivid accounts by reliable eyewitnesses that would gradually replace the false, often grotesque idea of Africa still rooted in the European imagination.

There is no evidence that John Leo ever met Ramusio. Separately, the two—a Muslim and a Christian—were developing a similar notion of what geography should be: not just maps and place-names but a more encompassing description of a territory that might include observations on local crops, on manufacture, on trade patterns, on systems of transportation, irrigation and communication, on the social and political organization of villages and towns, on religious practices.

Although they lived in an age when the struggle between Islam and Christianity was at its fiercest, John Leo and Ramusio seem to have shared the belief that the collection and dissemination of accurate, fact-based information, largely free of religious or political bias, could serve as the foundation of geographical knowledge. How easily the two of them—the writer and his future editor—would have engaged in fruitful dialogue. All the more so because Ramusio—despite the occasional dig at the prose—was surely receptive to John Leo's lyrical inclinations, delighting as much as his writer did in the fragrance of a rose garden in a mountain village or the warmth of a bowl of camel milk in the desert.

. . .

Another twenty years would go by before Ramusio was able to publish John Leo's manuscript and make it known to the public. But as he continued to gather material for a new geography of the world, his mind's eye could now behold a large swath of land across the African continent.

Absent from John Leo's description of Africa, however, was a vast, uncharted region south of Egypt and the Sudan, which he had apparently never visited: a mysterious Christian empire which Europeans generally referred to as Ethiopia.

CHAPTER FIVE

MEETING
PRESTER JOHN

I N THE AGE OF THE CRUSADES, EUROPEANS, FRIGHTENED BY THE ADVANCE OF ISLAMIC ARMIES IN THE EAST, SPUN a legend that proved so enduring that it shaped Western ideas about the geography of Asia and Africa for centuries. The legend was rooted in the story of the Magi, the three wise kings who came from the East, and grew around the notion that somewhere in the Eastern world lived a powerful Christian king who would one day come to the aid of Europe in the struggle against Islam.

The name of this legendary monarch was Prester John, "prester" being an old word for priest or presbyter (Prete Gianni, in Italian). As far as we know, the seeds of this story were first planted by one Patriarch John, head of the Christian Church of Saint Thomas in India, who visited Pope Calixtus II in Rome in 1122. Patriarch John described a mighty Christian state in which Pishon, the sacred river, flowed from Earthly Paradise. The capital of this state was Mylapore, where Saint Thomas's remains were preserved; it was so large a city, the patriarch claimed, that it took four days to walk around its perimeter.

Calixtus II was so impressed by what he heard that he implored Patriarch John to keep the information to himself while he was in Rome. But the Pope died and never got a chance to pursue an alliance with the powerful Christian king in the East.

Two decades later, another Christian emissary from the East, the Syrian bishop of Jabala, arrived in Rome bearing the woeful news that Edessa, the capital of a Crusader State and a Christian stronghold, had fallen to the Seljuks. The conquests of the First Crusade were now at risk. But all was not lost, the bishop assured Pope Eugenius III, because "one John, king and priest, who dwells in the East and is Christian but Nestorian," had defeated the Seljuks in a decisive battle near Samarkand and was coming to the aid of the Crusaders.

Perhaps the bishop was a little confused: the Seljuks had indeed been defeated—not by an imaginary Christian army but by an invading Mongol tribe from China. Not surprisingly, Prester John and his imaginary legions never came to the rescue of the Christian armies in the course of the disastrous Second Crusade (1147–1150).

But the legend of Prester John did not die. In fact, it surged back to life in 1165, when the Byzantine emperor Manuel Comnenus, the Holy Roman emperor Frederick Barbarossa and Pope Alexander III—the three most powerful men in Europe—received an extraordinary letter signed by none other than Prester John himself.

The letter—*Epistula Presbyterius Johannis*—described in glowing terms a fabulous empire located somewhere in India with glittering palaces and rivers of diamonds flowing from heaven. More important, the letter announced that Prester John was on his way to Jerusalem "determined to visit the sepulchre of our Lord with a very large army in accordance to the glory of our majesty."

The letter was a fake devised to promote a new crusade. But it was not considered a fake back then. It was copied and circulated widely, and the propaganda effect was widespread. Prester John loomed large again on the Eastern horizon.

The Pope decided to write back. He had heard that, though a Nestorian, Prester John was keen to embrace the Roman Catholic faith and to build an altar in the Church of the Holy Sepulchre in Jerusalem. So he encouraged him along that path, assuring him of his full support. Needless to say, the letter never reached its destination—papal emissaries wandered aimlessly in distant provinces for many years trying to deliver it. But it was leaked by the

Pope's entourage to publicize the new relationship between the Church and Prester John, its Christian ally in the East.

Yet Prester John again did not show up when the Third Crusade (1189–1192) and the Fourth Crusade (1202–1204) failed to recapture Jerusalem. By this time he was presumed long dead. Then, in 1221, as pressure for a fifth crusade was building up, Pope Honorius III received a letter from Jacques de Vitry, Bishop of Ptolemais, assuring him that David, an Indian king and a successor of Prester John, was on the march against the Infidel.

The only "king" attacking Islam at the time was the leader of the Mongolian tribes, Genghis Khan—hardly a Christian priest.

The picture was now more confused than ever. In 1253 King Louis IX of France sent out his own emissary, William of Rubruck, to establish contact with the Mongol tribes and see whether they had any connection with Prester John or his descendants. William's conclusion: whatever empire Prester John may have once controlled, it was now so reduced in influence as to be irrelevant.

A few years later, Marco Polo, the Venetian merchant and traveler, arrived on the Asian scene and went looking for traces of Prester John's Christian Empire in the great loop of the Yellow River. In the province of Tunduc, Polo found a man called George who claimed to be a descendant of Prester John. As we shall see later on, Polo came away unimpressed.

Prester John's days seemed numbered. But it wasn't the end of him yet: beginning in the fourteenth century and throughout the fifteenth century, as the campaign against Islam spread to Africa, the legend was reconfigured. His empire was no longer thought to be in India or in Central Asia, but in Ethiopia, a vast and vaguely defined territory south of Egypt which, according to the latest geography, occupied most of the southern part of the African continent. Europeans, so it was thought, had been looking for Prester John in the wrong place. It all made more sense now: Ethiopia, after all, had converted to Christianity as early as the fourth century.

· · ·

Portugal, the rising European sea power of the Renaissance, now led the chase for the elusive Christian king. In 1487 King João II sent an envoy, Pedro da Covilhã, to look for ways to open a new commercial route to the Spice Islands in order to break the Venetian monopoly in the Mediterranean (this was a decade before Vasco da Gama rounded the Cape of Good Hope). Da Covilhã's secret mission, though, was to make contact with Prester John's descendants in Ethiopia and forge a strategic alliance that would contain the expanding Muslim world. After a seven-year journey that took him across the Mediterranean, to Egypt, India, Madagascar and the Arabian Desert, da Covilhã finally reached the coast of Ethiopia and presented his credentials to the Negus, the Emperor, the man all the courts of Europe now referred to as Prester John.

The Negus never granted da Covilhã leave to return to his homeland, and King João II, who had grown obsessive in his quest for Prester John, died without knowing that his trusted envoy had found him at last. Years later, thanks to his closeness to the Ethiopian queen mother Elena, da Covilhã persuaded the new Negus to establish relations with Portugal by sending an envoy, Father Matthew, to King João's successor, Manuel I.

After a grueling journey from the horn of Africa to the Iberian peninsula, Father Matthew, the Ethiopian ambassador, reached Lisbon in February 1514. It is hard to exaggerate the impact this visit had on the young Portuguese king and his court: Father Matthew had traveled all the way from Ethiopia bearing letters in Persian, Arabic and Portuguese signed by the Negus. In the eyes of the Portuguese, this was the first true contact ever established between a European power and the legendary Prester John.

Father Matthew was received with great pomp at the court of Manuel I. It is worth noting that in the crowd of dignitaries that day was a twelve-year-old page, Damião de Góis, who was to play a crucial role in revealing the mystery of Prester John to Ramusio years later.

Manuel I sent Father Matthew back to Ethiopia with a Portuguese delegation headed by Odoardo Galvão, a diplomat and humanist.

The key figure in the group, however, turned out to be Father Francisco Álvares, a priest with a reporter's talent who ended up writing a fascinating description of the Portuguese journey to the court of Prester John.

Galvão and his men sailed around Africa and across the Arabian Sea to southern India, then headed north to the Red Sea. But on the way, Galvão contracted a fever and died in Kamaran, an island off the coast of Yemen. The mission could not proceed until a new ambassador arrived from Lisbon, and so the convoy backtracked to the Portuguese port of Cochin in southern India and waited.

It took several years for the new envoy, Rodrigo de Lima, to join the delegation, which proceeded at last to its final destination. Diogo Lopes de Sequeira, the naval commandant of the Portuguese colony in India, led a small fleet to the Red Sea, reaching the port of Massawa, on the coast of today's Eritrea, on April 9, 1520, Easter Monday.

The town was empty. The natives had fled to the mountains like they always did when Ottoman ships arrived. But when they heard the newcomers were Christians, they returned to welcome them and presented them with a gift of four oxen. The next day, seven monks from Saint Michael's, a monastery in the mountains twenty miles away, arrived to celebrate a Christian reunion that had been long in the making.

THE ROAD TO AXUM

Ethiopia was one of the oldest Christian nations, but the spread of Islam in the Middle East and North Africa had cut it off from the rest of the Christian world. Over time the Ethiopian Church developed autochthonous beliefs and rituals. It remained anchored to the faith in Jesus Christ but, unlike the Roman Catholic and Eastern Orthodox churches, believed in the union of his divine and human natures.

"This is truly a Christian land," Father Francisco observed as the jubilant monks surrounded the newcomers. The natives carried a small, simple wooden cross. All the Portuguese now wanted one too.

On the third day, the Barnagasso, the regional governor, appeared in Massawa at the head of two hundred horsemen and two thousand foot soldiers. He came in peace, and gave permission to the foreign party to head into the country to deliver their embassy to the Negus.

At this point the Portuguese delegation, headed by de Lima, comprised fourteen men, including the ambassador's deputy, a secretary, an interpreter, an organ player, a painter, a doctor, two servants and Father Francisco, who proved from the start to be not just a keen reporter, but a wise and level-headed observer, the only member of the delegation who would earn the trust of his companions as well as of the Ethiopians. Father Matthew, the returning Ethiopian envoy, was also part of the group, together with three assistants.

The presents for the Negus that had originally been brought from Portugal—fabrics, clothes, useless crockery and trunks full of Latin primers—had long been abandoned in Cochin in favor of a new set of more valuable gifts: a finely wrought sword, a gold dagger, a precious breastplate, a gold helmet, four rolls of fine Portuguese fabric, two muskets with munitions, a globe and an organ for church music.

The Barnagasso provided mules and camels for transport, and the traveling party was on its way into a vast terra incognita, with no real sense of where it was headed. The only one who was vaguely familiar with the terrain, Father Matthew, led the exotic caravan straight to Saint Michael's, the old monastery in the mountains.

There was about the place the melancholy feeling of a community not so much abandoned as quietly going to seed. The church, with high vaulted ceilings and a wide nave, was impressive, and the monastery and surrounding compound were solidly built. Yet the walls had long started to crumble. The orange and lemon trees, the vine-covered pergola, the old fig trees that had once made an agreeable garden now grew wild and untended.

The monks themselves looked haggard and dried up "like old wood." They fasted much of the year and subsisted on a meager diet of millet and honey. It was a pity, Father Francisco noted, "as the soil around here seems rich enough. But they don't do much with it."

Not everything was done according to canon. Instead of the traditional host, the monks took communion with a local focaccia. Religious chants resembled "shouting matches." Lamps were fueled with butter oil, and the blood of Christ was drunk from a rough copper cup instead of a silver chalice. Still, it was moving to experience the deep religious fervor that permeated this very old Christian outpost.

Father Matthew fell ill and died a few weeks after they reached the monastery. Now the Portuguese felt truly stranded as they headed back down the mountains and out into the highlands. The Negus did not have a fixed court; at a moment's notice he lifted camp and moved on with his royal cortège. So Ambassador de Lima's caravan traveled south from village to village with no clear destination, as if drawn from afar by the yet invisible Negus into his net.

The Ethiopian highlands were rich in deep, earthy colors. The soil was fertile, the fields neatly plowed and planted with millet, barley, chickpeas and lentils. Food was plentiful everywhere the Portuguese stopped for the night. They organized shooting parties to enrich their diet with meats. Birds were easy prey as the natives didn't shoot them.

The caravan managed an average of ten to twelve miles a day. Then the rainy season started, in mid-June, and the men were slowed down by frequent downpours.

One day an envoy of the Negus appeared out of nowhere on his mule. "The king sends his greetings," he announced, and hurried off.

Over several weeks the caravan crossed a vast plateau, then made its way into a hilly, verdant landscape. Quite suddenly the Portuguese came upon the remains of the great city of Axum, the capital of the once mighty Axumite Empire (fourth century B.C. to tenth century A.D.).

The name itself had an aura of legend. It was from Axum that the Queen of Sheba started her pilgrimage to Jerusalem in the time of King Solomon, with two camels loaded with gold. And it was in Axum that an Ethiopian queen later converted to Christianity.

The travelers stopped to admire the great Church of Saint Mary of Zion, built in the fourth century A.D. and said to have once held the Ark of the Covenant. The five vaulted naves, the terraced roof, the preciously inlaid pavement, the frescoed walls and its seven side chapels—all were still relatively intact. The church was destroyed twenty years later by the marauding troops of Sultan Ahmad al-Ghazi, a powerful Muslim conqueror, and was later rebuilt. Father Francisco's detailed description is the only one we have of the church as it was up until the early sixteenth century.

Saint Mary of Zion was flanked by two solid stone buildings that housed the monks and priests and their elders. Ethiopian emperors were crowned in the court facing the church facade, and Father Francisco duly noted the row of thrones carved in stone that had been used in the past and which were now partly crumbling. A big old sycamore in the center of the court shaded the entire compound. "I feel Prester John has deliberately sent us this way so that we could see these buildings," the priest mused.

The surrounding landscape was a jumble of old stone houses and towers. A few roughly hewn obelisks were still standing here and there but most of the taller ones lay broken and scattered in the fields. None of the natives could decipher the writing that was finely carved into the dark gray weather-beaten stone.

Beyond the ruins of the old city were new villages and well-tended vegetable plots. When the rain stopped and the skies cleared, men and women and even children from the villages came out to look for gold, poking the ground and upturning clumps of earth with a stick. Remembering the gold diggers he had seen at work in Spain in his youth, Father Francisco secured a wooden board and started to wash down clumps of earth looking for golden sparkles. He saw none, and soon concluded that perhaps he wasn't "doing things right."

LALIBELA

The meandering journey in search of Prester John continued into the region of Amhara. In September the convoy reached Lalibela, a town so deeply impregnated by religious faith that there seemed to be more churches than houses—churches of all sizes: large with high vaulted ceilings and multiple naves, or small and compact, but all solidly built and decorated with exquisite carvings.

The soft round hills in the background enhanced the simple grandeur of the town.

The Church of Our Savior, with its five naves separated by long rows of columns, was especially impressive. "No matter what angle one looks from," Father Francisco noted, "it appears to be made all

LA CHIESA DI SAN SALVATORE

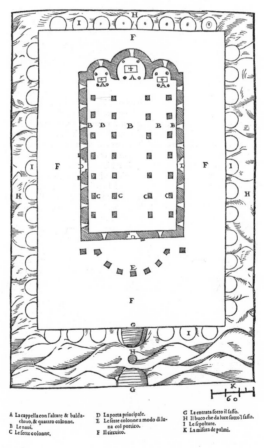

A La cappella con l'altare & balda-chino, & quattro colonne.
B Le naui.
C Le sette colonne.
D La porta principale.
E Le sette colonne a modo di luna col portico.
F Il circuito.
G La entrata sotto il sasso.
H Il buco che da luce sotto'l sasso.
I Le sepolture.
K La misura de palmi.

The floor plan of the Church of Our Savior in Lalibela,
as provided by Father Francisco Álvares and later published
by Ramusio in *Navigationi et Viaggi,* Book One

of one piece." The most astonishing sight, though, were the compact miniature churches carved directly into slabs of dark rock. "I had to go back twice to take careful notes," he wrote, "so strong was my desire that these excellent buildings be known to the world."

The caravan pressed forward across rolling green hills with wide-open views. The tired Portuguese—they had been on the road for close to six months—were not always welcome. In one village they were even stoned away by the suspicious inhabitants. And if they did not reach a village or a monastery before sunset, they had to camp out in the wild, staying up all night to protect themselves and their beasts of burden from the attacks of predators. But on the whole the caravan proceeded with surprisingly few accidents, greeted in most places by curious stares.

In one village, the local chief, eager to test Father Francisco's Christian credentials, quizzed him relentlessly before letting them pass through. "Where was Christ born?" "Where did he turn water into wine?" And then, "What road did he take to reach Egypt?"—clearly a trick question. The wary priest answered every query correctly, and the chief declared him to be a very wise and learned man, and kissed his face. Whereupon the priests in attendance threw themselves to the ground to kiss Father Francisco's feet.

A few days later—it was the middle of September—the road passed by a heavily guarded fortress. The Portuguese asked who lived in the castle. They were told that this was the place where the sons and nephews and grandchildren of the Negus were kept in custody so they would not threaten the throne. Those who tried to escape met a terrible end. The last to do so was the uncle of the Negus, who had his eyes carved out.

They hurried along.

Toward the end of September they reached the reedy shores of Lake Hayk, where they saw their first hippos. After months of boiled millet and lentils, they happily gorged on the local fish. "It had the face of a toad but it was the meatiest fish in the world," raved Father Francisco.

After several more days of travel, on October 8, they finally rejoiced at the sight of the royal camp shimmering in the distance. They had been on the road since April, and more than once they had wondered whether they would ever reach their destination. Or ever return home, for that matter.

The master of the royal house came out to greet them when they were still a few miles from their destination; he ordered them to set up camp right there where they were and to await instructions.

KING DAVID

They bivouacked for three days. On the fourth, they were finally summoned to court. Ambassador de Lima could not find his donkey—it had disappeared during the night—but he urged his companions to move along. He'd catch up with them soon enough.

Up close, the royal camp was quite a sight. A bright red pavilion on a riser was surrounded by a sea of tents. Four chained lions guarded the entrance. The Portuguese were led past the lions, through the main portal and into a vast courtyard crowded with royal guards. Nothing much happened for a long time. Finally an elderly priest wearing a white cloak came out:

"What brings you foreigners here?" he asked.

"We bring an embassy from the King of Portugal" came the reply.

The priest went back in and came back out three times. Then:

"Say what you wish and I shall refer to the king."

"We bring presents for His Majesty."

A royal messenger appeared on horseback, dismounted and asked the Portuguese, who were struggling with the confusing protocol, to get off their donkeys to receive the king's query:

"What presents have you brought?"

Father Francisco read the list of items, and the messenger, apparently satisfied, guided them beyond the courtyard to a great circle surrounded by a high hedge. Inside the circle there were many large tents, and beyond the tents stood the royal house, the Sagala: a long-house with a thatched roof.

Suddenly there was great commotion in the royal entourage: it had transpired that the Portuguese ambassador was not with the group.

"He is on his way," Father Francisco assured.

"Then you must pitch a tent and go no farther until he arrives," the messenger replied.

In the evening Ambassador de Lima trotted up on his donkey. Still, there was no royal summoning for several days. Eventually the Portuguese were told that their tent was in the wrong place and they would have to move it. Ambassador de Lima, a more short-tempered man than the ultra-patient Father Francisco, replied they had pitched it where they had been told to pitch it, and anyway they no longer had a crew with them to do the job.

A local crew was sent and the tent was moved.

It turned out the king wasn't in the longhouse after all, for on the last day of October they saw a cortège come down from the hills. A message came: the king had not looked at his presents yet but wanted to know whether the Portuguese had brought gold and silver crosses. Alas they had not: only wooden crosses.

The mood turned glum but the next day a surprise visit by Pedro da Covilhã, the envoy who had come to Ethiopia thirty years before looking for Prester John, lifted their spirits. Now an old man, da Covilhã was so moved to find himself in the company of his countrymen that everyone cried with happiness.

Then, one night, after being ordered to put on their official uniforms, the Portuguese were led into the inner sanctum. The king sat hidden behind a set of curtains. Nothing happened. After a while they were sent back to their tent.

Two days later, a new summons at midnight. Again, the king remained hidden behind curtains, but this time he initiated a tentative dialogue through his interpreter.

"Who is more cowardly," he asked, "the Moors or the Portuguese?"

"We are so well armed by our faith in Jesus Christ that we are not afraid of the Moors," the ever quick Father Francisco replied.

The king said he appreciated the presents but he would have liked to have more muskets and gunpowder. He admired the gold sword and asked for a fencing demonstration, which Jorge de Abreu, the best fencer in the delegation, was happy to provide. Next the king asked Emanuel de Mares, the organist, to play, and then he ordered everyone to dance. It was very late when they were sent back to their tent, but things looked promising now.

Father Francisco was summoned alone the next time, and told to come dressed as if to serve mass. From behind the curtain, the Negus asked the priest to explain what each part of the vestment symbolized. Then came a barrage of questions:

"Why were there two Christian churches, one in Rome and one in Constantinople?"

"How many bishops were there in the Roman Church?"

"Were priests allowed to marry in Portugal?"

"Did the apostles marry?"

"How many books did Saint Paul write?"

"How many prophets knew of the coming of Christ?"

The grilling went on into the night. Father Francisco answered patiently according to the views of the Roman Church. "You are true Christians," the Negus declared, putting an end to the interview. "You know about the Passion of Christ."

On November 19 the full delegation was led before the Negus. This time the curtains were lifted and suddenly there he was, sitting in his throne on a riser: a young man in his early twenties with a round face, big eyes, an aquiline nose and a sparse silky beard. He was of average height, his complexion light brown, "the color of a chestnut." He had a tall gold crown on his head and held a cross made of silver. A stole of blue taffeta covered half his face, and he wore a cloak of rich golden brocade over a silk shirt with large sleeves.

The legendary Prester John was alive and well. His real name was Lebda Dengel, son of Na'od; but he preferred to be known as King

David. Europeans, however, continued to call him Prester John for many years more.

The notion that King David would prove a powerful ally in the struggle against Islam faded fast. If anything, it was the Negus who now hoped the Portuguese would protect him from Muslim armies in the north and along the coast. In the ensuing discussions, he granted the Portuguese permission to build forts at Massawa and the Strait of Hormuz, and promised "men, horses, archers and supplies" if they sent a war fleet to protect his empire, adding that he would join the fight "in person." He appointed Father Zagazabo, a trusted cleric who had once traveled to Europe, as his ambassador to Portugal.

Once official letters of intent were written and signed, the Portuguese were eager to get started on the long journey home. But the Negus kept delaying permission to leave, and they began to fear that they would suffer the fate of da Covilhã. Meanwhile, they were forced to follow the court around the country.

Months passed, then years. On one occasion the Negus granted them leave to go, but when they reached the port of Massawa, the Portuguese ships that were to pick them up had come and gone.

Fortunately, Father Francisco diligently took notes during their peregrinations across the various regions of the Empire, from the border with the Muslim sultanate of Mogadishu up to Lake Tana, the source of the Blue Nile. In addition to vivid descriptions of the Ethiopian landscape, he drew up lists of trees and flowers, and birds and wild beasts; he wrote about the religious customs, the justice system, the royal court, the agricultural system, the social habits, even the regional diets. And whenever he came upon a church he liked, he took the time to sketch the floor plan to scale.

On April 27, 1526, six years after reaching Ethiopia, Ambassador de Lima and the rest of his men were picked up by a five-ship Portuguese fleet in the port of Massawa. They sailed down the Red Sea, stopping briefly at the island of Kamaran, off the Yemenite coast, where Father Francisco dug out the remains of Odoardo Galvão, the first ambassador, who had died on the way out to Ethiopia, to bring them back to Portugal. They then crossed the Arabian Sea to the coast of India and touched at the Portuguese ports of Goa, Cannanore and finally Cochin, where they loaded pepper and cloves, and set sail for Lisbon in January 1527.

They reached the Portuguese coast seven months later. A plague outbreak in Lisbon forced them to disembark farther north and then to travel overland to Coimbra, the ancient capital, where the new young king, João III, had moved the court temporarily.

Zagazabo, the Ethiopian envoy, presented his credentials to King João III and delivered a personal letter from young King David in which the Ethiopian monarch lamented the long isolation of his country. The Muslims were not his friends, he explained. "They only pretend to be so they can come here and sell their merchandise. But I get very little out of this relationship for they are greedy and they take all the gold. I don't fight them because I am afraid they will retaliate by destroying the Church of the Sacred Sepulchre in Jerusalem. I am very sorry for this state of affairs but what else can I do if no Christian king will come to my aid?"

It made no sense to him that the Christian kings of Europe squabbled and made war against one another. "You should band together! If I had a Christian king as a neighbor I would not part from him even for an hour." But if King João should ever decide to send his fleet to defend Christian Ethiopia, he would find a steadfast and resourceful ally in him, for he had "as many men and as much gold and supplies as there are grains of sand in the ocean and stars in the sky."

Meanwhile, he could use some immediate assistance. He asked for military advisers and weapons (swords and muskets); architects to design churches and good painters to decorate them; and specialized artisans, including wood carvers, goldsmiths and silversmiths, tile makers and printers.

"Please, help me," he wrote at the end of his letter.

The irony was not lost on the Portuguese. They had sought out the elusive Prester John hoping to find a powerful ally that would help them wrest control of the Red Sea from the Mamluks, who ruled the Arab world. Instead, they had found a weak monarch with a very long shopping list.

King David was left to fend for himself. In 1531, the aforementioned Sultan Ahmad al-Ghazi launched his Somali troops on a jihad. Ethiopia was ransacked. King David took refuge in the mountains and he died in 1540 in the monastery of Debre Damo.

Father Francisco went to work on his copious notes. The task ended up absorbing him for several years, but in the end he produced a long and detailed and immensely valuable description of his travels in Ethiopia. It had none of the self-aggrandizing prose or the exasperated exoticism of many travel narratives of the period. Father Francisco saw himself very much as a diligent reporter doing his job rather than the protagonist of a dramatic adventure. "I have described the events that occurred, the regions we traveled through, the qualities of the natives, their customs, their adherence to the principles of Christianity, without approving or criticizing their ways but leaving it to the reader to judge as he sees fit." He also vouched for the authenticity of his work at a time when false information circulated widely. "Those things that I have seen, I report as having seen, and those heard as heard," he assured, "and I swear upon my soul that I have not written a single lie—to lie to the reader is tantamount to lying to God."

In 1533, five years after his return, he was allowed to travel to Bologna to deliver King David's letter of submission to Pope Clement VII. On that occasion, he presented the Pope with a manuscript copy of his book on Ethiopia. News about the precious travelogue spread fast in humanistic circles in Italy and soon reached Ramusio, who was now eager to get a manuscript copy himself through his Portuguese connections.

Damião de Góis, whom we left when he was a pageboy at the court of King Manuel I, had grown up to become a highly regarded scholar in Lisbon. King João III sent him as his personal envoy to

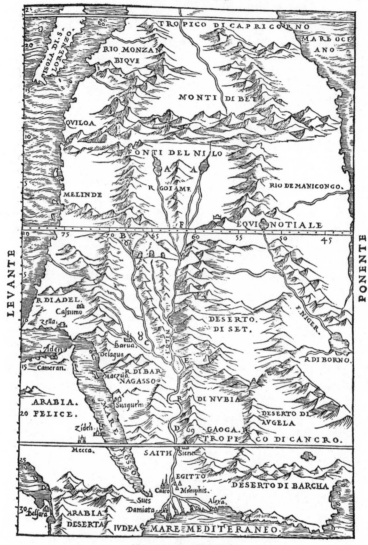

MEZZO DI

TRAMONTANA.

A.	Li fonti del Nilo	D.	Cancro
B.	Ariete	E.	La metà di Leon
C.	La metà di Tauro	F.	Libra

Viaggi.

Map of the Nile basin by Giacomo Gastaldi, with Egypt
and Ethiopia in the foreground, first published by Ramusio
in Book One of *Navigationi et Viaggi*

Antwerp, where he widened his network of intellectual friends across Europe. The king recalled him to Lisbon in 1533, in time for de Góis to meet Father Francisco before the priest left on his mission to Bologna, and to obtain from him a copy of the manuscript on Ethiopia.

The following year de Góis traveled to Padua to pursue his humanistic studies and was soon drawn into Ramusio's circle of friends. He must have been carrying the manuscript with him, because Ramusio says that he received his copy directly from de Góis.

Ramusio was overwhelmed by what he read. "Neither the Greeks nor the Latins nor anyone else had written anything worth our consideration about Ethiopia. Now Don Francisco Álvares has opened up that country and made it plain for us to see. Hope to God that we will one day know as much about many parts of the world we still know so little about as we now know about Ethiopia thanks to the writings of this man."

Trade, Ramusio always emphasized, was a function of geographical knowledge. Ethiopia, long neglected by Europeans, was strategically positioned between Egypt and the Arabian Sea, and in his view offered the possibility of easy access to India and the spice routes. "Trading with Prester John," he mused, perhaps getting a little carried away, "appears to be no less promising than the possibilities created by Signor Christopher Columbus's discovery."

CHAPTER SIX

INDIAN
JOURNEYS

IN THE LATE AUTUMN OF 1508 A SWASHBUCKLING ADVEN-
TURER BY THE NAME OF LUDOVICO DI VARTHEMA ARRIVED
in Venice to deliver a lecture at the Doge's Palace on his seven-
year journey to India and the legendary Spice Islands.

Varthema's presentation drew a lot of attention. Ten years had
gone by since Vasco da Gama had sailed around the Cape of Good
Hope, reaching the western coast of India and opening up a route
that broke Venice's monopoly on the spice trade in the Mediterranean. But the Portuguese were very secretive about what they
had found in India and how they were fortifying their presence in
the region. Official reports eluded even the most capable Venetian
diplomats. Here at last was an opportunity to hear a private citizen
give an eyewitness account of a vast area about which Venice still
knew very little.

For over two hundred years Venetian merchants had imported
spices, gems and precious fabrics from India and the string of
islands that form present-day Indonesia, thanks to caravans that had
threaded their way overland from the Indian Ocean to the Mediterranean. The spice trade in particular had long been at the heart of
Venice's commercial empire. The pungent aroma of cardamom, pepper, nutmeg, cloves, cinnamon and the many other exotic roots and

herbs that were sold at the Rialto had come to define the city's very identity. Yet India itself, not to mention the islands of the Indonesian archipelago, remained a blur in the mind of Venetians—a place of exotic tales and fabulous riches.

Early reports from the Portuguese reinforced that image. In one of the few documents that reached Venice after da Gama's breakthrough journey (and which soon found its way into Ramusio's collection of papers), an anonymous scribe painted this arresting picture of the Zamorin, the Hindu monarch in Calicut:

"His ears were pierced by little gold bars studded with rubies and diamonds, from which dangled two pearls the size of walnuts, one round and one in the shape of a pear. He wore golden bracelets, also studded with gemstones and pearls, around his upper arms and his calves, and a shining red ruby ring on one of his toes; the rings on his fingers were rubies, emeralds and diamonds—one as big as a lima bean. He was naked from the waist up and wore two belts of solid gold, covered with rubies. He sat on a silver throne which had two gold armrests, and the backrest was studded with gemstones and pearls."

Ramusio had only just returned from his diplomatic mission to France with Ambassador Alvise Mocenigo when Varthema came to town. He was still, at age twenty-three, in the very early years of his career in government. But Varthema's story left an indelible impression on him and is worth telling here in some detail.

Varthema himself was a compelling figure. He started out in life as a soldier. Inspired by da Gama's historic voyage, he quit the bloody battlefields of northern Italy and left his native Bologna "to explore a small portion of this earthly globe of ours," as he put it, "mindful that things seen are ten times as valuable as things heard."

Starting out in Venice, he sailed to Alexandria and traveled across the land of the Mamluks, stopping in Cairo, Beirut, Aleppo and Damascus—cities that were familiar to Venetian tradesmen, who had well-established commercial stations there.

In Damascus, Varthema did what Christian travelers did: he visited Saint Paul's prison cell and the house where Cain allegedly killed his brother Abel. He found the city to be so easy and pleasant that he decided to stay several months to improve his Arabic. Once he felt he was more or less fluent, he joined a caravan headed to Medina and Mecca disguised as a Muslim pilgrim by the name of Yunus—a fake identity he ended up keeping during most of his time in the East.

Mecca he found stifling: "I never saw such a crowded place." It wasn't just the heat and the number of people. "Nothing grows there—no grass, no trees, no fruit, nothing—and everything needs to be brought in from Cairo." But the pilgrim industry thrived. "Some go for penance, others for business," he quipped.

In the port of Jedda, Varthema found passage on a ship that dropped him off in Aden. His cover was nearly blown when he was accused of being a Portuguese spy and thrown into jail. The Sultan's wife, who had taken a shine to him, got him out of jail and "covered [him] with over a hundred kisses." Apparently, he resisted her charms, "knowing well what would have happened" if her husband had discovered the ruse.

Free again, he explored Yemen and Oman, then sailed from Muscat to Hormuz. He planned a journey across Persia, and on to the fabled city of Samarkand in Central Asia. But Persia was in the grips of civil war—Shah Ismail el-Sufi was fighting the Sunni Ottomans to impose the Shia faith—so he abandoned his plan. Meanwhile, in Shiraz, he ran into a merchant he had met at Mecca, a certain Cazazionor. Together they went north to Herat, in present-day Afghanistan, where the merchant lived with his family. Cazazionor forced Varthema to marry his beautiful niece. "Her name was Shams, which means sun ray. I pretended to be very happy but my mind was elsewhere."

The two companions were soon on the road again, eventually making their way back to Hormuz, where they found passage to India on a merchant ship.

Varthema and Cazazionor landed in Cambay, a rich trading city filled with ships and merchants from Persia, Tartary, Syria, the Barbary Coast, Arabia, Ethiopia. They traveled across the state of Gujarat and then down the coast to the cities of Goa, Mangalore, Calicut, Cannanore and Cochin.

Everywhere the atmosphere was increasingly tense. The arrival of the Portuguese on the western coast of India had disrupted the uneasy coexistence of the old Hindu kingdoms with the sultanates established by the Muslims. And as the Portuguese imposed their presence with force, the inevitable friction often led to deadly clashes between Christians and Muslims.

The two traveling companions had no particular destination. They followed the natural flow of circumstance, moving along from one great port to another, buying and selling merchandise to raise enough money to continue their journey. Like Varthema, Cazazionor traveled "for [his] pleasure, to see and learn more things."

They continued south to Coromandel, at the tip of India, found a passage to Ceylon and from there sailed on a junk across the Sea of Bengal to the powerful Hanthawaddy Kingdom in lower Burma. In Pegu, the capital, they were welcomed by King Binnya Ran, "a very humane and accessible monarch." And generous: he paid two hundred rubies for some coral Varthema and his friend had been trying to unload since leaving Ceylon.

Their vests lined with gemstones, they sailed down the Malay Peninsula to the fortified port of Malacca, which was ruled by a sultan the Portuguese were about to dethrone. They continued on to Sumatra, where the finest pepper was so plentiful it sold "like fodder back home." Joining a group of Christian merchants, they rented another junk and sailed eastward to the Moluccan Islands— Varthema was the first European to describe a nutmeg bush.

On the way back to India, they stopped in Borneo to look for camphor trees. On Java, where they spent five days bargaining for emeralds and silks, they heard with alarm that "there are men on this island who eat human flesh." It was apparently quite customary for a family to auction off a grandparent or an old uncle when they got in the way; the winning bidder would take the poor man home, kill him and cook him in a stew. The same treatment was reserved for young members of the family who were sickly and not much use. "Why leave this good flesh to the worms," Varthema was reportedly told when he inquired about this gruesome custom.

KILLINGS IN CALICUT

He and Cazazionor took leave of their Christian friends and sailed back to Calicut, on the western coast of India, where Varthema ran into Pietrantonio and Giovanmaria, two jewelers from Milan. They had arrived with Vasco da Gama a few years earlier to buy gemstones for King Manuel of Portugal and had stayed on, making a handsome living building pieces of artillery for the Zamorin, the local ruler. They went about town dressed like the natives, naked from the waist up, with only a wraparound cloth and sandals.

Overwhelmed by the emotion of running into two compatriots, Varthema revealed his true identity to them: he was not, as he was still letting on, a Muslim by the name of Yunus. He was Ludovico di Varthema from Bologna! The three of them "hugged and kissed and cried a lot."

The time had come to shake the hapless Cazazionor loose. Unwilling to tell him the truth—and to discuss the delicate matter of his "wife" in Herat—Varthema said he needed to be alone: he wanted to become a Muslim holy man and wished to retire to a mosque.

With Cazazionor out of the way, Varthema abandoned all pretense and resumed his true identity. But the aggressive policies of the Portuguese meant life in Calicut was no longer safe for European Christians. Even his new friends Pietrantonio and Giovanmaria could no longer count on the Zamorin's protection from the Muslims.

Varthema escaped north to Cannanore, where he sought refuge in a newly built Portuguese fort. He pleaded in vain for an expeditionary force to go fetch the two Milanese and bring them to safety:

he later learned that after weeks of clashes with the Portuguese, a mob of angry Muslims had marched to their house, captured them and slit their throats.

Giovanmaria's wife, a Hindu, managed to flee with her young son to Cannanore. Varthema paid eight ducats to purchase the little boy, had him baptized and named him Lorenzo for Lourenço de Almeida, son of the new Portuguese viceroy, Francisco de Almeida. The child died a year later of syphilis, a disease that had arrived in India a decade earlier carried by merchant ships from Europe.

Varthema's experience as a former man-at-arms turned out to be very valuable to the Portuguese in their struggle against the Muslims for control of the Indian coastline. He joined a fleet assembled by Lourenço de Almeida and distinguished himself in a bloody but victorious naval battle. His reward was a lucrative job in Cochin as the agent of European investors in India.

A year and a half later he was finally ready to go home—his Eastern jaunt was now in its seventh year. The Portuguese viceroy granted his request to take leave on the condition that he stay on for one more military engagement. The Portuguese obtained another victory at Ponnani, and Varthema was knighted on the battlefield. His godfather on that occasion was none other than Tristão da Cunha, the great Portuguese navigator, with whom he hitched a ride to Portugal.

Once back in Europe, Varthema wrote an account of his travels, which he hoped to publish in Rome, under the auspices of Pope Julius II. It was on his way there from Lisbon that he decided to make a detour to Venice, the city where he had started his journey to the East. The stopover was well worth it. The audience at the Doge's Palace listened to his enthralling presentation "in a state of stupor," according to one chronicler who was present. Varthema pocketed a generous fee of twenty-five ducats and headed on to Rome, where he finally got his story into print.

Itinerario offered a vivid picture of the Hindu kingdoms, caught

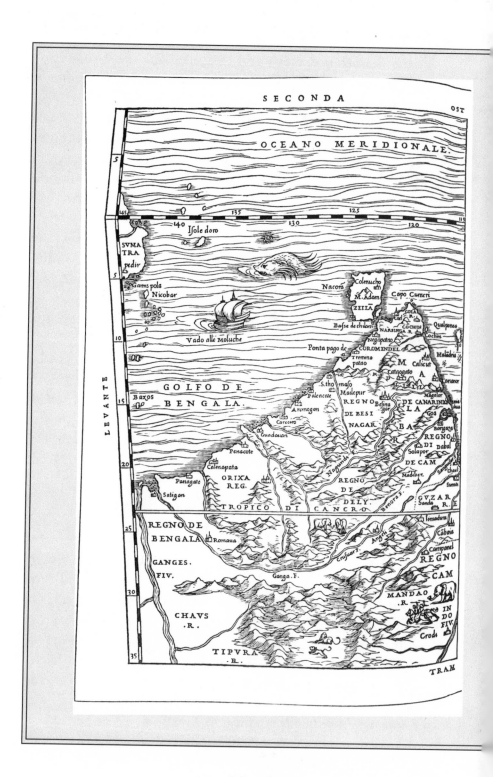

OCEANO MERIDIONALE.

SVMA
TRA
pedir

Ifole doro

Garms pola
Nicobar

Vado alle Moluche

GOLFO DE
BENGALA.

Baxos

Nacom

Colmucho

M. Adam

ZEILA

Baſſe de chilom

Ponta pago de

S.tho

Palcacote

Aremogan

Carecoro

Guadauan

Penecote

Calmapata

Panagate

Satigan

ORIXA
REG.

TROPICO DI CANCRO

Capo Cumeri

COLA

Cael
R.

NARSINGA R.

COCHIN

ochin

Qualpenes

Negapatno

COROMENDEL

Tremna
patao

Catnogato

maſo

Maslepir

REGNO

DE BESI

NAGAR

Magalor
Goa
Bangaza

REGNO
DI Dabal
Solapor

DE CAM

Madiber.

M Calicut

A

Cananor

DE CANARINII
LA
BA
R

GVZAR
Sanda R.

Chaul

Sumh

Maladria

Besma
gar

Napunda

REGNO
DE
DELY

Benora

REGNO DE
BENGALA
Romana

GANGES.
FIV.

Ganga. F.

Angik

Crisua 2.

Immadura

Cabaia

Compane

REGNO
CAM
MANDAO
.R.
IN
DO
FIV.
Crod.

CHAVS
.R.

TIPVRA
.R.

LEVANTE

Map of the Indian subcontinent by Giacomo Gastaldi,

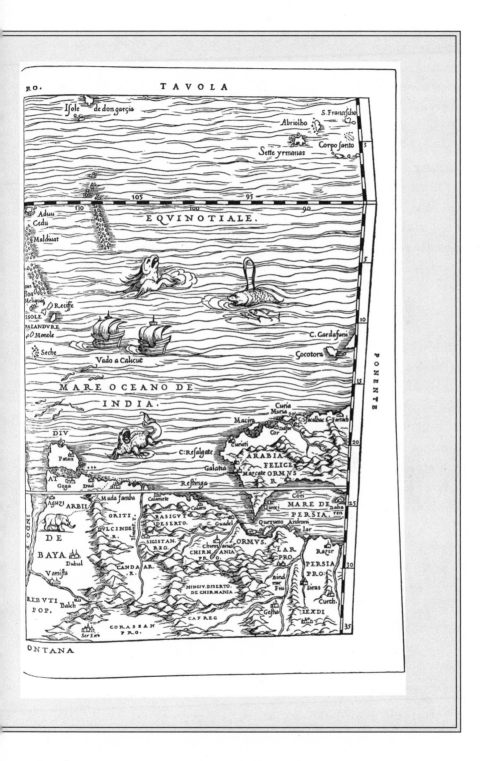

first published by Ramusio in Book One of *Navigationi et Viaggi*

between the arrival of the bellicose Portuguese and the imminent invasion of the Moghuls from the north. Varthema's observations about social and political mores came with colorful vignettes of everyday life and delightful digressions on how to train an elephant or the special qualities of mangoes. And all the while he was "on the road," gradually unveiling a world Europeans knew very little about.

"I have sought brevity so as not to bore the reader," the author declared in the early pages. Written in Italian vernacular and enlivened with dialogue in Arabic, the book was indeed breezy, well paced and, compared to the more plodding reports of official scribes, thoroughly entertaining. It was Renaissance travel writing at its best.

Itinerario sold well across Europe. Humanist Arcangelo Madrignani translated the book from the Italian into Latin. That version, in turn, was translated into Spanish and published in Seville. Ramusio obtained an early copy of the Spanish edition,* which he translated back into Italian because, he claimed, all the other editions were saturated "with errors and mistaken corrections." But he did not shy away from some heavy edits himself, deleting most of the expressions and dialogues in Arabic, which was what had given the book much of its flavor. Whether he did so for the sake of clarity or to avoid stirring the Inquisition into action, he didn't say.

Ramusio soon added a rare manuscript to his growing collection of travel narratives about India. The author was Duarte Barbosa, an enterprising official who had joined the second Portuguese expedition to India in 1500, led by Pedro Álvares Cabral.

Instead of returning with Cabral to Portugal, Barbosa settled in India to build a future for himself as a trader. He ended up staying fifteen years. He never became a rich merchant—he worked mostly

---

* Possibly from Andrea Navagero (see Chapter Seven). In his own writings, Ramusio used the Spanish spelling of the author's name, "Lodovico Barthema."

as a scribe and translator in Portuguese stations along the coast. But he traveled across India and came to know the territory as perhaps no other European did at the time.

Barbosa was a natural reporter who enjoyed interviewing men and women from different walks of life and different religions "about the ways and the customs of the country." He traveled to the major cities along the western coast—Cambay, Goa, Calicut, Cannanore and Cochin—and across the independent kingdoms of Gujarat, Bijapur and Decam, mapping out the territory. He had an easy, accessible style, whether he was writing about the Indian caste system, or describing the brick houses and lively villages in the countryside, or musing on the age-old tradition of chewing betel leaves, or explaining why black rice grown in the south was "better and healthier than white rice."

Barbosa eventually returned to Portugal, in 1517, carrying a full draft of a book. But he never saw it in print because his life, already so unusual, took an entirely unexpected turn.

While he was in India, his family had fallen out of favor with King Manuel of Portugal and so had moved to Seville. There, Barbosa's sister Beatriz had married another Portuguese exile, Ferdinand Magellan, who immediately enlisted his new brother-in-law in his ambitious effort to find a western passage to the Spice Islands. And so, after half a lifetime spent in India, Barbosa now embarked on a journey around the world.

The rest of the story we know thanks to Pigafetta. After the failed mutiny against Magellan at San Julián, on the South American coast, Barbosa was given command of the ship *Victoria*, which he held until he too was killed in the Philippines.

THE CABOT AFFAIR

In the vast and complex and wealthy world that Varthema and Barbosa brought to life so vividly, Venice was clearly not a player; from the moment da Gama opened a Portuguese route to the Spice

Islands, its far-flung commercial empire became dangerously vulnerable. And as the Portuguese consolidated their presence along the coast of East Africa and in all the major port cities of western India, Venetian merchants, who still depended on overland caravans to bring goods to the Mediterranean, seemed bound to lose whatever competitive advantage they still had.

Venice made an early effort to counter Portuguese expansion by reviving an idea that had long circulated at the Chancery: to build a canal from Port Said to Port Suez, connecting the Mediterranean Sea to the Red Sea and creating a shortcut to the Indian Ocean. In the spring of 1504 the Council sent a special envoy, Francesco Teldi, to convince the Mamluk sultan of Cairo that the Venetians could build a canal "quickly and easily"—and at their own expense. A fort at the two entrances of the canal would guarantee the Sultan control over what ships were allowed to pass. But as far as the Venetians were concerned, the objective was clear: "to allow as many [Venetian] ships and galleys through the canal as were necessary to block, obstruct and chase the Portuguese away."

Teldi fell ill and was replaced by Bernardino Giova, another seasoned merchant who was well connected to the Mamluk establishment. But the early instructions were canceled and the whole enterprise was eventually dropped. The Sultan was under pressure from the rising Atlantic powers not to give in to the Venetians, and he may have signaled his unwillingness to greenlight the project. Another possible explanation for the sudden change of heart is that, in the rush to find a way out of its predicament, the Republic had wildly underestimated the size and expense of the project.

A few years later, the news that Magellan had opened a western route to the Spice Islands—this time for Spain—was received with a sense of impending doom. In the end, the journey via the Pacific proved too long and costly to be competitive with the eastern route of the Portuguese; and in any case Spain was more interested in developing the new colonies overseas than financing risky expeditions around the globe. But as the world was opening up, Venice felt locked out by Portugal and Spain, the two rising sea powers.

With options running out, the Republic made one more attempt to break loose.

Even before the *Victoria*'s return to Seville with its bedraggled crew of survivors, the Council of Ten had secretly been in touch with Sebastian Cabot about the prospect of sending a Venetian fleet in search of its own route to the Spice Islands. Now it accelerated those talks, and Ramusio, at this point a thirty-seven-year-old seasoned official, was brought in to shepherd the process.

Sebastian was the eldest son of John Cabot, the Venetian navigator who had reached Newfoundland in 1497 while looking for China in the service of the King of England, Henry VII. Now a pilot major in Spain, Sebastian dreamed of finding the northwest route to the Orient that had eluded his father. But interest in a northwest passage was slack at the court of Emperor Charles V. So he offered his services to Venice. For love of the old country, he said.

His emissary, one Girolamo Bucignolo, was short on details when he arrived in Venice. Cabot would come in person to map out the voyage, he assured, but the Chancery needed to summon him on some pretext or other that would not raise the suspicions of the Spanish government.

Gasparo Contarini, the Venetian ambassador in Spain, was hastily instructed to arrange a secret meeting with Cabot "to see what he has in mind." Attached to the instructions was a letter pretending to summon Cabot to Venice to resolve matters related to the recovery of his mother's dowry.

Contarini was a capable and prudent diplomat, a humanist who had come late to public service after years of religious and philosophical studies. He viewed Cabot's plan with skepticism, but he dutifully invited him over for their first private talk on Christmas Eve of 1522. According to the ambassador's report, the interview did not go well. The plan seemed vague to him, and when he pressed Cabot for details, the pilot major insisted he would reveal them only in person to the Council of Ten once he got to Venice.

He wasn't going to force him to reveal his plans, Contarini replied, a little irritated. But he knew "a thing or two about geography," and given Venice's position on the map, he frankly couldn't see how such a voyage was feasible.

"If we build the ships in Venice they would have to sail through the Strait of Gibraltar to reach the ocean and both the King of Spain and the King of Portugal would prevent that," Contarini argued. Of course, one could build the ships outside the Mediterranean, possibly in the Red Sea; but then the enterprise would be at the mercy of the Ottomans. Besides, there was no guarantee they would obtain a sufficient supply of timber. And even if they did obtain it, how could their ships make their way safely to the Atlantic, given that Portuguese fortresses were everywhere in the Indian Ocean?

The only other possibility, the ambassador continued, was to build the ships in the Baltic Sea. But since Germany had declared allegiance to Emperor Charles V, that option was now also off the table. And in any case, there was no practical way of getting Venetian goods to the Baltic and spices back down to Venice.

"Still," the ambassador told Cabot, "you are the expert and I will defer to your judgment."

Cabot insisted that he knew "an easy way" of doing things: he'd navigated among those northern countries as a young man and was very familiar with them. He claimed to have turned down an offer from the King of England for the sake of his fatherland. He added, ominously, that if ever he chose to sail for England and found a northwest passage to the Spice Islands, there would be no other route left available to Venice.

"I shrugged at his words," the ambassador wrote at the end of his report. "To me the whole thing seems impossible." But he did not stop Cabot from going to Venice, and handed him the fake letter of summons prepared by the Chancery.

By the spring of 1523, Cabot was set to leave; but he requested a new letter of summons as too much time had elapsed and the first one felt stale. The new letter arrived in the summer of 1523. "He claims he will shortly ask leave of the Emperor to come to Venice," the weary ambassador reported. "The man assures me he can think of nothing else."

Months passed and Cabot did not ask leave. In fact, he was soon back at sea on orders from the Emperor to see if Magellan's route to the Spice Islands could not be completed more speedily after all.

That expedition turned into a fiasco, and Cabot's star dimmed. But it was not the last of his dealings with Venice—or with Ramusio.

CHAPTER SEVEN

NAVAGERO'S EMBASSY

IN THE SPRING OF 1524, RAMUSIO MARRIED FRANCESCHINA NAVAGERO, A DISTANT COUSIN ON HIS MOTHER'S SIDE. HE was nearly forty and Franceschina was in her twenties. Despite the age difference, it was a happy marriage troubled only by the difficulty of producing an heir.

Although Ramusio worked late hours at the Doge's Palace and frequently stayed over in Venice, he and Franceschina kept their home in Padua, in the large family house in via del Patriarcato that was filling with paintings and drawings and sculptures, as well as a notable collection of inscribed Roman marbles.

Ramusio finally fixed up the old farmhouse an hour outside Padua that he had inherited from his father. Villa Ramusia was now a simple but elegant two-story country house with a clean facade and a portico. The living quarters were on the first floor, the granary on the top floor. A courtyard separated the main residence from the barn and the animal shelters. All around were vineyards, orchards and vegetable gardens. The Valsugana, the old Roman road that linked Padua to the Alps and which was still an important thoroughfare for merchants traveling north, ran along the property.

Ramusio escaped to the country whenever he could. Not that he had much time for relaxation once he got there: the villa was a working farm, with extensive fields of wheat and corn that ran toward the hills north of Padua, and he was a hands-on landowner. He kept close track of the year-round farming activities, looked for ways to increase the yield of his crops and liked to experiment with new agricultural techniques. He kept his accounts in good order and went out of his way to fetch the highest prices for his goods at the fairs and markets.

He was also a keen gardener, and he liked to improve the surroundings by planting trees and laurel hedges and rosebushes. A collector of bulbs and seeds, he tried out new plant varieties in the flower beds or in the vegetable garden and the fruit orchards neatly laid out behind the house. He was among the first landowners in the region to plant corn brought over by the Spaniards from the New Indies and each year he set aside more acreage for the new crop, which seemed to have found its ideal habitat on the Venetian mainland.

Ramusio was usually in residence at Villa Ramusia during the summer. Old friends from Aldus's shop, like Bembo and Navagero, often visited, and they spent their time in happy, wide-ranging discussions about literary and philosophical matters, the natural sciences and geography. The latest member of what they called their "friendly and sweet academy" was Girolamo Fracastoro, the scientist in the group.

At the time, Fracastoro, an expert on infectious diseases, was focusing his attention on syphilis, a new illness that was wreaking havoc in Europe and was believed to have been brought over from the New Indies by Columbus's returning crewmen and later spread to Italy by French soldiers. It was Fracastoro who gave the disease its name, in a poem he wrote about its ravages—*Syphilis sive morbus gallico:* Syphilis, or the French Disease.

Although Ramusio thrived in the bucolic surroundings of Villa Ramusia, his job kept him firmly anchored in Venice, where he continued to gain respect and prestige as a high official in the Senate. In

1522 he was promoted to secretary general and his yearly salary was increased to ninety-four gold ducats.

The election in 1523 of the new Doge, Andrea Gritti—the popular hero who had saved the Republic in extremis in 1509 by recapturing the city of Padua—ushered in a period of prosperity and renewed confidence in the future. The arts flourished—Titian and Tintoretto, to name only two artists, were both painting in Venice at the time. The publishing industry thrived in an atmosphere of tolerance and intellectual vibrancy. The city itself was an open construction site, and the new architecture of the Venetian Renaissance found expression not just in the palaces that were replacing medieval buildings along the Grand Canal but in a sweeping urban renewal—*renovatio urbis* was the Latin buzzword of those years.

The shift from a maritime economy to a mainland economy was well underway, but sea trade was still a crucially important part of Venetian life, and as we have seen the Republic was struggling to hold on to its commercial empire after the opening of oceanic routes—this was the time of the secret negotiations with Sebastian Cabot to find a Venetian route to the Spice Islands. The Portuguese had already dealt a serious blow to Venice by breaking its monopoly over the spice trade; now the threat seemed to be coming from Spain. But what were the Spaniards really up to? What had they found overseas? Information coming out of Spain was scarce and unreliable. Thirty years after Columbus's first journey across the Atlantic, it was still hard to separate fact from fiction. In Venice some were convinced the Spaniards were spreading tall tales. "They are so bombastic," one senator declared, "that I am quite sure there is much less over there than what they claim."

There was, of course, quite a bit more. But in the early 1520s, the Spaniards themselves were still relatively clueless about the size and shape of the landmass they would soon take over.

Hispaniola (now the Dominican Republic and Haiti), the island Columbus had reached in 1492 on the first of his four crossings, and which was now governed by his son Diego Colón, remained the most significant Spanish colony in America. Spain had also subju-

Map of Hispaniola by Giacomo Gastaldi, first published
by Ramusio in 1556 in *Navigationi et Viaggi,* Book Three

gated and was in the process of colonizing the islands that we know
today as Cuba, Jamaica and Puerto Rico.

Vasco Núñez de Balboa, the first European to see the Southern
Sea, as the Pacific was known before Magellan, had established
a small colony in Darién, on the Central American isthmus, in
1513. The isthmus was seen as a crucial part of Spain's expansion
overseas—a possible gateway to the Pacific and trade with China,
the Malay Peninsula and the Spice Islands. But every attempt to
find a navigable strait somewhere along the narrow strip of land
had failed.

While the isthmus and the major islands of the Caribbean Sea
were fairly well mapped out, and Spanish ships sailed regularly into
what was now familiar territory, the mainland beyond that limited
area was still a terra incognita for Europeans. Juan Ponce de León,
the governor of Puerto Rico, had touched Florida to the north in
1513 but had not explored the region; a second landing in 1521 had
been repelled by the native population. To the south, the mainland's
northern coastline (today's Venezuela and Colombia) was known by

Spanish mariners, but no settlement had survived and the interior remained unexplored. Amerigo Vespucci, the Florentine navigator whose Christian name was used in 1507 by the German mapmaker Martin Waldseemüller to name the landmass, had sailed down the coastline to present-day Brazil. But while Vespucci's journey (1501–1502) was crucial in providing a sense of scale—he was the first to use the term "New World" (Latin *Mundus Novus*) in writing—still nothing was known of the interior, nor where this mysterious continent ended.

The latest news to reach Venice was about Hernán Cortés's encounter with the Mexica (Aztec). This was plainly not just another contact with natives whose culture the Spaniards considered primitive, as had been the case on the islands of the Caribbean Sea. As one astonished chronicler at the court of Charles V reported, "[The explorers] have found cities in which the subjects actually live according to the law, trade goods and walk around wearing clothes." Two of Cortés's emissaries brought back sophisticated artifacts and precious jewels that were put on display in Seville as evidence of a newfound civilization. Charles V took them with him when he traveled to Germany and England, impressing the courts in Europe with his small portable museum.

Still, the conquest of the Mexica Empire was a work in progress, and the shape and size of those territories was still extremely vague. Indeed, the Spaniards were still struggling to map not just the land of the Mexica but the mainland surrounding the entire Caribbean basin. And the relatively scarce information they had was jealously guarded by the Crown. Ramusio, faced with the great puzzle of the so-called New World, had been able to set only a very few pieces into place: the major islands of the Caribbean and parts of the isthmus and the Yucatán. So he was delighted when Andrea Navagero was named ambassador to Spain in the fall of 1523. It was a golden opportunity to gain a better sense of what the Spaniards had actually found on the other side of the Atlantic. With his best friend on his way to the court of Emperor Charles V, he looked forward to having his own trusted source of information.

LIBRARY FINES

Navagero was a surprising choice for such an important ambassa-dorship: patricians were expected to rise gradually up the ranks of government, whereas Andrea, at the age of forty, had never run for office before. But his peers held him in such esteem that, when he bid for the post in Spain, his candidacy quickly garnered a large majority in the Senate.

Bembo, alumnus-in-chief of Aldus's old publishing house, was quick to congratulate him for the honor of representing Venice at the court "of the greatest Prince the Christian world has had in a very long time." To be given this opportunity "at your first shot," he added, "is a sure sign of even greater things to come."

Navagero had been inducted into the Maggior Consiglio when he was only twenty years old—five years younger than the normal age at which a patrician joined the great assembly of the Venetian Republic. Many had bet on a rapid and successful career in govern-ment. But Navagero had put his love for Pindar and the classics first, spending far more time editing ancient Greek and Latin manuscripts in Aldus's shop than schmoozing at the Ducal Palace.

When the League of Cambrai had declared war against Venice, Navagero had gone off to be a soldier in the army of Bartolomeo d'Alviano, the charismatic general who led the Venetian resurgence after the crushing defeat of Agnadello.

General d'Alviano was close to Aldus's circle—he was a good client and was said to take his precious Aldine editions to the war front. He admired Navagero's literary talent as much as his valor in the field, and he soon took him under his wing. After d'Alviano was killed during the siege of Brescia in 1515, the whole of Ven-ice mourned him, and his protégé gave a stirring funeral oration in which he compared the general to the mythical warriors of antiquity.

D'Alviano continued to influence Navagero's life even after his death. The general died a rich man, and he bequeathed to Venice the funds for a public library that was to house the unique collection of Greek and Latin manuscripts assembled by the humanist Cardinal Bessarion. Before dying, d'Alviano had let it be known that he wanted Navagero to manage the collection. Not only did the Senate oblige; it also named Navagero the Official Historian of the Republic. The double job came with a combined income of two hundred ducats a year—no small sum for a poet-scholar who was always short of money.

The only portrait we have of Navagero was painted by Raphael in 1516. As the new director of the Bessarion library, Navagero saw himself as a roving ambassador of humanism. His first move was to travel to Rome to establish cultural ties with the entourage of the recently elected Pope Leo X, who was surrounding himself with some of the brightest intellectual stars of the period.

Bembo, the reader will remember, had left the court of Urbino to become a close aide to the new pontiff. Another migrant from Urbino was Baldassare Castiglione, who was at work on his masterpiece, *The Courtier*. Both had become close to Raphael, a native of Urbino, who had recently settled in Rome and was dazzling the city with his art.

Navagero traveled to Rome with friend and fellow humanist Agostino Beazzano. They stayed at the house of Castiglione, who guided them around the city. Official meetings were handled by Bembo, who had easy access to Pope Leo's entourage. Navagero discovered that his new position with the Bessarion collection carried great cachet in Rome's humanistic circles.

An avid sightseer, he wore down poor Castiglione with a thousand queries. He visited the ancient ruins that dotted the Roman countryside. And he insisted that his friends in Rome—Bembo, Castiglione, Beazzano and Raphael—accompany him on an excursion to Tivoli to see Hadrian's Villa, one of the most impressive sites of Ancient Rome (though at the time it was still thought to be the country residence of Emperor Augustus).

Before returning to Venice, Navagero sat for Raphael with his friend Beazzano for a rare double portrait which now hangs in the picture gallery at Palazzo Doria Pamphilj in Rome. It shows a big hairy man with a ruddy face, unkempt beard and mustache, deep lines beneath his dark green eyes and furrows down his cheeks (he is thirty-three in the picture but looks older). He is wearing a black turban-like hat and a black velvet gown. His brow is shiny and the curls on his neck glisten—he is sweating slightly. The impression is that he has just now turned his fiery gaze to the viewer as if caught, literally, in the heat of a conversation. Beazzano, with whom he is having that conversation, looks pale and delicate by comparison; with his bulging eyes, his pointed chin and his bobbed hairstyle, he embodies the humanist of the bookworm variety. Next to him, Navagero looks positively Homeric, a poet-warrior from antiquity.

The library Navagero was hired to run did not yet exist, but the books and manuscripts that were to serve as the initial nucleus—including more than a thousand priceless Greek and Latin codices—lay crammed into forty-eight crates, gathering mildew in a dank storage room at the Ducal Palace.

Cardinal Bessarion had brought the collection to Italy after the fall of Byzantium and had later donated it to the Venetian Republic with the proviso that it be used to create a public library for the study and dissemination of Greek and Latin culture.

The construction of the library was postponed while the Republic was consumed by its policy of expansion on the mainland, and then by war against the League of Cambrai. General d'Alviano had wanted to give Bessarion's collection a dignified home, but his death had slowed things down further; work on the grand building designed by Francesco Sansovino—the Biblioteca Marciana—would not start for another twenty years.

Still, Navagero had plenty on his hands as he tried to organize the distribution of books. The main problem: readers rarely returned what they borrowed. Precious volumes soon found their way into private libraries or on the stalls of booksellers around Saint Mark's

Square, often with Cardinal Bessarion's own annotations scribbled in the margins!

It was not a promising start. The fact that no one even knew the exact content of the crates did not help. So Navagero reorganized and indexed the entire collection with the help of Ramusio, who worked upstairs in the Senate chambers and came down when his day job was over. Meanwhile, they put in place a punitive system of fines that has been, in varying forms, the bane of university students and researchers ever since. Ramusio took on the unpleasant task of collecting the money. Thanks to Bembo, they also obtained a brief of excommunication from Pope Leo X for those who did not return books.

Unsurprisingly, books and manuscripts started to reappear, and gradually the library began to function in a more orderly fashion. It was still a makeshift operation, but at least Bessarion's treasure was finally receiving proper attention.

The work at the library left Navagero with little time for his second job—writing an official history of the Republic. There were grumblings in the Senate. "We pay him handsomely," one senator griped. "And what has he done so far?" But when Doge Loredan died in 1521, Navagero delivered a funeral oration so widely praised that his standing as one of Venice's preeminent men of letters was never higher.

Three years later, the ambassadorship to Spain was practically his for the asking.

Navagero was replacing Gasparo Contarini, the veteran diplomat who had conducted the fruitless negotiation with Sebastian Cabot two years before. The balance of power in Europe was now shifting in favor of Spain. Charles V was vying for control of the rich plains of northern Italy. The Venetian Republic wanted to contain Spain's growing influence in the region and protect its own possessions in the northeastern part of mainland Italy. To this end, it agreed in July 1523 to a peace treaty with Spain that awaited ratification. Navagero's brief was to get the peace treaty approved and carry forth a policy that satisfied Spain without alienating France, Venice's traditional ally.

Navagero promised Ramusio that, in addition to his official duties, he would use his time in Spain to do some serious
intelligence-gathering about the new Spanish territories overseas.
The two struck a deal. In exchange for regular reports by Navagero,
Ramusio would run the Bessarion collection for him and take care
of Navagero's topiary garden on the island of Murano.

Navagero left clear instructions: he wanted a grove of trees
planted, and a new laurel hedge, and a row of cypresses and more
rosebushes. "There is nothing I care more about," he said, "than to
have [the garden in Murano] well planted by the time I return."

LUSH GARDENS AND MYRTLE HEDGES

Navagero's departure turned out to be a drawn-out affair. He and
Lorenzo Priuli, the junior member of the two-man delegation, were
hesitant to leave. Spain and France were on the path to war over
northern Italy and traveling was complicated. Furthermore, the
plague was spreading in Genoa, the port city from which they were
supposed to sail to Barcelona. But after three months, Gritti, the
new Doge, became impatient and told Navagero and Priuli to leave,
lest they be stripped of their appointment.

They were finally off in July 1524, traveling to Padua, Vicenza,
Verona and Mantua, carefully sidestepping plague-ridden enclaves.
In Parma, Priuli was stricken by a severe illness—whether it was the
plague or tertian fever is unclear, but he was bedridden for three
months. Navagero went ahead on his own, to Livorno instead of
Genoa, where the plague was decimating the population. But in
Livorno he could not find a passage to Spain: the few shipowners
who were making the crossing were asking exorbitant prices because
war now seemed imminent (one captain asked for eight hundred
ducats!). He remained stuck there during the months of October,
November and December. Meanwhile, Priuli recovered and joined
Navagero in Livorno.

In February 1525, Francis I crossed the Alps at the head of the
French army, invaded the Po valley and seized Milan from the out-

numbered imperial forces. The Venetian government quickly dispatched new orders to Navagero and Priuli: they were to slow down and wait for the final outcome of the hostilities before heading to Spain.

Charles V was not about to give up control of northern Italy to the French. The imperial army, beefed up by a contingent of twelve thousand German-speaking mercenaries, crushed the French army at the Battle of Pavia on February 24, 1525. During the fighting, Francis I was thrown off his horse. Charles de Lannoy, commander of the imperial army, found him on the ground, took him prisoner and sent him off to Spain.

The imperial forces regained control of Milan and the rest of northern Italy. Navagero and Priuli were now instructed to accelerate their mission to Spain, to get the peace treaty ratified but also to plead for the liberation of the French king. By April the plague around Genoa subsided and the two envoys finally sailed to Barcelona with their secretary Giovanni Negro, two servants and three horses.

They very nearly didn't make it across. The sea was so stormy, Navagero later wrote to Ramusio, that the heavy cog was "tossed about like a gondola." During the perilous crossing "even our very experienced mariners lost all hope of survival." He described seamen on their knees in the whipping spray imploring a few trembling friars to take their confession. "I had always thought *montes aquarum* [mountains of water] was meant as a poetical image but it describes exactly what I saw."

Navagero's best horse died during the crossing, and the other two could hardly stand when they landed north of Barcelona. "We were half dead ourselves . . . [eager] to embrace land and leave the sea behind us."

Back in Venice, Ramusio was relieved to read that his friend Navagero was alive and well, if a little shaky. He immediately informed Bembo. "Thank God he survived the storm," Bembo replied. "In the end this peregrination across Spain will serve him well because he will finally learn to appreciate the man he is."

. . .

Barcelona, evenly spread out along the shore against the high hills of Collserola, was a welcome surprise: fine-looking stone houses, richly adorned churches and "lush gardens with myrtle hedges and orange and citron groves." Navagero absorbed his new surroundings with Ramusio always in mind. He diligently reported place-names to his friend back in Venice, and distances and geographical markers. At every opportunity, he drew connections with the geography of the Ancients. Wasn't the broad low hill that overlooked the harbor, which the locals called Mongivi, the Mons Jovis—Mount Jupiter—which Pomponius Mela, the great Spanish geographer of the first century A.D., mentioned in his *Chorographia*?

The Catalans, although subjects of the Spanish Crown, had managed to preserve a form of self-government that allowed them to run their country pretty much as they pleased, Navagero noted. They also had considerable trade advantages and could levy all sorts of taxes on visiting foreigners—including ambassadors! "They have obtained so many privileges that the [Emperor] can hardly be said to rule at all here," he wrote to Ramusio. "When the Court comes to Barcelona, the local government charges dishonestly high rental fees on all the houses taken up by the imperial retinue; so whatever taxes the Catalans pay come straight back into their pockets every time the Emperor comes to town."

Charles V and his itinerant court were in Toledo, in the heart of Spain. Navagero and Priuli secured fresh horses and transport mules "at huge expense" and set off on a four-week journey to their destination. The small party traveled on dusty tracks and rocky trails across an impervious terrain under a scorching sun. They stopped a few days in beautiful Zaragoza, on the banks of the Ebro, then headed on to Guadalajara, Alcalá and Madrid, and then south until they finally came in sight of glistening Toledo, clamped to a rock over the Tagus and surrounded by dry, harsh mountains.

The two Venetians were made to wait three weeks outside the city walls before they were allowed to make their official entry. Eventually a delegation led by Diego Colón, governor of Hispaniola and the son of Christopher Columbus, rode out to greet them. At the time, Colón was under investigation for tax fraud by the Council of the Indies and he had returned to Spain to press his case at court, where he knew he had the favor of the Emperor.

Navagero was thrilled to be welcomed by the son of the legendary Admiral of the Ocean Sea. And he was especially happy to recognize, behind Colón, two very familiar faces: Gasparo Contarini, the outgoing Venetian ambassador, who was a childhood friend, and Baldassare Castiglione, whom he had not seen since his visit to Rome in 1516. Castiglione, who had with him a nearly complete manuscript of *The Courtier,* had landed a job as nuncio of the new Pope, Clement VII, in Spain. Although Charles V had a very fraught relationship with Pope Clement—and one which was only going to get worse—he enjoyed the company of Castiglione, whom he described as "one of the finest men in the world."

Navagero and Priuli presented their credentials to the Emperor, Priuli making an elegant speech in Latin. After the crushing victory at Pavia against Francis I, Charles V now dominated much of northern Italy. Priuli prudently couched his oration as an homage to the victor, but it was in no way an act of submission: the Venetians reaffirmed the independence of the Republic and the preservation of its own traditional sphere of influence in the Italian northeast.

The Emperor reacted with impatience. As Grand Chancellor Mercurino Gattinara, his powerful Piedmontese adviser, later explained to Navagero and Priuli, Charles V now considered all of Italy as *"cosa sua"*—his own property. "As a true Italian," Gattinara strongly recommended that they accept "a full deal" with the Emperor as he alone was capable of guaranteeing peace in Italy. He further suggested the Venetian Treasury pay the Emperor 120,000 ducats to seal the deal. The two Venetians remained vague. Priuli, as planned, headed back to Venice. But as he passed through Madrid, he made a point of paying his respects to the King of France, Francis I, who was still in prison and very ill.

Navagero, meanwhile, took over the ambassadorship from Contarini and settled into his new life in Toledo. The city, he told

Ramusio, was a tumble of close-fitted houses. The streets were twisted and narrow and densely populated. In contrast to Barcelona, there were no squares or gardens in which to walk about. Yes, there were fine houses built around patios, in the local manner; there were palaces. But the buildings did not look out to the surrounding landscape. "There are few balconies and they tend to be small because the summer heat is intense," he reported. "Inside, the rooms are lit only by what little light comes through the door."

The atmosphere, he said, was compressed and suffocating.

The sweeping view of the Tagus valley below offered a measure of relief. Orchards and vegetable plots, drenched by great wheels drawing water from the river, were spread out as far as the eye could see. This was "la huerta del Rey," the King's vegetable garden, he explained. "Fruit trees are everywhere, and the plots are neat and well tended and provide an array of produce for the city markets, including eggplants, cardoons and carrots, which they feed to horses."

Beyond the orchards, the Tagus flowed into a wide and fertile plain known as the Vega. A truncated Roman aqueduct stood in the fields like the skeleton of a gigantic dinosaur. In ancient times it had carried water from the river all the way up to Toledo. How the Romans had managed such a technical feat was a mystery that still baffled the Emperor's engineers. Not far from the aqueduct, moss-covered outcroppings were all that remained of what must have been a sizable Roman arena. And scattered everywhere were more time-eroded vestiges that Navagero could not identify.

Among the ruins in the Vega, one crumbling and distinctly un-Roman building stood out: an old castle built by Muslims in the early Middle Ages, when they ruled over much of Spain. One legend had it that Galiana, the beautiful daughter of a sultan, lived in the castle at the time of the Paladins. Christians and Muslims fought over her. When King Alfonso VI finally conquered the castle, his soldiers discovered an idyllic setting with gardens and fountains. Inside the castle they found astrolabes, compasses and other sophisticated instruments made of gold and silver, and a water clock with an elaborate mechanism no one could understand.

. . .

Ramusio was pleased to hear that Navagero was now in the company of friends and enjoying the views from Toledo. He thanked him for the vivid descriptions and the history lessons. But he was getting a little impatient: where was the information on the Spanish discoveries that Navagero had promised? Navagero replied apologetically that it was impossible to find "printed books on matters pertaining to the Indies." He asked Ramusio for a little more time: he was making the right connections at court, and thanks to yet another Italian humanist who had become "a very close friend," he was finally getting a better sense of things. "Soon I shall be sending more material than you'll be able to handle."

PETER MARTYR

This new "close friend" was none other than Pietro Martire d'Anghiera, Peter Martyr in English. We met him earlier: he was the man in charge of supervising the debriefing of Elcano and Pigafetta after the return of the *Victoria* in 1522. Over the years, Martyr had interviewed the major pilots, explorers and conquistadores who had returned from the New Indies, collecting and editing their reports. And even though he had never crossed the ocean himself, he had accumulated a vast amount of knowledge about the Spanish colonies.

Although an outsider, Martyr had done very well for himself at the Spanish court, rising to become a close adviser first to Queen Isabella, then, after her death, to King Ferdinand, and finally to young Emperor Charles V.

Martyr grew up in Arona, a small town on the shores of Lake Maggiore. He left home in his early twenties, a bright, well-read young man looking for adventure. After a stint in the army, he headed to Rome. The Spanish ambassador to the Holy See, Íñigo López de Mendoza, was struck by his sharpness and convinced him to travel back to Spain with him. There Martyr joined the Spanish army and participated in the last phase of the Reconquista, the war to expel the Muslims from Spain. In 1492 he was present at the siege of Granada, the last bastion of Al-Andalus.

Martyr left the military, joined the clergy and widened his social connections by teaching humanities to the sons of Spanish grandees. He enjoyed great favor at the court of Ferdinand and Isabella. After acceding to the throne, young King Charles set about organizing the Council of the Indies, the powerful agency that oversaw relations with Spanish-controlled territories overseas. He appointed Martyr to the Council and gave him the additional title of Official Historian of the Spanish Possessions Overseas.

By the time Navagero met him in Toledo in the spring of 1525, Martyr had become a semi-retired éminence grise at the court of the Emperor. A diminutive man with a sunken face, a long wispy gray beard and a drooping mustache, he was a year shy of his seventieth birthday and was suffering from liver disease. He received Navagero in his house, surrounded by books, piles of manuscripts, exotic artifacts and a collection of stuffed birds.

Martyr was in the process of bringing up to date the official chronicle of the Spanish expansion overseas. He had divided the material in sets of chapters called "Decades." The narrative was built around Christopher Columbus's four journeys to the Caribbean.

Although partial to Columbus, Martyr took his role as official historian seriously. In his view, the Columbian epic was marked by dazzling feats and woeful failures. Columbus was unrivaled as a navigator and discoverer, and had opened up the New World to exploration and conquest. But he had been an ineffective administrator. He had allowed the rapacity of his men to go unchecked. He had turned his gaze aside in the face of rampant violence against the natives. And when the search for fabled "rivers of gold" had proved disappointing, he had promoted a dubious plan for shipping slaves instead.

A bad administrator with questionable moral values, he was even worse as a geographer. On his first journey out, Columbus had imagined, quite plausibly, that he was headed to Asia—he had even carried with him official letters addressed to Asian rulers, including one to the elusive Prester John! But ten years later, after his fourth trip to the Caribbean, he was still convinced, against all evidence, that he had found his way into Marco Polo's world. He continued to annotate obsessively his worn copy of Polo's *Travels,* and he never abandoned the idea that Hispaniola was a part of Japan, the Caribbean mainland was the Malay Peninsula and the Orinoco in Venezuela was one of the four sacred rivers that bathed the Earthly Paradise in the East. In spite of his lifelong quest for new frontiers, Columbus remained stuck in a Polo-inspired oriental fantasy.

Still, Martyr felt his shortcomings had been allowed to obscure his outstanding achievements. Columbus's Spanish rivals had carried out a relentless campaign of denigration against him during the last years of his life (his return to Spain in shackles to stand trial on charges of embezzlement after his third journey to the Caribbean was surely the most humiliating episode of that campaign). For them, the Admiral of the Ocean Sea had become "the Pharaoh"—an avid manipulator, interested only in promoting his own family.

The effort to destroy Columbus's reputation did not subside after his death in 1506. On the contrary, his enemies accused him of having been not only a villain and an embezzler but an impostor who had falsely claimed he had "discovered" the New World when in reality other pilots—Spanish pilots—had been there before.

A fabricated story to that effect had circulated in Spain soon after Columbus's death, and according to Martyr was still making the rounds twenty years later.

Long before 1492, so this yarn went, a shipowner from Andalusia who happened to be a friend of Columbus's was sailing his caravel between Spain and the Canary Islands when his ship was hit by a terrible storm and carried westward by the winds until he and his crew were shipwrecked on an island on the other side of the ocean. Although they had lost many men at sea, they were able to repair the ship and eventually sail back. More men died of disease or hunger, and by the time they reached Madeira only the shipowner and two or three men were alive, barely. Now it happened that Columbus lived in Madeira at the time (true fact) and so the mysterious Andalusian found shelter in the house of his old friend, with whom he shared charts, portolans and travel logs. The surviving crew members died within days and eventually so did the shipowner. Now Columbus was left with all the information he needed to mount his own expedition and earn all the credit.

As Official Historian of the Spanish Possessions Overseas, Martyr was in a position to debunk this tale and restore the reputation of the Genoese admiral by placing him squarely at the center of the epic journey across the Atlantic.

A version of Martyr's first three Decades had appeared in print in 1516 with the title *De Orbe Novo*. The book was the most comprehensive account of Columbus's four journeys across the Atlantic. It also included Balboa's discovery of the Pacific, Pedrarias's forced colonization of the Darién isthmus, and the exploration of the continental coastline (Venezuela and Colombia) by Alonso de Ojeda and his rival Diego de Nicuesa, who had both been looking for a passage to the Spice Islands.

Although the book was nearly ten years old, it was still the most authoritative source of information on the early phase of the Spanish expansion overseas. It is likely Navagero began to translate the original Latin version into Italian while he was in Spain.

Meanwhile, Martyr had brought the narrative up to date, writing five more Decades. All were in Latin and in manuscript form. The material covered the Spanish landings in the Yucatán by Francisco Hernández de Córdoba and Juan de Grijalva and their initial contacts with the Maya civilization; the founding of Panama City by Pedro Arias Dávila; and the latest account of Hernán Cortés's conquest of Mexico, based on letters Cortés wrote to the Emperor and on a number of interviews with men who had returned to Spain.

Martyr's seventh Decade was especially intriguing because it mentioned a far-flung region roughly where South Carolina is today, which the Spaniards had recently visited. Lucas Vázquez de Ayllón, a judge in Hispaniola, had sponsored the mission of a certain Francisco Gordillo to sail north and explore the coastline on the mainland, make contact with the natives and treat them amicably.

Gordillo was joined by Pedro de Quexos, an unscrupulous slave trader who convinced him to trick some seventy members of a friendly tribe located at the mouth of the Pee Dee River into boarding their ship and to take them back to Hispaniola. A special commission headed by Governor Diego Colón ordered the captives freed. But with no place to go, they wandered the streets of Santo Domingo begging for food and shelter. According to Martyr, they were dead within two years. Except one, who learned Spanish, was baptized Francisco de Chicora and went to work for Judge Ayllón as an assistant and translator.

Ayllón traveled to Spain with de Chicora to obtain permission to colonize the region at the mouth of the Pee Dee—permission which was granted to him. Once back in Santo Domingo, Ayllón organized an expedition to establish a small settlement that was already being called New Andalusia. Predictably, de Chicora disappeared as soon as they hit shore.

Martyr's Decades were not a unified narrative but rather a series of reports, like the one on Ayllón, which he constantly amended, improved and updated. So the reality of the "New World" was being unveiled in slow stages, one small piece at a time.

The many private conversations Navagero had with the ailing Martyr were just as important as the official reports in shedding light on the Spanish activities overseas. There is no reason to doubt him when he tells Ramusio that he and Martyr had become very close. And one can easily imagine Navagero in Martyr's company: two Italian humanists speaking the same language, talking into the night about the latest geographical findings.

Ramusio was pleased that Navagero was speaking regularly to Martyr but wary of having to rely too much on someone who certainly spoke with authority but had never crossed the Atlantic himself, never seen the places he spoke about. And so he urged his friend to find a source that could provide them with credible eyewitness accounts of what the Spaniards were finding on the other side of the ocean.

As it happened, the man they were looking for had just arrived in Toledo. And he too spoke very good Italian.

BABY DRAGONS AND GIANT TOADS

Gonzalo Fernández de Oviedo y Valdés was a Spanish official who resided in Santa María la Antigua, a fifteen-year-old township in the Darién region; he had sailed back to Spain to brief the Emperor on the state of things in the fledgling colony.

Oviedo was born in a family of the minor nobility around 1478 and raised at court, where he took service as a page to Don Juan, the son of King Ferdinand and Queen Isabella. His course seemed set, but after Don Juan's premature death in 1497, young Oviedo left

Oviedo described iguanas as "baby dragons" that made for an excellent roast. Ramusio published this print in 1556 in *Navigationi et Viaggi,* Book Three, using an earlier wood engraving published by Oviedo in *Primera parte de la Historia general y natural de las Indias, islas y tierra firme del mar oceano.*

the court and traveled to Italy as a soldier of fortune, with an eye to improving his education while living in the country of humanism.

He landed in Genoa, spent time in Milan, where he met Leonardo da Vinci, and then settled in Mantua at the court of the Gonzaga; there he befriended Andrea Mantegna, the great Renaissance painter famous for his studies on perspective. Oviedo later visited Rome, which was then in the hands of his corrupt fellow Spaniards, the Borgias. And he traveled south to Naples and Palermo, also under Spanish rule.

In 1502, after five years in Italy, he returned to Spain, fell in love with Margarita de Vergara, married her and was heartbroken when she died giving birth to their son. He remarried and his new wife, Isabel de Aguilar, gave him two more children. He took on a variety of jobs in the Spanish administration to support his young family. But his wanderlust returned and now he yearned to explore the territories overseas—he was apparently inspired by the accounts of his friends Bartolomeo and Diego Colón, respectively a brother and a son of Columbus.

In 1513 he sailed to the New Indies as an inspector in charge of controlling the production of gold ingots. He landed on the coast of present-day Colombia and traveled to the province of Darién, in the Central American isthmus, which was ruled by Pedro Arias Dávila, a cruel despot who had put to death his own son-in-law, Vasco Núñez de Balboa, the first European to see the Pacific. Oviedo stayed a little over a year—long enough to draft a damning report about Dávila's ruthless repression of the natives, write a proposal for the reorganization of the colony *and* compose a chivalric novel, *El libro de Don Claribalte,* which he published upon his return to Spain.

However, no one in Spain had much interest in his plans for the colonies. King Ferdinand died in 1516 and the court was consumed with the accession of the new young king, Charles I, the future Emperor Charles V. Oviedo had only one desire: to return to the Spanish possessions overseas. In 1520 he finally obtained a new administrative assignment and crossed the Atlantic together with his wife and three children. He settled in Santa María la Antigua,

A typical hut built by natives in the New Indies. Print published
by Ramusio in 1556 in *Navigationi et Viaggi,* Book Three,
from an earlier wood engraving by Oviedo.

the township which Balboa had founded a decade earlier in the
Darién region. At considerable expense, he built a roomy two-story
house with a pleasant veranda overlooking a garden with orange and
lemon and citron trees, all imported from Spain and irrigated by the
stream that ran through the property.

Oviedo soon found himself at odds with Dávila not only on
account of the governor's despotic ways but also because of the latter's decision to build a new township farther north, where the isthmus reached its narrowest point (present-day Panama City), thus
abandoning Santa María la Antigua del Darién. Meanwhile, events
in his personal life took a heavy toll: he lost a child shortly after
settling in the new house, and a year later he lost his wife, Isabel.
Despite these reversals, he diligently carried out his responsibilities.
And he started work on *A Natural and General History of the Indies,* the
massive book that eventually made his reputation. Inspired by
Pliny the Elder's ten-volume *Natural History,* Oviedo had in mind an

Hammocks, Oviedo wrote, were "comfortable and easily
transportable." He suggested they be adopted by European armies
so that soldiers didn't have to sleep on the ground. Print published by
Ramusio in 1556 in *Navigationi et Viaggi,* Book Three, from an
earlier wood engraving published by Oviedo.

encyclopedic opus on the geography, the fauna, the flora of the New
Indies, and on the native peoples and their customs.

After marrying again—to Catalina de Ribafrecha—Oviedo left
his two surviving children behind with his new wife and sailed once
more to Spain to denounce Dávila's ways and to try to scuttle his
plan to move the township farther north. Oviedo, by now quite
knowledgeable about the overseas territories, was hoping to inherit
Peter Martyr's job as Official Historian of the Spanish Possessions
Overseas. Since his *Natural and General History of the Indies* was still

a work in progress, he arrived in Toledo armed with a handwritten summary (*Sumario de la natural historia de las Indias*) he had hastily put together for the Emperor. Even in its abbreviated form, the *Sumario,* which Oviedo privately published while he was in Toledo, was the most comprehensive and detailed description of life in the New Indies available in Spain at the time. And though it did not get him Martyr's job—at least not yet—it certainly raised his profile at court.

The primary purpose of the *Sumario* was to create for the Emperor a vivid picture of his possessions in the New Indies. In this Oviedo succeeded brilliantly. To read the *Sumario* is to immerse oneself in a world at once wildly exotic and yet realistic and thoroughly convincing. His writing was precise, even methodical, but never dull; his literary skills combined with his genuine passion for the topics he wrote about made for an absorbing narrative. In this Oviedo resembled other travel writers of his generation, like al-Wazzan and Father Francisco Álvares, who, despite very different backgrounds, were interested in describing the world as they saw it.

Oviedo evoked to great effect the tropical landscape of the Caribbean region, whether he was describing the thick steamy jungle, the rich arable soil or the lush exotic fruit trees. He delighted in writing about the wildlife—there were plenty of tigers and jaguars and pumas. But the unusual native species, like tapirs and pecaris, drew his attention the most. Wild rabbits and hares provided a protein-rich diet, he wrote, but armadillos and iguanas, which the Spanish colonists called "baby dragons," also made an excellent roast. Wild turkeys were tastier and more tender than Spanish ones. Monkeys were everywhere, and so were "smelly opossums." He warned against vipers and scorpions and "giant toads" and spiders "the size of an open hand." Crocodiles and alligators were always lurking in the swamps and one learned very quickly "to be careful when wading rivers."

The climate, hot and humid with torrential downpours, made it hard to grow European grains, he explained. But sugarcane, brought over from the Canary Islands, did very well. He rhapso-

Canoes were built out of a single tree trunk and came in all sizes.
According to Oviedo, they often capsized, but the natives were good
swimmers. Print published by Ramusio in 1556 in *Navigationi et Viaggi*,
Book Three, from an earlier wood engraving published by Oviedo.

dized about native species: maize, cassava and especially "the delicate and pleasant-tasting" sweet potatoes, which the natives called
batata. Not to mention the great variety of luscious tropical fruit like
the juicy guanábana, the pinkish guayaba and the papaya, "fleshy as
a cantaloupe." Coconut oil was excellent for making corn cakes and
also as a remedy against kidney stones. Pineapples had the oddest
carapace yet tasted so delicate and sweet. Prickly pears were plentiful and very delicious but—beware!—"your piss will become as red
as blood and give you a scare." A plantain looked like a banana but
tasted "like the bone marrow of a roasted ox."

The list of exotic fruits went on but he reserved the place of
honor in this rich gallery for the mighty avocado: "They call it a
pear but it is not a pear, it weighs a pound and at its core is a pit
like a chestnut. The pulp has the consistency of butter." After one
has picked these delicious pears that are not pears off their tree, one
must wait for them to slowly ripen. "Careful not to wait too long,
however, or they will take on a very sad appearance."

In the *Sumario,* Oviedo made his first attempt to describe the lives of Caribbean natives, including their cooking and drinking habits and leisure time activities—an entire chapter was devoted to their skill in a fast-moving team sport in which they passed a ball using head, shoulders and hips. He discussed their social and political organization, the role of the *cacique,* the importance of women in the community. He wrote about their weapons and how they used them in battle; he illustrated hunting expeditions and ingenious fishing techniques. He also dwelt on the cannibalistic practices of certain tribes.

Unlike his great rival, Father Bartolomé de las Casas, Oviedo did not believe natives should be allowed to live in the new Spanish

The fruit of the plantain looked like a banana but tasted
"like the bone marrow of a roasted ox," Oviedo wrote.
Wood engraving published by Oviedo in Seville and reprinted
by Ramusio in Book Three of *Navigationi et Viaggi.*

colonies as free men and women. He thought them inferior beings
who should be subjugated and governed for their own good in a
state of semi-slavery. But he abhorred the repressive and needlessly
cruel measures of Governor Dávila—the constant beating and rap-
ing, the gratuitous killing, the lack of even a semblance of human
compassion—which he continuously denounced in his dispatches to
Spain. As he saw it, those policies were a major cause of a distressing
phenomenon: the spread of mass suicides among the natives.

Traditionally, warriors used cyanide from cassava roots to poison
their arrow tips before going into battle. Now, Oviedo wrote in a
grim passage, entire families ingested the same deadly poison to take
their own lives.

The *Sumario* circulated widely in Toledo and made a strong impression at court. Oviedo's reputation as a chronicler of the overseas
colonies grew and he was given permission to publish his work in
print during his visit. Navagero himself drew heavily on Oviedo's
writings during his time in Spain, and he took back to Venice a copy
of the *Sumario*. Perhaps more important, he laid the groundwork for
the fruitful relationship that blossomed a few years later between
Oviedo and Ramusio.

IMPERIAL WEDDING

Navagero looked forward to Seville, the booming gateway to the
new Spanish colonies. However, life at court was still consumed by
the crisis between Spain and France, and his presence was required
in Toledo. He was to keep lobbying for the release of Francis I without irritating Charles V. But the Emperor was driving a very hard
bargain: he insisted on getting all of Burgundy (roughly a third
of France) and a free hand in northern Italy. Meanwhile, Francis I
wasted away in a tower in Madrid, wracked by debilitating migraines
and weakened by syphilis. An abscess in the head brought him close
to death.

The French delegation finally acquiesced to the Emperor's demands, initially without the consent of the king. But in January 1526, Francis I relented and agreed to sign the treaty, and seal the deal by marrying the Emperor's recently widowed sister, Leonore. Charles, fearful the French king would renege on his word, imposed an insidious last-minute condition: the king's two sons from his first marriage, François, age eight, and Henri, age seven, were to be brought to Spain as hostages. Once released from prison, Francis I returned to France already plotting his revenge.

The treaty signed, the Spanish court moved to Seville for the wedding of Emperor Charles V and Isabella of Portugal. After having spent six months in Toledo, Navagero was glad to get back on the road. He and his secretary joined the migrating caravan just as the orange groves were beginning to blossom. Riding west along the Tagus, they reached the city of Talavera, then turned south toward Andalusia.

They had not gone very far when news reached them that Diego Colón was dead. His health had taken a turn for the worse during the winter and he was very ill when the court left Toledo. His friends, including Oviedo, had discouraged him from traveling to Seville. But he had insisted, fearing for his position if he did not stay close to the Emperor. After barely a day on the road, he took shelter in the house of a friend in the town of Puebla de Montalbán, just twenty miles west of Toledo. He died three days later, leaving his wife, Doña María, and his seven children back in Hispaniola. His heirs were unable to settle the suit brought against him at the Council of the Indies for another ten years. In the end Diego's eldest son, Luis, was made Admiral of the Indies and Marquis of Jamaica, with a yearly stipend of ten thousand ducats—a pittance compared to the original agreement negotiated by Columbus in favor of his descendants. In exchange, Luis agreed to drop all future claims of the family in the New Indies.

Riding horseback in the rugged Spanish landscape and spending nights in primitive taverns along the way could be taxing, but Navagero was soon sharing with Ramusio the excitement of approaching Seville from the north. The hills overlooking the city were covered with sweet-smelling orange and lemon trees. Beyond the hills, olive groves extended in the plain for thirty leagues or more. "The olives are more beautiful and delicious than any I have tasted before," he wrote enthusiastically. Always delighted to find vestiges of antiquity scattered in the landscape, he described to his friend back home the crumbling remains of a Roman temple and the ruins of what looked like ancient public baths. Parts of an old amphitheater were scattered in the fields as well. All the marble had been removed, the stones were out of place and the steps were worn by time. It looked, he wrote, "like a gaping mouth from which the teeth have been pulled out."

And finally Seville, bathed in the sharp light of the Atlantic. Navagero found the city enchanting, with its pleasant open streets (in contrast to Toledo), splendid palaces and sun-drenched gardens. To his delight, it had not entirely lost its Islamic atmosphere. The new cathedral incorporated elements of the old mosque on which it was built. Next to it was a cloistered courtyard with porticos and chapels; at the center, an orange grove and a plashing fountain. Opposite the compound was a wide terrace of shiny white marble, with steps leading down to the street. The terrace was very crowded and he was told this was the principal meeting place for gentlemen and merchants. The area was known as "The Steps": auctions and sales and games of every kind took place there in a festive atmosphere.

Next to the cathedral rose the tall, majestic Giralda. Originally a minaret, it had been converted to a bell tower after the Catholics had taken over the city. There were no stairs to the top. Navagero had to walk up a steep ramp. "It's like the one we have inside the steeple of Saint Mark," he wrote to Ramusio. "In the old days the muezzin rode up to the top on a mule."

Behind the cathedral was the fabled Alcázar, where the Muslim kings had lived. It was a Garden of Eden of glistening marble, clear running water and patios filled with orange and lemon trees. "There cannot be a more pleasant place in all of Spain."

Seville was a peaceful and unrushed city, but the harbor down by the Guadalquivir, with its crowded docks and busy shipyards, its sailors and merchants and drunks, was a clamoring chaos where large oceangoing ships, carried upstream from the mouth of the river by powerful tides, disgorged their exotic treasures.

At the center of that lively confusion was the Casa de Contratación de las Indias, the agency responsible for all shipping operations to and from the New Indies, which was spread out in several office buildings near the waterfront. The agency selected and trained pilots, assigned ships, charted itineraries, assembled crews. It supervised the drawing of new maps and the updating of old ones, and kept a detailed record of life in the Spanish possessions based mostly but not exclusively on the reports of returning pilots. It also served as a customs house for incoming and outgoing merchandise.

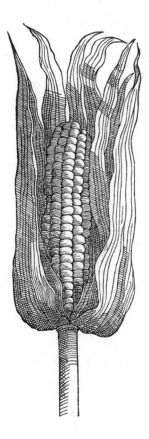

Oviedo rhapsodized about the qualities of maize, a native species that Ramusio was soon growing on his estate on the Venetian mainland. Wood engraving published by Oviedo and reprinted by Ramusio in 1556 in *Navigationi et Viaggi*, Book Three.

Ships sailing west across the Atlantic, Navagero explained to Ramusio, carried grains, wine and oil as well as everyday clothing items that were still not being produced overseas, such as shirts, frocks, even socks and underwear. Incoming ships returned with gold and less perishable produce like sweet potatoes, which Navagero said tasted like chestnuts, and pineapple, which reminded him of "quince, peaches and slightly of melon."

Returning ships also carried small numbers of natives from overseas; they were usually brought over under the supervision of religious orders. Down at the harbor in Seville, it was easy to run into clusters of them. "They have large faces and pressed noses like Circassians," Navagero wrote. "The color of their skin is ash gray." They were usually on their way to some building or other of the Casa de Contratación, chaperoned by a couple of friars. But left to their own devices, they invariably divided up into two teams and played their favorite ball game. "They are not allowed to use their hands or feet and mostly use their hips—an unusual game but they are very good at it."

The wedding of Charles V and Isabella took place on March 11, 1526, at the Alcázar palace. The bride was the daughter of King Manuel I of Portugal and the Emperor's first cousin on his mother's side. From the earliest age, Isabella had been determined to marry the Emperor—*aut Caesar aut nihil* was her motto: the Emperor or nothing. But Charles V had initially spurned her in favor of Mary Tudor; it had seemed at the time like a more politically convenient match, which would have cemented an alliance with England. But after the Battle of Pavia (1525) and his crushing victory against Francis I, Charles V was less interested in an anti-French alliance with England. He canceled the engagement with Mary Tudor, who would go on to become Queen of England, and went back to the initial candidate, his cousin Isabella.

In Seville, Charles V set up his quarters at the Monastery of Saint Jerome, on the north side of town, where Spanish kings often rested before their formal entrance into the city. Navagero was able to visit the gardens designed around orange and citrus groves and enclosed by elegantly manicured myrtle hedges. "The river flows by and gives a special grace to the place," he wrote to Ramusio. "The monks seem to lack nothing, immersed as they are in that fulsome beauty that only nature can provide. An easy path will surely lead them to paradise."

Isabella's triumph was clouded by the recent death of Charles V's sister Elizabeth of Denmark. The court was officially in mourning and the wedding ended up being a relatively subdued affair. Still, despite the doleful circumstance—and the fact that he hardly knew his bride—Charles was immediately taken by Isabella's looks and her lively intelligence.

He decided they would spend their honeymoon in Granada, the former jewel of Muslim Spain in the heart of Andalusia. The court followed, and so did the diplomatic corps.

THE ALHAMBRA

Granada was spread out over three separate hills in a beautiful green valley where two rivers came rushing down the snowcapped Sierra Nevada: the Darro flowed placidly through the city while the Genil rushed down, skirting its southern limit.

The Spanish had taken Granada from the Muslims after a bloody siege more than thirty years before, yet it was still in many ways an Islamic city.

Navagero had barely settled into his quarters—"a small house but pleasant and nicely ventilated"—when he headed out to explore the fabled Alhambra, the fortified citadel on the highest of the three hills where the Muslim sovereigns had once lived. After an invigorating walk in the crisp mountain air, he entered the now abandoned palace and wandered through the cool rooms lined with the finest white marble and decorated with gilded stucco and arabesque. Streamlets of fresh mountain water murmured along the walls. The empty suite of rooms led to a garden where a miniature aqueduct, flanked by myrtle hedges and sweet-scented orange trees, ran through a succession of patios, until it reached the final one, the Patio de los Leones, which had at its center a fountain with four spouting lions. "If one person whispers in the mouth of one of the lions," Navagero wrote to his friend like a child enraptured, "and another person sets his ear at the mouth of another lion, he hears every word distinctly."

Floating below the garden were the billowing domes of the Alhambra baths, where the sun shone through little holes scattered "like a thousand eyes." A secret door led to the Generalife, a Moorish palace next to the Alhambra with its own gardens and groves. From a balcony, Navagero peered down at an eight-foot-high hedge which evidently a dutiful gardener still tended to, for it was "clipped so evenly at the top that it formed a myrtle lawn suspended in midair." Nothing seemed to be lacking in this perfectly beautiful and pleasant place, he mused, "except someone who might take enjoyment from it and live here quietly and happily, with no other desire but the pleasure of study." Ah, if he could only re-create the same atmosphere of those Moorish gardens in his own garden in Murano! And how *were* things proceeding in Murano? Was the laurel planted? And the topiary garden clipped? Was Ramusio making sure that the trees and plants and roses were getting enough water? "You agreed to take care of Murano out of your own free will," Navagero reminded his friend back home, "and now you must stick to the task if you wish to be respected as the man you are." In Venice, Ramusio must have smiled upon reading the letter, for it was always a pleasure for him to ride out to the island by gondola to check on the progress of Navagero's garden.

On the way down from the Alhambra, the scenery was not so glorious; the signs of decay were everywhere. Navagero walked by crumbling old palaces and empty fishponds and shapeless myrtle hedges—wistful remnants of the recent past. But the Alcaicería, the Muslim quarter at the bottom of the hill, was teeming with life: a warren of narrow crowded streets lined with the shops of merchants selling earthenware, fabrics, produce, dried fruits, colorful spices and many different types of nuts. "Imagine our Rialto," he wrote to Ramusio, evoking the busy marketplace by the Grand Canal.

Navagero was impressed by the stylishness of Muslim women, who wore "shirts that come down just over the navel, colorful trousers known as Zaragolles, striped stockings and open-toed slippers." Their breasts, he pointed out, were large and slightly sagging, which was considered a desirable thing. "They dye their hair black with a smelly tincture and paint their fingernails the color of skin. They wear a turban. And a long white scarf falls sideways to the ground. They lift it to cover their face when they do not wish to be recognized."

In the small valley beyond the Alcaicería, the river Darro slinked smoothly past boulders and rocks. Scattered along the banks were simple Moorish houses and their small gardens with "water fountains, myrtle hedges, bushes of musk rose and other sweet-scented flowers." Every house, every garden, Navagero noted, "has its own special grace." The land was neatly tilled, and where it was not planted it was thick with ilex groves. Fruit trees were plentiful: prune, peach, fig, quince and apricot. He tasted a cluster of *glindas garofales,* juicy, succulent cherries that were "the most delicious in the world." Pomegranates grew in every garden, and grapes, including one variety with no pips. The olive trees were so large the groves looked "like oak forests."

Navagero imagined the country must have been even more beautiful when it was ruled by Muslims. In the years leading to the last act of the Reconquista in 1492, the Spanish Crown had agreed to keep the Inquisition out of Granada for forty years to provide a period of transition during which the Muslim population would be safe. The city had become a haven for Muslims fleeing other parts of Spain. When Navagero arrived, the forty-year furlough was coming to an end, and many families were leaving, most of them migrating to North Africa. His own mood turned melancholy as he mourned the passing of a great culture. He felt that the arrival of the Spaniards in that beautiful city did not carry great promise: "Already a number of houses have been abandoned and gardens have gone to seed. Soon there will be no one left to take care of the land. The Moors are the ones who till and sow. The Spaniards hardly plant at all. One seldom sees them at work in the fields. They prefer to go off to war or to the New Indies to seek their fortune."

The excitement that came with exploring Granada was suddenly dampened by the death of his new friend Peter Martyr, who had opened many doors for him and had been good company. The title of Official Historian of the Spanish Possessions Overseas did eventually go to Oviedo, who returned home to Santa María la Antigua to resume his duties as a colonial official.

A DREADFUL LITTLE PLACE

In early December 1526, after a prolonged honeymoon, Charles V left his beloved bride in Granada and traveled north to Valladolid followed by the imperial court. The political situation was deteriorating rapidly. Not surprisingly, Francis I was conniving to forge an alliance with Milan, Florence and Venice to retake northern Italy. The so-called League of Cognac had the support of Pope Clement VII—the Spaniards dubbed it the Liga Clementina. Infuriated by this turn of events, Charles responded by preemptively invading Italy.

Navagero, who had followed the court to Valladolid, now found himself marginalized since Venice was backing the French. Even more uncomfortable was the position of his old friend Baldassare Castiglione, the papal nuncio, whose unabashed admiration for the Emperor was leading the Curia to question his effectiveness as a diplomat.

Navagero would have liked to return to Venice, but he was now, like the rest of the diplomatic corps, at the mercy of the Emperor. The plague broke out in Valladolid and the court moved to Palencia, some thirty miles north. Foreign envoys were housed in an old Franciscan monastery in the town of Paredes de Nava, fifteen miles away; they went back and forth for several months between Paredes and Palencia, pleading vainly for peace as the imperial troops in Italy headed south. In early May, Charles's troops conquered Rome and sacked the city during the five-day rampage described in Chapter Four. The Pope, the reader will remember, remained holed up in Castel Sant'Angelo, his fortified residence overlooking the Tiber.

Negotiations between Charles V and Clement VII dragged through the summer and early fall. In mid-October the plague was not abating and Charles V ordered the court to move farther north, to the medieval city of Burgos. "A melancholy city under a melancholy sky," Navagero wrote forlornly. "It is always cloudy and freezing cold. They say Burgos suffers misery for all of Castile."

The only solace was the company of Castiglione and the fellow ambassadors of Milan, Florence and England.

The intense personal rivalry between Emperor Charles V and King Francis I continued to dictate the course of events. In November 1527 the Emperor and the Pope finally hammered out a peace agreement. The Pope withdrew his support for the League of Cognac, which Francis I had cobbled together to contain Charles V's growing power in Europe. Faced with a weakening of the anti-imperial front, France turned to England for help, and in January 1528 the two countries declared war against Spain. Francis I ordered the Spanish ambassador Íñigo López de Mendoza in Paris detained. Charles V retaliated by having not just the French ambassador arrested but also Navagero and the other diplomats whose countries had joined the League of Cognac. They were transferred under military escort (fifty guards and thirty knights) to the medieval fortress at La Poza de la Sal, north of Burgos. Navagero was miserable: "It is a dreadful little place perched on some rocky mountain. There is not a pleasant building in sight. We spend our days in the fortress, heavily guarded." Though not as heavily as the French, who had to suffer the night guards sleeping in their antechamber.

The ambassadors remained incommunicado for four months at La Poza. At the end of April, Francis I released de Mendoza and an exchange was set up to take place in Fuenterrabía, on the border between Spain and France. A small convoy of bedraggled diplomats made its way into the Pyrenees on foot and on mules up steep, rocky paths covered with mud. All of them were relieved to leave La Poza behind. Navagero, for one, regained his good spirits as they traveled across Basque country, wading mountain rivers, traversing pristine oak forests and bivouacking in small stone villages surrounded by apple orchards that produced delicious cider.

Navagero had one regret: his dear friend Castiglione, whose company he had cherished during his four years at the court of Charles V, had decided to stay behind. Castiglione had come to admire the young emperor and considered Spain his country of adoption. He had completed the manuscript of *The Courtier* and was anxious to get it published; many copies in manuscript form were circulating in Europe and he feared pirated editions would soon appear in print. He dreamed of publishing *The Courtier* in Venice, the city of books, where he had so many good friends. Aldus Manutius was dead, but his son Paolo was upholding the prestige of the house. Once Navagero was safely back in Venice, Castiglione hoped he and Bembo and Ramusio would see to it that his book, the work of a lifetime, was properly published.

It took ten days for Navagero and his companions to reach Fuenterrabía, the border town on the Atlantic. They crossed the bridge over the river Andaja (now Bidasoa) and walked over to France as free men; then it was on to Bayonne, where Navagero was able to send a dispatch to Venice informing the government that he was alive and safe. What a relief it was, "and how wonderful to see people laughing and dancing and being merry—how different they are from the Spaniards."

SUMMER IN PARIS

To his chagrin, Navagero was not allowed to travel straight back to Venice. His government instructed him to head to Paris, acquaint himself with the king's entourage and only then—after a journey through France—make his way home.

So off he went. On June 9 he was in Bordeaux, where he admired the vineyards and tasted "the most excellent wine." He then traveled across Cognac country, reaching Poitiers, with its ancient Roman aqueduct and the ruins of the old amphitheater, on June 19. He moved on to Tours and the Loire valley with stops at the royal châteaux of Blois and Amboise. On June 24 he was in Orleans, where he admired the impressive defensive walls, the beautifully built houses and the wide, straight avenues; he duly paid homage to the bronze statue of Joan of Arc. Then it was on to Chartres and from there to Paris, which he reached on June 27. He wrote back enthusiastically about the cathedral of Notre-Dame, the island of Saint-Louis, the two solid bridges across the Seine—one made of wood, the other of stone—and the long barges bringing into the city a profusion of merchandise. He regaled his friend back home with vivid descriptions of the wide and busy streets, the fine buildings ("though the facades could use a little work") and the shops filled with the richest selection of goods. There was such a lively hustle and bustle everywhere that one hardly noticed whether or not the court was in residence at the royal palace. "This is the grandest, most beautiful, most opulent, most populous city—and the only one that can be compared to Venice."

After a summer in Paris, developing a network of contacts at court and nursing a battered foot, he finally headed home in mid-August, stopping in Lyon for ten days before winding his way on the back of a mule up the steep, rocky tracks of the Alpine pass at Moncenisio. He descended into Piedmont slowly, following the switchback trail "like a snail turning on itself a thousand times." Afterward, it was a straight journey across the Po valley, stopping in Alessandria and Piacenza, then skirting Cremona to avoid another outbreak of the plague, and entering the Republic near Brescia. He reached Venice on September 24, 1528.

· · ·

Ramusio was overjoyed to have his friend back. Navagero had made good on his promise, coming home with a treasure trove of first-rate material on the New World: not just Martyr's precious *Decades* and Oviedo's fascinating *Sumario,* but also the private notes he had accumulated during hours of conversations with Juan García de Loaysa and the other members of the Council of the Indies, as well as with swashbuckling explorers like Pánfilo de Narváez and Esteban Gómez, not to mention poor Diego Colón.

Navagero, for his part, was happy to find the garden in Murano fully grown and resplendent in the late summer's golden light. Ramusio also handed him back the keys to the library, which he had kept in good order and running.

Navagero was widely praised for the way he had conducted his difficult ambassadorship. "This first embassy has given you an outstanding reputation," Bembo assured him. "Surely the fatherland will show its gratitude." But Navagero was a changed man. His experience in government, while rewarding in many ways, had ultimately disappointed him. While still in Spain he had confessed to Ramusio that a career in government was not for him. "The truth is I have never been so lacking in [political] ambition. There it is . . . I don't despise statecraft, and I think I have shown that I am not entirely inept in this field. But what I have done is enough for me. My true ambition lies elsewhere. I've never been so sure of myself."

Navagero longed to return to a life of letters and also to cultivate his interest in botany: "If I am to be happy, the garden in Murano must always come first." But he was not a rich man. His appointment as official historian had lapsed. He needed a steady income to maintain his property on the island. The prestigious office of the Riformatori dello Studio di Padova, which included responsibilities in the fields of culture, higher education and publishing, was open to candidates. It seemed like the perfect job: he would be able to devote his time to the subjects he loved while remaining close to Murano.

Navagero was also eager to translate the work of Martyr and Oviedo, and get the two works into print as soon as possible.

His plan, however, was soon derailed; he was unable to garner the votes in the Senate for the job he wanted. Instead, to his great concern, in January 1529 the peculiar alchemies of Venetian politics led him to be nominated ambassador to France.

In his endless struggle with Charles V, Francis I was pouring troops back into northern Italy. The French army easily took Milan, but instead of consolidating its control of northern Italy it went chasing the imperial army down south and besieged Naples, a Spanish dominion. Francis I was also thinking of invading Spain to free his two sons.

Navagero was sent rushing back to France to dissuade the French monarch from widening the conflict. He traveled at full speed in wretched weather across the Po valley and over the freezing Alps, reaching the Loire valley in early April. Francis I greeted him at the castle of Blois. Navagero, exhausted and feverish, retired to his lodgings. He never did manage to press his case. His condition worsened day after day and he died on May 8, 1529.

The news reached Venice four days later and was greeted with disbelief. Ramusio was inconsolable at the loss of his closest friend. Navagero's brother Pietro traveled to France and returned with the coffin, which was entombed in the small church of San Martino, on the island of Murano, next to the garden Navagero had so lovingly nurtured.

Bembo wrote a sonnet in memory of his friend. It ended with these lines:

The pain is sharp
but now I see you
consorting with those ancient souls you loved so dearly
and I find my consolation.

CHAPTER EIGHT

IN THE LAND
OF BIRU

R AMUSIO, STILL GRIEVING FOR HIS LOSS, WAS NEVER-
THELESS EAGER TO EXAMINE THE RICH MATERIAL ON
the overseas territories that Navagero had brought back to
Venice. But the Senate entrusted him with an unusual dossier that
required his immediate attention.

In November 1530 a flamboyant character by the name of David
Reuveni arrived in Venice preceded by a dubious reputation. He
went about town dressed in oriental clothes, claiming to belong to
a lost Jewish tribe in the Arabian Desert. He said he was the son of
a certain King Solomon of Tabor and the brother of the current
King Joseph, who ruled over 300,000 descendants of the tribes of
Ruben, Gad and Manasseh. His mission was to lead the Jews back to
the Promised Land, and he had come to seek the support of European princes—while astutely dangling the prospect of an alliance of
Christians and Jews against Islam.

Reuveni was the guest of Guido Rangoni, a military commander
from Bologna who lived in lavish quarters at Palazzo Contarini del
Bovolo. He petitioned the authorities to spend the winter in the city
and reside outside the Jewish ghetto. Meanwhile, he attracted attention with his flashy attire, his frequent public ablutions, his street
preaching. Ramusio was asked to make sense of this curious man—

his knowledge of geography and foreign languages made him ideally suited for the task.

It turned out Reuveni had been on the road for some time. From the Arabian port of Jeddah he had crossed the Red Sea to Ethiopia and then had traveled north through the Sudan and Egypt, following the course of the Nile. Pushing along the coast, he had stopped in Gaza and Hebron, and finally Jerusalem, where he had roamed the streets as a self-proclaimed prophet and miracle-maker. After returning to Egypt he had sailed from Alexandria to Venice on the ship of a wealthy Venetian merchant. He hadn't stayed in Venice at first. Instead he had gone straight to Rome to meet Pope Clement VII. The Pope had been noncommittal but sufficiently intrigued by the man to send him with letters to visit King João of Portugal. His visit in Lisbon was not a success, and he was back on the road traveling to Spain, France, northern Italy and finally to Venice again, where he planned to persuade the Republic to support his design.

Ramusio interrogated Reuveni over several days, hoping he might turn out to be a useful source of geographical information. But the mysterious visitor failed the most basic tests—for one, he could not come up with the names of the major rivers in the region he claimed to come from. Ramusio soon lost interest. He found the man to be obsessed and a little crazed ("like an alchemist is about gold")—the sort of person any serious geographer should stay clear of. Whether Reuveni was a true impostor or a spy seeking to damage the Republic, Ramusio couldn't say. "For sure Jews love him like a Messiah," he wrote at the end of his official report to the Senate. "I don't have much else to add."

His inconclusive findings were nevertheless enough for the secretive Council of Ten to swiftly expel Reuveni. He moved on to Regensburg in Germany to try his luck with Emperor Charles V, who was visiting his Habsburg domains. This did not end well; Reuveni was arrested and sent to Spain, where he faced the Inquisition in Llerena, a town in Extremadura. It is possible that he died there.

．　．　．

Once the Reuveni matter was settled, Ramusio was finally free to turn his attention to the treasure trove Navagero had brought back from Spain. And he immediately went to work on an Italian translation of the books by Peter Martyr and Oviedo—Navagero had begun to work on those texts when he was in Spain, but according to Bembo it was Ramusio who did most of the translating and the final editing.

Following Navagero's death, Ramusio wrote to Oviedo quite out of the blue with questions about the New Indies, and specifically about the new colony on the isthmus, called Panama, where Oviedo had lived. The two continued to correspond on a regular basis, and an unusual transatlantic friendship blossomed. They even became business partners.

In 1537 Ramusio, Oviedo and a third investor, Antonio Priuli, launched a company that specialized in the export of "liquors and sugars" from the New Indies to Europe. The deal was for six years minimum, renewable. All the relevant papers were later destroyed in a fire at the Chancery, so it is impossible to know how successful the business turned out to be, but it seems to have thrived through the 1540s and possibly the early 1550s.

In addition to keeping Ramusio informed about their business activities in the Caribbean, Oviedo continued to be his principal source on developments and discoveries in the New World. Ramusio introduced both Pietro Bembo and Girolamo Fracastoro to Oviedo, and they in turn corresponded with him. As Fracastoro put it to Oviedo, "All Ramusio's friends love you just as much as he does."

In 1532 there was a happy and to some degree unexpected development in Ramusio's private life. After eight years of marriage, Franceschina gave birth to a baby boy. He was named Paolo, for Ramusio's father, and soon nicknamed Paolino. His belated arrival brought great joy to the house on via del Patriarcato. Ramusio was already forty-seven when his son was born. Despite the pressing demands of his daily job at the Senate and the tiring commutes between Venice and Padua, he was from the beginning an attentive and tender father.

The next four years of solid work and sweet domesticity were probably the happiest of his life. It was an especially gratifying period for Ramusio the editor, culminating with the publication in 1534 of the Italian edition of Peter Martyr's history (the first three Decades of *De Orbe Novo*) and Oviedo's *Sumario*.

During the same period, news reached Venice that Francisco Pizarro had conquered an empire perhaps even richer than Mexico.

Pizarro had arrived in the New Indies in 1509 and had settled in Panama, where he'd quickly amassed a fortune. But he was not the retiring type. Like Cortés, he saw himself as an empire builder, and he was determined to discover and conquer a country of his own.

Balboa's sighting of the Pacific in 1513 had opened the way to territories south of New Spain, down the western coast of what Ramusio later described as "a big chunk of the New World." Pizarro set his eyes on a mysterious kingdom which the natives south of Panama called *Biru,* and which was said to be rich in gold and silver.

After a few exploratory trips down the coast of Colombia, Ecuador and northern Peru, Pizarro sailed to Spain, where Charles V granted to him the rights to all lands south of Tumbez, a town on the northern edge of the Inca Empire, for a length of two hundred leagues (it turned out the Inca Empire was twice as long). Pizarro was also given the titles of Captain General of the expeditionary force and Governor of whatever land was conquered.

He left Panama in February 1531. A year later he established a first Spanish township in San Miguel, on the river Chira, near present-day Piura, and remained there until September, when he advanced inland toward the highlands. The Inca Empire was in the throes of great internal strife. Huascar and Atahualpa, the two oldest sons of the late Emperor Huayna Capac, were locked in a bloody civil war.

Huascar controlled the southern part of the empire, Atahualpa the northern part, where Pizarro and his men established their base.

On November 15 the Spanish expeditionary force—sixty horsemen and ninety foot soldiers—arrived in the northern capital, Cajamarca, and quickly took control of the city. Atahualpa was headquartered in a military camp nearby. Pizarro sent his brother Hernando and one of his captains, Hernando de Soto, to meet Atahualpa and lure him back to Cajamarca. As one chronicler wrote, the two emissaries rode so menacingly close to where Atahualpa received them that the *latu*—the fringe of red wool that dangled from his headgear and symbolized imperial power—"flapped and fluttered in the warm air blowing from the horses' nostrils."

The two Spaniards persuaded Atahualpa to come meet Pizarro in Cajamarca, where he was preceded by a colorful procession. Clad in a dress made of the most delicate wool and decorated with gold trimmings, Atahualpa was carried on a litter padded with parrot feathers and studded with gemstones in gold and silver settings. In addition to his royal escort, Atahualpa was followed by an army of as many as eighty thousand men.

Pizarro, his captains and most of his men were hiding in buildings facing the central square. When the procession reached the square, Atahualpa found no one waiting for him except a Dominican priest who assured him that the Christians who had arrived were his friends. Then, in a flash, the Spaniards opened fire against the crowd with their artillery and burst out of their hiding place "with such fury that the natives, terrified by the gunfire and the rearing steeds, retreated to the mountains and many never came back down."

Pizarro had Atahualpa arrested and strangled to death. In his place he installed Atahualpa's younger brother Tupac-Hualpa. Soon the plunder of gold and silver began in earnest.

The first eyewitness report that came out of Peru was written by Cristóbal de Mena, a disaffected Spanish captain who sailed back to Spain with other veterans in 1533. His account was printed in Spain in April 1534. De Mena was critical of Pizarro, and even accused the Captain General of holding back a substantial quantity of gold owed to the Crown. A second report, by Pizarro's secretary Francisco Xerez, appeared later that year and was much more supportive of the Captain General. Ramusio translated both texts into Italian and had them printed side by side in late 1534 in the belief that the cumulative effect of the two differing narratives would ultimately benefit the truth. It was a typical example of Ramusio's neutral approach to geographical knowledge. His principal objective was to provide readers with credible information gathered in situ—those "things seen" Ludovico di Varthema had spoken of so many years before upon his return from India. And in the case of Peru, about which nothing was known in Europe before Pizarro's campaign, he clearly felt it was better to publish both accounts than to choose one over the other.

The three books Ramusio worked on in the 1530s—Martyr's *Decades,* Oviedo's *Sumario* and the volume on Peru—provided readers in Europe with the broadest, most up-to-date narrative on the geography of the New World. Ramusio was not an apologist of empire, and he certainly did not sugarcoat the cruelty and bloodshed the Europeans inflicted on the native population (and among themselves). Nor did he believe in a crusading mission of the Christian powers. If there was a rationale for making contact with unknown territories and peoples—in this he remained profoundly rooted in the Venetian ethos—it was not exploitation or plunder or religious conversion, but commerce. And commerce depended on reliable information.

Pizarro had opened up an immense new territory that stretched from Panama all the way down to the Strait of Magellan. It was finally possible for Europeans to get a sense of the true proportions of the southern part of the New World, divided from north to south by the high chain of the Andes and traversed by the great water system of the Amazon.

What lay to the north of what was called New Spain, however, was still largely a mystery.

By the mid-1530s, Cortés had invaded and mapped the territory from Panama to the mouth of the Colorado River. His old idea of projecting Spanish power across the Pacific had quickly faded after Charles V had renounced any rights to the Moluccan Islands. South of New Spain was now Pizarro's territory. Cortés had no choice but to keep pushing north.

Was there land or ocean beyond Mexico? Did the New World link up with Asia? And if not, how far was Cathay?

These questions were still unanswered in 1536 when the long-lost conquistador Álvar Núñez Cabeza de Vaca reappeared, a haggard waif in rags, after a harrowing nine-year-long journey across the entire width of North America.

Cabeza de Vaca had joined Pánfilo de Narváez's disastrous expedition to Florida in 1527. Marooned in the swamps, the survivors headed west hoping to reach New Spain, which was much farther than they imagined. Cabeza de Vaca lost touch with his companions and wandered in the wilderness, barely surviving until he was taken in by a native tribe. He slowly made his way across the Mississippi basin and into present-day Texas, New Mexico and Arizona, until one day he ran into a slave-seeking Spanish expedition.

Cabeza de Vaca returned to Seville in 1537 and wrote a riveting account of his journey of survival (it was published in Spain in 1542 and Ramusio translated it into Italian; it is still very much in print today).

So there was land to explore north of Mexico. But Cortés would not be the one to lead the way. Charles V, wary of his power and ambition, decided to replace him. Cortés was allowed to launch one last expedition in 1539 before his final return to Spain. A three-ship fleet led by Francisco de Ulloa sailed up the coast of Baja California until the 32nd parallel, reaching the mouth of the Colorado River before turning around.

Antonio Hurtado de Mendoza, the man Charles V chose as the Viceroy of New Spain, was not a conquistador like Cortés or Pizarro but a loyal servant of the Crown and a capable administrator. Picking up where Cortés had left off, he organized a number of expeditions to the territory north of New Spain.

Spanish ships sailed up the Pacific coast of North America all the way to Oregon without reaching the end of the continent. In 1539, Marco da Nizza, a Franciscan friar sent north by Hurtado de Mendoza, made contact with Pueblo and Zuni settlements in the American southwest. He returned the following year with an expedition led by Francisco Vázquez de Coronado that marched to present-day Kansas searching for elusive empires.

Meanwhile, Hernando de Soto, a veteran of Pizarro's campaign in Peru, was now sent to retrace Cabeza de Vaca's meandering journey backward through present-day Arizona, New Mexico, Texas, Arkansas, Oklahoma and Mississippi, where he eventually died from illness and sheer exhaustion.

The push northward petered out before the Spaniards were able to provide a plausible configuration of the New World, and Ramusio understood he would have to find information on the northern part of the continent from other sources.

CHAPTER NINE

SAILING TO
HOCHELAGA

O NE OF THE MANY HATS RAMUSIO WORE WAS THAT OF
THE DOGE'S OFFICIAL FRENCH TRANSLATOR AND INTER-
preter. He had become fluent in the language when he
had traveled to France with Ambassador Alvise Mocenigo soon
after joining the Chancery as a twenty-year-old junior clerk. Over
the years he had nurtured those early contacts with humanists at
the court of Louis XII, Francis I and Henry II. So it was to those
French connections that he now turned, hoping they could help
him pick up the thread abandoned by the Spaniards. For the French
had recently explored the eastern coast of North America and had
sailed up the Saint Lawrence River.

Ramusio's friends in Paris—nameless "literary gentlemen"—
leaked to him two invaluable documents.

The first was Giovanni da Verrazzano's letter to King Francis I
detailing his journey up the entire length of the eastern seaboard,
from South Carolina to Nova Scotia—an extraordinary achievement, which provided perhaps for the first time a real sense of how
vast the northern part of the New World might be. "Even vaster
than the Old World," Verrazzano surmised.

A well-educated Florentine sea merchant living in France, Verrazzano had persuaded Francis I to sponsor an expedition with a

twofold aim: find a "French" route to Asia while exploring the possibility of establishing a French presence in the New World, in order to contain Spanish expansion. Although the French king had given his blessing to the operation, it was Verrazzano's fellow Florentine merchants in Lyon, eager to gain easier access to Chinese silks, who had actually financed it.

In early 1524 Verrazzano sailed across the Atlantic aboard the *Dauphine* and made landing in South Carolina (possibly at Cape Fear). He followed the coast to present-day Virginia, sailed across the Chesapeake Bay and up to the Hudson estuary. Everywhere he stopped, he was warmly greeted by native tribes. The pleasant landscape of New England left him enchanted. He imagined French farmers growing wheat, grapevines and olive trees there one day. He even took time to explore the local fauna and flora, delighting in the different "wild roses, violets and lilies, not to mention the many other scented flowers that we are not familiar with." The islands along the granite coastline of Maine reminded him of the Dalmatian coast in the Adriatic.

Verrazzano returned to France and wrote a glowing report to Francis I, describing an idyllic country, peaceful natives, and a rich and verdant nature: a country ready to be colonized by the French. Verrazzano also believed that he had found a possible opening to the Pacific along the Carolina coast; in 1527 he crossed the Atlantic again, at the head of a fleet of five ships, looking for that elusive passage to Asia.

The expedition was over before it even began. Verrazzano went ashore on a small island in the Lesser Antilles and was killed by a tribe that was said to practice cannibalism.

Years later, Ramusio was the first to publish Verrazzano's initial report to Francis I, giving it a wide audience outside of France. In an introductory note, he did not spare his readers the details of the gruesome end suffered by Verrazzano, "roasted and devoured" in full view of his helpless mates, including his younger brother Girolamo.

According to Ramusio's informers in Paris, Verrazzano had

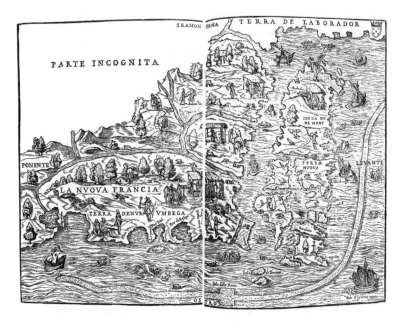

Jacques Cartier found a passage just south of Labrador and sailed into what later became known as the Gulf of Saint Lawrence. This early map of the region was published by Ramusio in Book Three of *Navigationi et Viaggi*.

pushed hard to persuade the king to send colonizers to settle along the coast, "where the climate is mild and the soil is rich and there are beautiful rivers and natural harbors." But a decade passed before Francis I was ready to sponsor another expedition to the New World.

Which brings us to the second document Ramusio obtained from his Parisian connections: a complete manuscript of Jacques Cartier's report on the first of his three journeys to Canada.

Every summer, fishermen from Brittany crossed the ocean to fish in the waters around Newfoundland. In 1534, Cartier, looking for a passage to Asia, sailed north, up Newfoundland's eastern coast. He found the landscape of "rough and broken rocks" very bleak and inhospitable—"the kind of place God might have reserved for Cain." But after hugging the craggy shore for several days, he reached the tip of Newfoundland, found a passage just south of Labrador and sailed into the vast expanse of water that would later be known as the Gulf of Saint Lawrence.

Cartier did not find the estuary of the Saint Lawrence on his first trip. He sailed down the coast of Labrador, reversed track when he reached the island of Anticosti, then headed south along the coast of New Brunswick. Although, like Verrazzano, he did not find the passage he was looking for, he was enchanted by the country that was opening up to him. Unlike Newfoundland, the mainland was more welcoming, the soil was fertile, the woods rich with timber. He listed elms, yews, ashes, willows and all manner of conifers. Wild sweet peas and grapevines grew everywhere, and the fields were filled with strawberry and raspberry bushes.

The natives along the coast, who belonged to the Mi'kmaq peo-

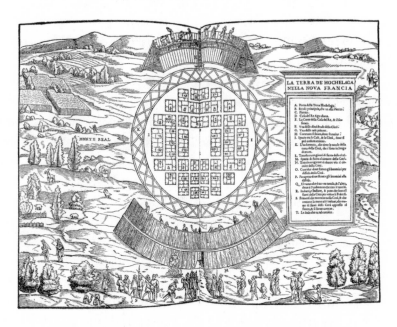

The population in Hochelaga was hardworking and peaceful, according to Jacques Cartier, who encouraged Francis I to establish a French colony there. This drawing was printed by Ramusio in *Navigationi et Viaggi*, Book Three.

ple, were friendly and curious about the small presents Cartier had brought along—especially knives and mirrors. The peace was disturbed only once, when Cartier had a thirty-foot cross planted in the ground roughly near Sandy Point on the coast of New Brunswick facing Anticosti. The words VIVE LE ROY DE FRANCE were carved in capital letters. Chief Donnacona, wearing an old bearskin, was soon on the scene with his sons; he delivered "a long sermon" telling Cartier with sounds and gestures that he had no business planting a cross on his land without his permission. Cartier tried to explain that it was merely there as a signpost as they intended to return soon. Somehow the issue was resolved amicably and Cartier expressed the wish to take two of the chief's sons, Taignoagny and Agaya, back with him to France. Donnacona gave his consent and a large party came over to bid a festive farewell to the two young men.

The following spring, as promised, Cartier returned to the region aboard *La Grande Hermine,* a sturdy one-hundred-ton carrack trailed by two smaller ships. This time, after following the southern coast of Labrador, Cartier sailed around the northern tip of Anticosti and into the wide estuary of the Saint Lawrence, where huge whales gamboled along the three ships.

Taignoagny and Agaya, now back in familiar waters, guided Cartier and his men upstream. Everywhere, now, the landscape was green and lush and the soil very soft and the hunting grounds rich with wildlife.

They came to the settlement of Dacona, near present-day Quebec City, where the two young brothers were reunited with their father, Chief Donnacona. The Frenchmen, leaving the big galleon behind, sailed upstream aiming to reach Hochelaga, a large settlement situated where Montreal stands today. They were greeted amicably along the way, even joyfully, as natives came down to the shore, the women holding their babies, and touched the newcomers. As recounted by Cartier, the journey to Hochelaga resembled an itinerant party—one to which the Europeans had invited themselves.

Hochelaga itself was a settlement of some fifty houses enclosed by a tall, tightly fitted wooden fence. Cartier noted that the population worked the land, fished and hunted, and lived a peaceful, productive existence. "It would be so easy to domesticate them," he concluded in his report to Francis I, encouraging the creation of a French colony in those territories—a New France to rival New Spain in the south.

Cartier and his men headed back down the river and set up winter quarters in a natural harbor at the confluence of the Saint Charles and the Saint Lawrence rivers, not far from Chief Donnacona's base. They were snowed in until the following spring and were decimated by what appears to have been a virulent strain of scurvy: "I have never seen anything like it," Cartier reported with clinical precision. "The men couldn't stand up, their legs were swollen, their veins black as coal and their skin was covered with blood-red splotches; the disease moved from the lower parts of the leg to the thighs, the hips, the arms, the shoulders, and the neck; the mouth smelled foul, the gums rotted and teeth fell."

In mid-April, after the ice had melted and the river was again clear, the survivors sailed to France. With a ruse, Cartier seized Chief Donnacona and took him to France as Exhibit A in a campaign to persuade Francis I to invest in a large-scale settlement plan. Nine other members of Donnacona's tribe, including two young girls, were taken to France against their will.

The ship reached the harbor of Saint-Malo, in Brittany, in July 1536. During his time in France, it appears Chief Donnacona lived in relative comfort at the king's expense. He was, briefly, an object of fascination as he entertained his listeners with tales of gold and rubies and other riches, including spices that did not exist in North America. King Francis I himself received Chief Donnacona and interviewed him at length.

Cartier made one more journey to the New World, in 1541. But by then Francis I had lost interest. No gold, no silver, no new passage to Asia had been found; sending over a few French farmers seemed hardly worth the effort.

Chief Donnacona spent the remaining years of his life in France; he died around 1539, two years before Cartier's third and last journey to the New World. The other captives had also died by then, except one of the two girls. It does not appear she sailed back home with Cartier. Presumably she remained in France, but her fate is unknown.

CHAPTER TEN

THE RETURN
OF MARCO POLO

RAMUSIO'S IDYLLIC WORLD CAME APART WHEN HIS
BELOVED FRANCESCHINA DIED OF A SUDDEN ILLNESS IN
the winter of 1536, leaving him bereft and alone with four-
year-old Paolino.

It fell once more to Bembo to console his younger friend. "I know
from experience," he wrote, "how bitter the loss of one's sweet and
faithful companion can be when one is getting older and needs her
more than ever."

Bembo had recently lost his own "faithful companion," Moro-
sina della Torre, a courtesan he had met in Rome when he was a
young secretary to the Pope; she had followed him back to Padua
and given him three children out of wedlock.

"But always remind yourself," Bembo added, "how blessed you
are to have Paolino."

Ramusio now faced the task of raising his son as a single parent.
He couldn't take him to Venice with him—he wasn't set up for that.
But neither did he want his little boy left to the care of others in the
big house in Padua, hours away from him. So he reorganized his
commuting schedule to spend as much time as he could with his son
in via del Patriarcato; and he started homeschooling Paolino from
the earliest age.

Later on, when the boy turned twelve and was ready for higher education, Ramusio established a small, in-house *pedagogium* where his son and a few other boys were taught Greek, Latin, mathematics and geography, of course. The principal teacher was Giovita Rapicio, a humanist from the prestigious Scuola di San Marco who came highly recommended by Bembo and Fracastoro. Ramusio himself taught geography, with the assistance of his friend Giacomo Gastaldi, a Piedmontese cartographer who had recently settled in Venice and was making his reputation as one of the finest mapmakers of his time. Both Gastaldi and Rapicio lived in the Ramusio household with the students.

But all of this was yet to come. Meanwhile, at the Senate, Ramusio's energies were increasingly consumed by tensions with the Ottoman Empire. After the trauma of Agnadello two decades earlier, Venice had pursued a policy of peaceful relations on the Italian mainland. But now the eastern front was under threat as Suleiman the Magnificent chipped away at the intricate network of colonies that formed Venice's empire in the Mediterranean. Already in 1533 a Turkish fleet had threatened the island of Crete, a centerpiece of Venice's sea dominions. The Venetians managed to destroy the enemy ships on that occasion. But Suleiman was soon at it again, attacking smaller colonies in the Aegean Sea and finally crossing over into the Ionian Sea and laying siege to the island of Corfu, another important Venetian stronghold—and much closer to home than Crete. Only a local outbreak of the plague led Suleiman to lift the siege and sail back to Constantinople. But the reprieve was temporary, and in 1538 Pope Paul III gave his blessing to a Christian coalition in support of Venice. The allied fleet met the enemy off the port of Prevesa, in the Ionian Sea, and suffered a humiliating defeat. Venice was forced to cede control of the Peloponnese to the Ottomans—a major blow to its Mediterranean empire.

In addition to his daily responsibilities at the Senate, Ramusio was again busy with library duties. Bembo, who had recently published *Prose della volgar lingua,* his foundational work on a modern Italian language, had inherited Navagero's double job as official historian of the Republic and director of the Bessarion collection. It was not long before he pleaded with Ramusio to give him a hand in managing the distribution of books. The burden became even greater in 1539 when Bembo, at the height of his literary prestige, was made a cardinal; he moved to Rome and delegated all library duties to his friend. "You're the only one I can trust with the keys," he explained. Still, he was soon reproaching Ramusio for his laxness. "It has come to my attention," he wrote in an especially stinging complaint, "that every day people come to ask you for books and that you easily give in even to those noblemen who refuse to pay the standard deposit fee. This is the easiest way to lose books; it will not reflect well on either of us. My orders are strict: the deposit must be twice the value of the book. If someone refuses to pay, have him copy the manuscript in the library under your supervision. And if he is of such rank that you should feel incapable of denying him what he seeks, then tell him you are merely following my orders."

In spite of the heavy workload and his new responsibilities at home, Ramusio continued to collect and edit fresh material for his geographical studies. After concentrating on the New World during the 1530s, in the new decade he turned his attention to Asia.

Venice had always looked to the East. Venetian merchants had traded in Asia Minor for close to three centuries. But beyond Asia Minor was a terra incognita—a vast landmass stretching all the way to China, hard to penetrate and never properly mapped by Europeans.

Marco Polo, of course, had traveled to China in the late thirteenth century, at the height of the Mongolian Empire, when global trade had flourished and European and Middle Eastern merchants went searching for new markets deep into Asia.

Polo's account of his journey to China was one of the most widely known books in Europe. But for a long time it was read as a work of the imagination, much like John Mandeville's *Travels,* which *was* a fictional memoir of roughly the same period.

It wasn't only because of the wondrous content of Polo's book that readers saw it as largely made up. As Ramusio observed, copyists had taken so many liberties with the text over time, had made so many changes and introduced so many errors and plain falsehoods, that in the end they had contributed to the notion that the book was "a fabulous tale with not the slightest basis in reality. In other words, a dream."

At the onset of the Age of Discovery, however, geographers and explorers began to take a second look at Polo's account of his journey as they searched for clues about the East. The Portuguese mined it for geographical information as they planned a route to the Spice Islands. And Columbus, as we have seen, owned a heavily annotated copy, which he took with him on his third trip to the New World, still convinced that the territory he had discovered overseas was the easternmost part of Asia.

But it was Ramusio who, after long and painstaking research, finally established that Polo's *Travels,* far from being "a fabulous tale," was a remarkable fact-based narrative—and therefore an invaluable tool for mapping out the vast Asian landmass.

By the time Ramusio turned his full attention to Polo's work in the 1540s, the original version of the manuscript had long been lost. The standard text—and the only version ever printed up to that point—was a Latin translation done by a Benedictine monk, Francesco Pipino, in the early fourteenth century, when Polo was still alive. It was published in Antwerp in 1485 (Christopher Columbus's worn copy belonged to that batch). Ramusio owned a later edition, printed in Basel in 1532, on which he went to work. A few later versions were available to him for comparison, but he was looking for something older, something closer to the original Polo manuscript, to do a proper collation. And to his own surprise, he found what he was searching for in the house of a friend who happened to live only minutes away from the Chancery.

This person came from a distinguished family of Venetian merchants, the Ghisis, who had thrived in the days of Marco Polo. The last descendant—Ramusio's friend—had in his library a very early version of Polo's book, also in Latin. The manuscript was so old, in fact, that Ramusio believed it might have been translated directly from the original, perhaps even by Marco Polo himself.

Ghisi was very protective of this family heirloom. Nevertheless, he invited Ramusio to study the precious codex and compare it to Pipino's version. One can imagine the thrill Ramusio must have felt as he eagerly immersed himself in Polo's exotic world. In a way, it was like being back in Aldus's shop when he was a young humanist collating precious manuscripts of the classics. Only now he was identifying place-names, calculating distances and mapping mountain ranges, rivers and cities in order to provide cartographers with reliable data. And his eyes could not have traveled on the wings of a more piercing gaze than Polo's.

A VIAL OF SACRED OIL

Travels begins not with Marco but with his father, Niccolò, and his uncle Maffio, two experienced Venetian merchants who had long plied the commercial routes in the Mediterranean before opening the way to Cathay.

In the 1250s the Polo family established a trading post in Crimea, and more precisely in the port city of Soldaia, present-day Sudak, on the northern coast of the Black Sea. The oldest brother, Marco the Elder, ran the business and resided there. Sometime around 1260 the two younger brothers, Maffio and Niccolò, briefly joined Marco the Elder, and then pushed eastward, looking for new markets in the rich region of the Volga.

These were the westernmost lands of the great Mongolian Empire founded by Genghis Khan in the 1220s and consolidated by his sons and grandsons—an empire that stretched from the Pacific to the Mediterranean.

Just as Maffio and Niccolò were about to turn around and make their way back to Venice, war broke out in the region, forcing them to make a loop in a southern direction that eventually brought them to Mesopotamia. At this point, lured by commercial routes as yet unknown to them, they traveled farther away from home, leaving Persia behind them and following the caravans north into present-day Uzbekistan. Drawn by the powerful gravitational force of eastern-bound trade routes, the two brothers headed deeper into the Mongolian Empire, until they reached Bokhara, a great trading center on the road to China.

There Maffio and Niccolò met an envoy of Emperor Kublai Khan, grandson of Genghis Khan and founder of the Yuan Dynasty that ruled China. It did not take long for the man to persuade the two Venetians to follow him back to China to meet the Emperor in person.

After a yearlong journey, they arrived at the court of Kublai Khan. Impressed by their tale and curious about the Christian world, the Emperor appointed them his personal ambassadors to the Pope. They were to travel to Rome and then return to China with one hundred wise men of the Christian Church willing to make the case before him that Christianity was the superior religion; the Emperor also asked for a small vial of sacred oil from Christ's sepulchre in Jerusalem.

It took the Polos three years to make the journey back from China to the Mediterranean. In the port city of Acre, the last stronghold of the Crusader States in the Holy Land, they learned from the Pope's resident ambassador, Tebaldo da Piacenza, that Pope Clement IV was dead. What to do? Tebaldo suggested they wait around for the election of the new Pope to make their embassy. The election promised to be a long-drawn-out affair, so the two brothers sailed to Venice in the meantime, to see their loved ones. They had been away seventeen years.

In Venice, Niccolò learned that his wife was long dead. She had been pregnant when he had left the city, and he now met his sixteen-year-old son, Marco, who had been raised by his uncles. Niccolò took a second wife, Fiordelise Trevisan, who gave him another son, Maffio.

Deliberations in Rome dragged on. After two years there was still no Pope. The two brothers decided they could no longer wait, and they began the long and arduous journey back to China. This time Niccolò took with him his son Marco.

Their first destination was Jerusalem, where they managed to obtain some precious oil from the Holy Sepulchre to give to Kublai Khan. They then headed north to Anatolia, and were still on their way when word reached them that a new Pope had finally been elected. And the choice had fallen on none other than their old acquaintance, Tebaldo da Piacenza. The new Pope, who took the name Gregory X, was still in Palestine. He summoned the Polos back from Anatolia and gave them a letter for Kublai Khan. But Pope Gregory X dispatched only two churchmen (instead of one hundred)—men of such little stamina they abandoned the caravan at the first difficulty.

THE ROAD TO THE HINDU KUSH

The Polos headed once again to the kingdom of Kublai Khan in what turned out to be a slow, three-year-long, meandering journey through Anatolia, Persia, Afghanistan, Uzbekistan, the Pamir plateau and across China.

During the nearly twenty years Marco ended up spending in Asia, he took copious notes that later found their way into his book. He always reacted to his surroundings with the eyes of a merchant looking to make a good trade. But the range and depth of his observations, the quality of his anecdotes reflected the skills of a consummate travel writer who could re-create in a well-turned paragraph the worlds he visited.

The second journey of the Polos into Asia began around 1272 at the seaport of Layas, a busy harbor in the northeast corner of the Mediterranean which they reached by sea from Acre. Their caravan moved slowly north across Anatolia to Erzurum, near the Black Sea, then east, past Noah's Mount Ararat, "a very high mountain," Marco wrote, "where fresh snow falls upon old snow and cannot be climbed to the top." In the lower parts, however, "the pastures are so rich and abundant from the snowmelt that they fill up with cattle from all the neighboring regions."

Heading south across the mountains into Kurdistan, the Polos stopped for a while in Mosul, a mostly Christian city in present-day Iraq, famous for delicate cotton fabrics of plain weave which Venetians called *mosuline* (today's muslins). It was famous too, Marco added wryly, for the "wretched brigands who live in the mountains and gladly steel from merchants."

Then it was on to the ancient metropolis of Tabriz, in what is now northwestern Iran and which, under Mongolian rule, was fast becoming an important commercial center. Marco found it a very pleasant city, surrounded by gardens and orchards filled with a great variety of fruit trees. Merchants from as far away as Europe and India traveled there to buy and sell fabrics, pearls and precious stones. "Traders can make a lot of money here," he pointed out. But the wealth, he noted, did not trickle down and "the local population remains poor." Despite their reduced circumstances, Armenians, Georgians, Persians and Arabs managed to live in relative harmony. There was a strong Christian community, but Muslims were making many new converts by practicing what Marco described as unfair religious competition: "It is enough for a man to say that Mohammad is God's emissary on Earth to be promised salvation."

The natural thing to do from Tabriz would have been to push eastward, rounding the southern shore of the Caspian Sea. Instead the Polos made a four-month-long detour, traveling down the length of Persia to the Arabian Sea. Perhaps they wanted to gauge the possibility of finding a sea passage to India, even as they explored the commercial possibilities Persia offered.

The country, it turned out, was rich in grains—wheat, barley, millet and oats grew plentifully. Nearer the towns and villages, the land was covered with vineyards and a great many fruit trees, especially peaches, apricots, pomegranates, quinces and date palms. The cities were busy with traders and artisans. Horse breeding was a major commercial activity in many of the regions they visited along the way.

In Yazd, in central Persia, Marco admired the gold-embroidered silk gowns known as *yazdi*. After eight more days on the road, through extensive groves of date palms filled with partridges and quails, the Polos reached the city of Kerman, famous for the high-quality turquoise quarried in the nearby mountains. Local artisans used turquoise gemstones to decorate "saddles, bridles, spurs, swords, bows, quivers, and other hunting and warring gear." Textile workers specialized in luxury fabrics designed "for the curtains and coverlets and cushions of the sleeping places of the rich."

After another week on the road, moving across a pleasant countryside where herdsmen tended their flocks, the Polos made their way into the high mountains of the Jebal Barez. The temperature dropped and, despite their heavy furs, they suffered from the bitter cold. Eventually they descended into a plain where the climate was again hot and dry, and after a few days they reached Jiroft, a city which the Mongols had laid to waste only a few years before and was now "of little consequence," despite a noble past.

The countryside surrounding the ruins of Jiroft, however, was very inviting. A wide array of fruit trees attracted pheasants, partridges, turtledoves and black francolins. Fields of wheat were plowed by the mighty zebu, beautiful white oxen with their characteristic hump. When he first saw one from a distance, Marco thought he was seeing a fat-tailed sheep the size of an ass. "Also, they are excellent to eat."

From Jiroft, it was a five-day journey across a wide plateau, and then down through a treacherous road to a lower plain where the land was flat and covered with date palms. A hot wind blew in from the sea. At land's end they saw the great seaport of Hormuz clustered on an island just off the coast.

Hormuz teemed with traders who had sailed from the western coast of India bringing spices, medicinal herbs, gemstones, pearls, gold jewelry, fine fabrics and elephant tusks. The merchandise was sold and then loaded on caravans that were assembled on the coastline beaches. From Hormuz, the goods traveled to Asia Minor, Europe and Africa along well-worn commercial routes. The boats made their return voyage to India with all manner of artifacts in their holds, but they mostly carried back Persian-bred horses brought down to Hormuz and kept in huge corrals along the coast until they were sold and taken on board the waiting ships.

If the Polos had hoped to sail to India themselves on one of those transport ships, they quickly changed their minds. They knew how to build a boat—they were Venetians!—and one expert look at those vessels was enough to convince them that they were "of the worst kind and dangerous for navigation." According to Marco, they were built without nails (the wood was too hard); instead, the planks were "sewn" together with a special twine made with the filaments stripped from coconuts. The ships were not properly caulked and were prone to leaks. The shipbuilders often resorted to ingenious solutions; but this did not change the fact that they were bound to go down "in the slightest tempest."

So the Polos turned around and made their way back to Kerman. From there, a three-day journey northward got them to Kuhbanan, an agreeable town with mild temperatures, where Marco, by now a vigorous twenty-year-old, eyed some very nice mirrors made of polished Indian steel—and the women reflected in them, "who in my opinion are the most beautiful in the world."

They continued north for another six days across the green pastures, hills and dales of Khorasan until they entered a harsh desert, the crossing of which was only to be attempted "with a very substantial supply of water."

The exhausted caravan emerged in present-day northern Afghanistan. The Polos rested in the city of Shebargan, where they tasted "the most delicious melon in the world." Years later Marco still recalled the local custom of cutting the melon in thin spiraling slices and leaving them out to dry until they tasted "as sweet as apples."

The next stop on the Polos' eastward march was the noble city of Balkh, or what remained of it after Genghis Khan's armies had sacked and destroyed the old citadel and butchered the population.

Balkh was the ancient seat of Zoroastrianism and Buddhism before the advance of Islam; it was also the city where Alexander the Great allegedly married Roxana, the daughter of a local nobleman. According to Marco, it was still possible to get a sense of what the city had been by walking amid the grandiose ruins and across the now empty, spacious squares.

But there was no time to tarry. The caravan pressed on along a narrow valley between two spines of the Hindu Kush range that ran parallel to the course of the river Oxus. After twelve days the Polos arrived in Taloqan, a prosperous town at the foot of the mountains, in today's northwestern Afghanistan. A great mud castle looked down on the cluster of houses around the busy market square; farther down, a fast-moving river was lined with poplar trees that shimmered in the cool mountain air. Almond trees and groves of pistachios grew in profusion. But Taloqan was better known in the region for its rich salt mines—"the purest salt in the world—so hard it can only be broken with iron picks."

After another three days heading east across the Hindu Kush range, the Polos entered a fertile valley where the Panj River, a tributary of the Oxus, flowed gently among scattered plane trees. This was the valley of the Ishkashim, a proud, independent people who spoke their own language. The land was rich and they harvested wheat and barley. A favorite local pastime was hunting porcupine. Not always an easy chase: "These animals roll themselves up into a ball and shoot out their quills, wounding the men and their dogs."

Beyond the valley of the Ishkashim, the caravan snaked its way in rugged, uneven terrain until it arrived in the Kingdom of Badakhshan. It was a traveler's paradise. "Between the lofty mountains," Marco wrote, "are wide plains covered with rich grassland where sheep graze in flocks of two, three, four hundred. Large streams of the purest water come spurting out through clefts in the rocks, and in these streams are trout and many other fine fish."

The region was famous for the quality of its deep blue lapis lazuli and the purity of its rubies, both of which were heavily mined in the surrounding mountains. Although Marco doesn't say, the Polos probably took the opportunity to make a few trades. Gemstones were a practical asset—easy to carry and easy to convert.

In Badakhshan the men dressed themselves with the skins and furs of wild animals. They were excellent horsemen and archers. This was horse breeding country and the horses were very sturdy and fast. Their hooves were so hard they didn't need to be shod. It was said they descended from Bucephalus, Alexander the Great's legendary steed.

The Badakhshani were also good tillers of the land. They grew wheat of the finest quality and a type of barley without a husk. They had no olives but extracted oil from sesame seeds, which Marco swears was "better and more flavorful than any other." Across the region, the villages and small towns were busy with the banter of tradesmen and the tinkering of artisans. Silversmiths and copper-smiths in particular produced refined artifacts.

The Polos ended up staying in Badakhshan much longer than planned. Marco fell ill and, although he gives no details about his ailment—in his writings he was very reserved about his private life—it must have been fairly serious, for they stayed a whole year in the end.

When people fell ill in Badakhshan, it was customary to take them high up into the mountains for a few days. "The air is so pure and healthy that they soon recover," Marco explained. Eventually, he too was taken to the highlands and there he got well enough to travel again.

The Polos had been on the road for two years already and still had a long way to go before reaching their destination. The crossing of the Kingdom of Badakhshan itself required twelve days. They traveled another three days along the track, which now veered northeast along a narrow corridor that followed the Panj River and led them to the region of Wakhan.

The landscape was now stark against the deep blue sky: steep barren mountains, silvery green poplars along the banks of the river, the occasional mud village and always a few flocks of sheep here and there nibbling at the rocky terrain. The track continued to rise gently as they headed up toward the Pamir plateau, where three great mountain ranges meet—the Hindu Kush to the east, the Himalayas to the south and the Tien Shan to the north. It was a grueling climb. "Mountain after mountain you slowly ascend," Marco noted, "until you come to a region which is said to be the highest in the world."

It took twelve days to cross the windswept Pamir highland at a fairly constant altitude of thirteen thousand feet. They followed the course of a wide river flanked by pastures so rich "the leanest cattle would turn fat in ten days." In these wide-open expanses Polo spotted the great sheep of Pamir, with its spectacular spiraling horns "sometimes six palms in length." Five centuries later, Edward Blyth, a British zoologist at the Asiatic Society of India in Calcutta, would name that particular subspecies after Polo (*Ovis ammon polii*).

INTO THE MONGOLIAN EMPIRE

After their descent from the Pamir, the Polos came to a crossroad. One track went north. It would have led, after forty days of slow travel across rugged regions inhabited by rough, primitive tribes, to Kashgar, a busy commercial city that owed its prosperity to its position at the junction of the great caravan roads connecting Asia and Europe. Marco gives a brief description of Kashgar—the handsome gardens, orchards and vineyards; the great textile industry; the large presence of Muslims. But he is probably reporting what his father and uncle had seen on their earlier return journey from China.

Instead, coming down from the Pamir, the Polos most likely turned east at the crossroad and followed the southern rim of the Taklamakan Desert, a vast, sand-shifting basin that stretches just north of Tibet for about six hundred miles. The track followed a narrow strip of land between the Tibetan plateau and the desert proper and passed through ancient cities where the Polo caravan stopped to trade and stock up on supplies.

This region had once formed the Kingdom of Khotan, a prosperous Buddhist state that was wiped out in the eleventh century by Turkic conquerors who had converted to Islam. By the time the Polos arrived, the region had been invaded by the Mongols and was now ruled by the Great Khan. But the population, Polo noted, remained predominantly Muslim.

Khotan, the ancient capital, was still a rich city. The fields around it produced good quantities of cotton, hemp and linseed, as well as wheat. Every farm had its vineyard, and orchards with pomegranates, pear and apricot trees, and mulberries. The streets were filled with the din of artisans. It was a merchants' dream of a city "and there is everything one needs in greatest plenty."

Farther down the road was Kharcan, once a thriving center that had been "laid waste" by the Mongols. Much of the population had left and the city was semi-abandoned. The rivers and streams nearby, tributaries of the Kharcan River, were full of jasper and chalcedony, and the gathering of those gemstones was one of the few activities still practiced there.

From the sandy old city of Kharcan it was another five days across more arid terrain before they reached the town of Lop, on the edge of a salt lake that extended into the western part of the vast Gobi, which Marco calls the Great Desert (*Gobi* is the Mongol word for "desert").

Lop was the last bastion of Islam on the road to China, and the major gathering place for caravans intending to cross the Gobi—a journey that required weeks of preparation. Marco estimated that it took several months to cross the desert lengthwise. It was an extremely hazardous journey as water was hard to find along the way. "Travelers must load a number of stout asses and camels with provisions and merchandise before they venture out," he warned. In addition, evil spirits inhabited the desert and lured travelers to their destruction with mysterious voices and songs. Or so the Polos were told. They prudently kept to the route that skirted the southern rim of the desert and kept them in view of the Tibetan plateau.

After a month the caravan reached Sachion (Dunhuang), the first in a string of towns along an open passage that ran south of the Gobi and north of the Tibetan plateau and is known today as the Hexi Corridor. This well-traveled "funnel" was, and still is, the main point of entry when one travels overland from Central Asia into China.

The region was an important center of Tibetan Buddhism. Sachion was crowded with gilded temples and monasteries. Buddhist monks were suddenly everywhere, and Muslims were now a small minority. The Polos were entering a new world.

The landscape softened as they continued their eastward journey. The sandy, rocky terrain on which they had traveled since coming down from the Pamir receded. Now the countryside was dotted with farms and villages and fortified towns.

The largest of these was Succuir (Jiuquan), a prosperous trading center surrounded by fruit trees loaded with pears, apricots, peaches, and apples that made good cider. Cantaloupes and watermelons grew in the fields. But the principal staple—the product for which the region was known by merchants far and wide—was rhubarb, a medicinal plant that grew wild in the nearby mountains and was widely used against stomach pains and gastrointestinal troubles.

Although highly prized in Asia, rhubarb had only recently appeared in apothecaries in Europe, thanks largely to adventurous Muslim traders. But demand for it was growing, and its commercial potential was certainly not lost on the Polos. "Here it is produced in large quantities," Marco noted with interest. "Merchants buy loads of it and ship it to all parts of the world."

In late spring, farmers came down from the mountains, their carts overflowing with mounds of leafy rhubarb which they sold to local middlemen. The root and underground stem of each plant was then cut and laid to rest on wooden planks for a few days. Once the rich yellow and red juices had congealed properly, the pieces were hung to dry in the wind until they were ready to be shipped, usually after a couple of weeks.

Ramusio learned these particular details about how rhubarb was treated not from Marco but from a Persian merchant who happened

IL RHEVBARBARIO

Demand for rhubarb was growing in Europe in the time of Marco Polo. This sketch, possibly by Ramusio himself, was published in 1559 in Book Two of *Navigationi et Viaggi*.

to be passing through Venice at the time when he was studying the Ghisi manuscript. His name was Chaggi Memet, and he too had traveled to Succuir in a caravan, much the same way the Polos had nearly three centuries before. Over lunch on the island of Murano, Memet entertained Ramusio and a few of his friends with stories about his travels in Asia. With Marco's account still fresh in his mind, Ramusio was enthralled by his guest's detailed description of the rhubarb market, which had greatly expanded since the days of the Polos. In fact, Memet happened to have with him a sketch of the rhubarb plant, which Ramusio copied and later had printed.

The Polo caravan made progress through the Hexi Corridor. Ten days after leaving Succuir, it arrived in Campion (Zhangye), "a large and magnificent city" made of stone houses, each with its vegetable garden and private orchard. And everywhere one looked there were beautiful golden temples and monasteries and representations of the Buddha. "Some of these were made of wood, some of stone, some of clay; and all were carved and gilded and polished in a masterly style," wrote Marco. One reclining Buddha was at least ten paces long. "Behind it were smaller figures that looked like disciples in the act of reverent salutation."

Marco was struck by certain religious customs he learned about in Campion, including an unusual ritual surrounding the birth of a son: "After the child is born the father rears a sheep, and after a year the sheep is brought before the Idol and sacrificed. The flesh is boiled and laid out as an offering and the family prays to preserve the boy in good health. Once the Idol has absorbed all the juices of the flesh, the family takes the remains back home and feasts on them. Priests are given the choicest morsels: head, feet, intestines, skin. The bones are set aside and placed in an urn."

The dead in these same provinces were burnt, Marco went on, but only when astrologers said the constellations were properly aligned. This could take some time, and the corpse, meanwhile, would begin to decompose. "They place it in a coffin made with boards a palm thick in order to contain the smells of putrefaction. The coffin is then sealed with pitch and lime and rubbed with sweet-scented gums and camphor, and finally covered with silk fabric. Food and wine are placed on the table where the coffin lies long enough for the dead person to feed itself and for its spirit to satisfy itself with the aromas of the victuals."

It sometimes happened that astrologers advised not to take the coffin out of the house through the front door if celestial signs were not propitious. And if the windows were too small, which was often the case, the only way to get the coffin to the pyre was to tear down a wall.

It is perhaps worth noting that whenever Marco described religious practices that surely must have seemed very strange to him, he avoided the use of derogatory terms and never used a superior tone. His writing was always factual and detached—a reporting style that Ramusio surely appreciated.

As for sex, Marco went on, monks "abstained from the indulgence of carnal and sensual desires," but among the general population "unrestricted intercourse was not considered a serious offense." According to the accepted rule, if the woman took the first step, it was all right to have sex, but not if it was the man—which might seem to some readers today as an early and rather enlightened application of the principle of consent. However, Marco added, "this custom did not prevent men from having a great number of wives—as many as thirty in some cases—so long as they could afford it."

The population was generally vegetarian (except when it came to certain religious sacrifices!) and had little inclination for war. They were farmers, artisans and merchants. The friendly, peaceful atmosphere provided a welcome respite from the grueling fatigue of travel. The Polos were also pleased to discover that, although they encountered few Christians, the town of Campion alone had three churches where they could worship their God.

They settled down and stayed a whole year. The Christian churches had little to do with their decision. "Business required it," Marco explained. And although he didn't say so specifically, it is hard to imagine what else could have kept them there for so long, if not the exciting possibilities offered by the rhubarb trade.

In Ramusio's time, travel to China was restricted, and the passage of caravans all the way through the Hexi Corridor no longer permitted. Memet, the merchant visiting Venice, told Ramusio that he had not been able to go beyond Campion. But in the Polos' time, during Mongol rule, trade was active and the road into China open and well-traveled.

Leaving the Hexi Corridor behind, the caravan entered a vast new province called Erginul (Qinghai), which took twenty-five days to cross. The towns and villages were pleasant and prosperous. Now that they had left the rougher regions of Central Asia, the physical features of the artisans and tradesmen with whom they interacted also changed. "The men are fat and their noses small," Marco noted. "Their hair is black and they have no beard save for a few scattered hairs on their chin. The women of the higher classes are fair of skin, well formed and free of superfluous hairs."

The road traversed wide-open plains moistened by gently flow-ing rivers—the headwaters of the Yellow and the Yangtze rivers are both in the region. Wild yaks "so large as to be comparable to elephants" grazed the rich pastures. The merchant in Polo was quick to notice the fine quality of their long, shaggy hair. "It is white and black and lies flat on the body; but on the shoulders it is white and woolly, and stands upright as high as three palms, and is softer and more delicate than silk." Many years later, when Marco returned to Venice, he brought back samples of yak wool. "It was greatly appreciated by all who saw it."

Even more alluring, from a merchant's point of view, were the herds of musk deer that roamed the plains. They looked like small antelopes long in the tooth, "with their four husk-like teeth—two above and two below—that were no less than three inches long." The local custom was to kill the animals on nights of full moon. "The sac of coagulated blood containing the precious gland is sev-ered and put to dry the next day in the sun," Marco explained. Those desiccated glands produced "the powerful perfume" that was so sought after not just in courts across Asia but in Europe as well.

Marco marveled at all the valuable goods they were finding. He saw his first white camels in Egrigaia (Ningxia), a rich province they reached after eight more days on the road. Local weavers used the silky hair of those rare animals to make camlet, a delicate fabric that was the height of luxury in Venice. Rich merchants paid very dearly to line the collars of their winter cloaks with it.

Soon the caravan reached the province of Tenduc (Hohhot), where Europeans believed Prester John's empire was located. The Polos made their way to the capital of this legendary kingdom with great anticipation. The visit, however, was a letdown. The Mon-gols had long taken over the province. True, a Christian king, a man named George who claimed to be fourth in descent from the original Prester John, was allowed to rule the fiefdom in their name. The Great Khan even gave royal daughters in marriage to George's sons and nephews to keep the little puppet state going. But Marco warned against lingering illusions: what was still referred to in Europe as Prester John's empire was only a small "portion" of what people imagined back home. And in any case, the kingdom now belonged to the Great Khan.

MEETING KUBLAI KHAN

News of the Polos' return reached the Great Khan, who sent a squadron of guards to escort the caravan during the last leg of the journey. From King George's little fiefdom it was only three days to Cianganor, an idyllic imperial hunting estate with silky streams and placid lakes dotted with swans. The Great Khan enjoyed hunting there because it was near Mongolia and he felt closer to his family roots. The low green hills around the lodge were filled with pheasants, partridges and quails. The fields were regularly sown with millet and other grains so the birds were well fed when the Great Khan visited the estate with his hawks and gyrfalcons.

Cianganor was still weeks away from Cambalu, the new capital of the empire, where the Great Khan resided. But the Polos were invited to rest at his hunting estate as long as they pleased before traveling to the capital, where he awaited them.

Marco was deeply impressed by the beauty of the estate. He was especially taken by the multitude of colorful cranes. He counted at least five varieties. One was black as a raven, with large wings; another was like the white cranes that were common back home; a third one was smaller, with handsome streaks of red and blue; the fourth was large and gray, with a black head and red crest. The most dazzling of all was a large crane with very long wings and feathers with eyes like a peacock's, but shiny and golden; the head was a stark black against the red crest, and the neck was black and white. "It was truly stunning," he wrote, perhaps referring to the red-crowned crane, a species that is highly endangered today.

Cianganor was a first taste of the magnificence that awaited the Polos. After three more days on the road, they reached the Great Khan's fabled summer residence in Xanadu (Shangdu), where again they were invited to stay as long as they liked.

For all their traveling, they had never seen anything so splendid. The vast imperial palace was built with the finest marble and a selection of the handsomest stones. The interior halls and chambers were entirely gilt. Marco was dazzled by "the elegance of the design and the skill of the execution."

The palace faced the town of Xanadu, while the back looked out onto a vast walled park that Marco reckoned was no less than sixteen miles long all around. Inside the park were rolling green meadows freshened by springs and rivulets, and handsome groves and woods. A variety of animals "of the deer and goat families" roamed the estate and served as prey for hawks and other rapacious birds the Great Khan kept on the grounds. When he was in residence and went riding out on the estate, he was in the habit of asking his retinue to bring a small leopard along. At a whim, the leopard was released, and within instants it would kill a stag, a goat or fallow deer. The prey was then fed to the hawks. "In this manner the Great Khan amuses himself," Marco reported.

Scattered across the imperial grounds were beautiful horses "white as snow." Marco claimed, no doubt exaggerating, that the Great Khan kept ten thousand of those horses in his stables, adding that "they were highly revered and no one dared stand in front of them even when they were at pasture in the meadows." The mares' milk was thought to be a divine beverage; only members of the imperial family—direct descendants of Genghis Khan—were allowed to drink it.

When the Great Khan was in Xanadu, during the months of June, July and August, he stayed in the imperial pavilion, an architectural marvel built in a grove at the center of the grounds. The building was supported by a colonnade of finely gilded pillars. Around each one, a golden dragon entwined its tail while its head supported the extended roof. The entire edifice, including the roof, was built with large bamboo canes, three palms in girth, well varnished and so closely knitted together that the edifice was perfectly waterproof. The roof was made of canes that were cut at the joint, split in two and laid alternately concave or convex to form natural gutters. The pavilion was so light it had to be held down with silk cords—two hundred of them—lest it blow away with a strong wind. It was put together with such ingenuity that every component could easily be taken apart, removed and set up again, at the Emperor's pleasure. The spot where the pavilion had been put up when the Polos visited was so idyllic, the air so pure and the temperature so mild, Marco observed, it was no wonder the Great Khan liked to use it in the summer.

Kublai Khan finally received the Polos in the new winter capital, Cambalu (a distortion of *Khanbaliq,* the "City of the Khan"; it was situated where Beijing stands today), some two hundred miles east of Xanadu. Here the imperial family lived in a large palace inside a fortified citadel, with elegant gardens, fishponds and swans. The rest of the city, still largely under construction but growing fast, was built like a chessboard, with straight avenues and cross streets. Civil servants and foreign diplomats were housed in Taide, a nearby satellite city.

The Great Khan was apparently very pleased to see the Polo brothers return after so many years. True, he was disappointed that they hadn't brought with them one hundred learned Christian scholars, as he had requested; but he was delighted with the bottle of precious oil from the Holy Sepulchre, which they had carried all the way from Jerusalem.

Niccolò brought forward his twenty-two-year-old son, who bowed deeply and lifted his gaze to see "a man of average height, well proportioned, with a rosy complexion, dark eyes and an elegant nose."

A REPORTER IN CHINA

Marco Polo's meticulous description of his journey to China helped Ramusio fill in huge gaps relative to the Asian landmass. And the more he cross-referenced place-names, recalculated distances and verified the information Marco provided, the more confident he grew that he was on solid ground: Marco's narrative was turning out to be not just a fascinating tale of adventure but the greatest source of factual information about Asia. One can imagine the excitement with which Ramusio turned to studying the next section in Polo's *Travels,* which still today reads like an extensive, eye-opening reportage on China. And this despite the occasional embellishment or unfounded rumor inserted to enliven the narrative.

The Great Khan, who was now around seventy years old, had in the space of three decades enlarged and consolidated the most powerful empire of its time, an immense territory that stretched from the China Sea to Central Asia, administered by a well-organized government and an efficient bureaucracy.

Marco, who had already picked up the rudiments of the Mongolian language along the way, must have impressed the Great Khan with his mature demeanor and his intelligence, for he was soon serving him as a personal envoy.

He ended up staying in China sixteen years and learned several more languages and acquired a great familiarity with the sprawling machinery of government. He traveled extensively across the country on official missions, recording geographical data and mapping out the territory, always looking for new ways of advancing the family business. He visited the silk factories in Xian, the salt mines in Tingu (Changzhou), the stud farms in Yunnan, the arms manufactures in Yangui (Yangzhou), the sugar factories in Unguem (Minhou) and the great port cities in southern China.

He was fascinated by the efficient use of paper money, which did not exist in Europe. In China it had been around for at least two hundred years, but the Great Khan had vastly extended its use to facilitate trade throughout the empire. "It now circulates in every part and no one dares refuse it," Marco reported.

Paper money was produced on a massive scale thanks to the ubiquitous mulberry tree that fed the silk industry. "The bark is stripped and separated from the thin membrane that lies between it and the trunk proper," he explained in one of his fascinating asides. "This membrane is then steeped and pounded in a mortar until it is reduced to a pulp and made into paper. Then it is cut up in pieces of different sizes. A number of officials add their name and stamp their seal, after which the chief official affixes the royal seal which has been dipped in vermilion. When the notes wear themselves out they are taken to the mint, where, at a cost of three percent of their value, they are replaced with new ones."

Infrastructure was also key for such a large-scale trading economy. The Mongols built an elaborate transportation system—roads, bridges and canals—that allowed goods and people to move relatively quickly along navigable waterways and well-serviced roads often lined with poplar trees. Comfortable inns were usually available along the way.

A reliable transportation network ensured an efficient postal system: information from the center of the Empire to the periphery traveled quickly by horse and even by foot messengers, who ran short distances—about three miles—to ensure rapidity. The swift passage of these runners was announced by the tinkle of the bells tied to their feet.

In Marco's view, the Great Khan's policy of religious tolerance was another important factor in facilitating trade. Buddhism was the main religion in the Empire, but Muslim and Christian minorities lived in relative harmony. And this, he wrote, created a healthy atmosphere for commerce.

Marco became an unabashed admirer of the Great Khan (and since he wrote about him long after he had left China, there is no reason to believe his admiration was not genuine). He described him as a benevolent ruler who promoted good government by instituting sound domestic policies. He dwelt on the welfare policies aimed at helping the poor, including the distribution of free meals and clothes for the indigent. In the countryside, he added, the government was quick to offer aid to farmers whose crops were damaged or destroyed by natural calamities—storms, rains, floods. In the worst cases, farmers were granted a one-year tax reprieve while the government stepped in to provide enough grain to feed the livestock and provide seeds for the next crop.

A network of more or less reliable civil servants governed the far-flung empire, and it is easy to imagine why the Great Khan would value the opinion of a trusted outside observer. But in his writings, Marco was often vague about the precise nature of the missions he was asked to undertake.

This we know: in the late 1270s, a couple of years after the Polos arrived, the Great Khan sent Marco on a four-month-long fact-finding mission to Sichuan and Yunnan, the two great regions in southwestern China that had been recently subjugated by the Mongolian army.

The gateway in and out of Cambalu, the capital, was a massive bridge ten miles west of the city that stretched over the Hun-ho (or "Muddy") River for a length of about one hundred paces. It was a grandiose structure. The ascending bridge rested on twenty-four marble arches; the upper level was decorated on each side with lofty columns standing on marble tortoises and topped with the figure of a lion.

Beyond the bridge, the road continued for about thirty miles and then bifurcated into two main arteries, one headed west to northern China, the other to southern China.

Polo took the southern route and traveled on horseback across a flat countryside dotted with fortified towns and small villages surrounded by well-tended fields, orchards and mulberry groves. He diligently took down place-names and distances (days of travel), and wrote brief descriptions, mapping the territory every step of the way.

After crossing the Yellow River at Cacianfu (Puzhou), he headed south across the rich agricultural plains of the Wei River basin until he reached Quezanfu (Xian), the ancient capital of the once great kingdom of Shanxi, then an important trading center for silk fabrics, ruled by a son of the Great Khan. Marco continued on his southbound journey into the rugged mountains of the Tsin Ling Shan range. A narrow twisting road took him through gorges and over lofty peaks and into thick forests filled with tigers, bears, lynx, fallow deer, antelopes and stags.

It took him twenty days to get across the range. Whether he was traveling alone or as a member of an official delegation is unclear. In any case, he never complained about the physical discomforts of traveling and he insisted he found "convenient accommodations" in small mountain villages along the way.

At last the road led into the plains of Sichuan, a vast region irrigated by the sprawling Upper Yangtze River system that flowed down from the Tibetan plateau. Sichuan, conquered by the Great Khan some two decades earlier, was a prosperous land. The capital, Sin-din-fu (Chengdu), was fast becoming an important trading center. A tributary of the Yangtze flowed through the busy city, bringing in large barges filled with exotic goods. The focal point of commercial activity was a long covered bridge that stretched across the river. A row of marble pillars supported a tiled wooden roof decorated with vivid red paintings. The whole length of the bridge was lined with small shops and warehouses. On one end, a larger building housed the officers who collected duties and tolls.

The use of paper money was not yet widespread in distant Sichuan. Instead, local merchants used little gold rods for large purchases and so-called salt money for everyday expenses. Salt was mined and boiled until it formed a paste that was then cut into small cakes, flat on the bottom and convex on the top. The cakes were then hardened on hot tiles set by the fire. The production of these salt cakes, which were worth two pence each and carried the stamp of the Great Khan, was strictly controlled by government officials.

Marco was surprised to discover that Sichuan was a large producer of cloves, a staple that commanded large sums on the Rialto and was usually associated with the tropical climate of the Spice Islands. "The tree is small," he observed. "The branches and leaves

resemble those of the laurel shrub but are somewhat longer and nar-
rower. The flowers are white, as are the cloves themselves, which
darken as they ripen." The main export, however, was ginger. "It is
produced here in large quantities and shipped to the entire province
of Cathay."

The local wine was "excellent," he noted, even though it was not
made with grapes but wheat and rice and a mixture of spices.

From Chengdu it was another ten days to the banks of the Yangtze
River, which separated Sichuan from Yunnan. Before the Mongol
invasions, Yunnan was divided into seven different kingdoms; now
it was ruled by Essen Temur, one of Kublai Khan's grandsons and,
according to Marco, "a wise and virtuous man."

The capital, Yachi (Kunming), was built on the eastern shore of
Lake Dian, some five days south of the Yangtze River. It was a lively
city. The streets were lined with the shops of artisans and trade was
brisk. As in Sichuan, the use of paper money was still limited: cow-
rie shells imported from bordering Vietnam were the currency of
choice.

Much of the flat land around the city was covered with rice fields;
and rice was the main staple of the local diet, together with fish
from the lake.

The region was famous for its horse breeding farms, and horses
were Yunnan's main export to its southern neighbors: India, Burma
and Vietnam—countries Kublai Khan had tried in vain to conquer
by sending large armies, and which were now important trading
partners.

Yachi was the last official stop on Marco's fact-finding mission in
southwestern China. Before heading back north, he decided to
make a ten-day detour to Dali, an ancient city nestled between Lake
Erhai and the mountains of the Cangshan range. Dali had once been
the capital of a kingdom of the same name but had been largely

destroyed by Kublai Khan's army during the Mongolian conquest. It was now being rebuilt under the supervision of one of Kublai Khan's sons. Trade-wise, the province offered little of interest. But Marco never forgot his time in Dali because it was where he saw his first crocodile. He called it a serpent for lack of a more specific word: "It moves along the shore like a heavy trunk dragged in the sand. The jaws are wide enough to swallow a man, the teeth are large and sharp, and their whole appearance is so formidable that neither man nor animal can approach it without terror."

Instead of confronting the beast, hunters preferred to lay traps by planting wooden stakes tipped with sharp iron spikes in the sand. "The serpent's flesh," Marco explained, "was considered a delicacy and sold at high prices."

A TURN IN SOUTHERN CHINA

The Sung Dynasty ruled southern China for three centuries before it was swept away by the Mongols. In 1268, only seven years before Marco arrived at his court, Kublai Khan had sent a large army led by his trusted commander Ching Hsiang ("the Hundred-Eyed") into the territories south of the Yellow River. The old Sung monarchy had lost the taste for war. The king fled, cities fell one after the other, and the Hundred-Eyed and his men easily took the Sung capital, Hangzhou—the Celestial City.

With one relatively brief campaign, Kublai Khan had more than doubled the size of his empire and brought about the reunification of China. Southern China, which Marco referred to as Manzi (*Mantse,* the Mongolian word for "barbarian"), was a rich, highly developed country; it was divided into nine provinces interconnected by a network of roads and canals and busy port cities along the coast.

In the early 1280s Marco was sent on an official mission to the city of Yangui (Yangzhou), in the heart of southern China, apparently to act as substitute for the local governor (although, as we shall see, there is no proof that he did).

He traveled to his destination at a leisurely pace, taking notes, as he always did, on the landscape, the towns and cities he visited, the products of the land and of the local artisans. In Changlu, he stopped to study the production of crystallized salt, which was exported to the rest of the country. Farther south, in Changli, a city in the heart of the Shantung district, he observed the making of the delicate silks for which the province was famous.

The road south roughly followed the Grand Canal, which connected southern and northern China and was crowded with loaded barges of all sizes. Trade flourished in all the towns and cities along the great waterway. It sometimes seemed to Marco as if the entire region was one giant commercial district—a merchant's paradise.

Six days after leaving Changli, he arrived in Tandinfu (Dongping), once the capital of Shantung. The city had been the scene of a recent insurrection on the part of one of Kublai Khan's own lieutenants, but was once again peaceful and very agreeable— a place where one might even want to settle. "The gardens which surround it, filled with handsome shrubs and excellent fruits, make it a delightful place to live. And silk is produced in wonderfully large quantities."

But duty called.

Three days after leaving Tandinfu he arrived in Jining, another great city on the Grand Canal, where "the sheer number and size of vessels continually passing to and fro laden with goods of the greatest value was astonishing."

After another two weeks across flat rich country dotted with thriving small towns and villages, Marco reached the city of Coiganzu, on the banks of the Yellow River, which he reckoned was at least a mile wide at that point, and teeming with commercial ships.

The river marked the border between Cathay (northern China) and Manzi (southern China). There was a strong military presence in the area. The Great Khan kept a large navy—as many as fifteen thousand vessels, according to Marco—anchored in a harbor farther downstream, in the delta of the Yellow River. Each vessel could carry fifteen horses and up to twenty armed men, not counting the crew. These ships were mostly used to transport troops up and down the coast with great speed in case of popular unrest.

The road into Manzi was a well-paved causeway built on a levee that ran across wide lagoons deep enough for navigation. The Hundred-Eyed had sailed into those waters with his invading force some twenty years before.

Once on firm ground again, Marco resumed his journey, heading now in a southwestern direction to his final destination: the wealthy and powerful city of Yangzhou, on the north bank of the Yangtze River.

Yangzhou was the capital of a vast province with jurisdiction over twenty-seven other cities, according to Polo's count. It had a vibrant cultural life, bustling marketplaces and busy workshops. But the economic backbone of the city was "the manufacture of arms and military equipment of all kinds that served the many troops stationed in this part of the country."

The province was ruled by a "baron" or governor named by the Great Council but usually handpicked by the Great Khan himself. Marco didn't explain why he was sent to Yangzhou, only claiming that he "acted as governor for three years by special order of the Great Khan." Was he there simply to replace an untrustworthy official? Or to manage the all-important salt marshes east of the city? Or to supervise the production of arms? Not long before Marco was dispatched to Yangzhou, the arsenal had exploded and a raging fire had caused the death of more than a hundred people and crippled production capacity. Was his presence there somehow related to that event?

Whatever the nature of his mission, it was important enough to keep him there for three years. During that time he had occasion to travel extensively down the Pacific coast. He visited the porcelain manufactures in Tingui (scholars have not identified this city), where, he said, the earth was exposed to wind, sun and rain for forty years before being treated and refined and baked. "It seems the artisans work for their children and grandchildren . . ." He reported on the abundance of ginger and galangal in the former kingdom of Concha (Fujian), and on the great sugar plantations and refineries introduced there by the Great Khan. He visited the garrison city of Fuju (Fuzhou), on the banks of the Min River, where the Emperor kept another large army to quash possible insurrections. And he followed the coast down to the sprawling port city of Zaitun (Quanzhou), so busy it was "impossible to convey an idea of the number of merchants operating there or the quantities of goods passing through."

The amount of pepper that was unloaded in Zaitun was "one hundred times greater than the amount that reached Alexandria on its way to Europe," Marco declared emphatically.

Indeed, one of the challenges he faced was in providing his audience at home with a sense of the extraordinary scale of things—the size of the cities, the great number of people, the number of ships sailing up and down the large waterways, the sheer quantity of goods being moved across the Empire.

Of all the cities Marco visited, none impressed him more than Kinsai (Hangzhou), the old capital of the Sung Dynasty. It was a truly splendid city of canals and well-paved avenues spread out along the shore of the West Lake. Hangzhou was more populous than any city in Europe or the Middle East—some 1.6 million families lived there according to Marco's reckoning, or one million according to recent estimates.

A main avenue ran through the city, with lovely houses on both sides and pagoda-style mansions with gardens. The avenue was paved with bricks and flagstones, but a central lane was covered with gravel and reserved for carriages, while a turf track on the side was exclusively for official messengers on horseback.

The side streets led from the avenue to ten large squares that served as major marketplaces. Shops and private houses lined each square; merchants kept their warehouses along the river that marked the boundary of the city. Barges sailed upstream from the seacoast, delivering merchandise that came all the way from India.

Market stalls overflowed with the greatest selection of vegetables and fruits. Game was especially plentiful: roebuck, fallow deer, hares, rabbits, partridges, pheasants, francolins and quail, even ducks and geese from the lake. Butchers sold quartered oxen and calves and kids and lambs in addition to poultry. And the fishmongers had so much fish brought in every day from the seaports on the coast that it seemed impossible they could sell it in a day. "Yet it was gone in just a few hours."

The market squares were flanked all around by tallish buildings. The ground floor usually housed a craftsman's shop or a store that might sell wine, spices, drugs or rice. Families lived on the top floors. The streets were crammed at all hours of the day with shoppers and strollers "while rich masters put on airs and strutted about proudly."

Despite the crowds, the streets were clean. And so was the citizenry: public baths, where men and women made their daily ablutions, were widely available.

Courtesans were restricted to certain quarters—in theory. In practice, they were all over town "and more numerous than I dare report." They lived in well-furnished houses with servants and were "richly adorned and perfumed." Visits to these pleasure palaces left quite a lasting impression on Marco: "These highly accomplished women are masterly in the art of caressing and fondling, and of shaping words for their customers. Strangers who have once tasted their charms are left in a state of bewilderment, and never forget them."

The West Lake, Hangzhou's main attraction, offered a peaceful contrast to the busy pace of life in the city. Tall leafy trees along the water's edge shaded temples and handsome monasteries. Marco described two islands in the middle of the lake. On each one was a large compound made of several pavilions with elegant reception rooms and dining halls. These popular public spaces were leased for weddings, anniversaries and other celebrations. The meals were catered, but china, silverware and service were provided in-house.

Pleasure boats drifted leisurely on the lake, often leaving a swath of music and laughter in their wake.

MISSIONS ABROAD

During his time at the court of Kublai Khan, Marco was sent on diplomatic missions outside China and reported on distant territories which he either visited or were described to him.

He never made it to Cipangu (Japan), the neighboring country Kublai Khan had tried and failed to conquer. But Marco's mention of its "inexhaustible sources of gold" enflamed the imagination of navigators later on, most notably that of Columbus. This despite Polo's dire warning that "when the natives seize an enemy who cannot raise his ransom, they kill him, make a stew and eat him with gusto as they find human flesh to be the tastiest in the world"—a dubious allegation that may have been part of a broader campaign by the frustrated Chinese to discredit their fiercely independent neighbor.

Marco did sail to the South China Sea and discovered "a whole new world." On one trip south he visited the Kingdom of Ziamba, in present-day Vietnam, reporting on such disparate topics as the widespread use of elephants for travel and transport, the medical properties of aloe and the quality of black ebony. And also on a peculiar form of paternalism the King of Ziamba liked to indulge in: When a young girl was old enough to be married off, she was presented to him. If he found her to his liking, he took her in for a while. When he tired of her, he gave her a dowry with which to find a suitable husband. It was no wonder, Marco noted, that the king was said to have more than three hundred sons and daughters.

He went on to describe a very large island some 1,500 miles south of Vietnam, probably Borneo. There is no evidence that he actually visited the island, but he probably heard from other merchants what a spice treasure it was, with pepper, nutmeg, cinnamon, galangal and cloves growing plentifully.

On a later fact-finding mission, Marco traveled farther south to the island of Samara (Sumatra), with a small fleet and some two thousand mariners and soldiers. Contrary winds forced him to stay longer than expected—five months in all. He set up a fortified camp to keep away "beastly people who like to eat men."

The island, which was in large part Muslim, was divided into eight kingdoms. Marco apparently managed to visit six of them, taking note of unusual local mores. He claimed, for example, that in the Kingdom of Dragoian, in the north of Samara, when someone fell ill the parents called in the soothsayers and asked them if the sick person was going to die; if the answer was yes, they sped things up by suffocating the poor victim; then they cooked the corpse "and gobbled him up, sucking the marrow from the bones to leave no living matter behind." According to Marco, the bones were later placed into a small wooden box and buried in the mountains to keep vermin away.

References to one form or another of cannibalism would not have surprised Ramusio. Stories of tribes eating human flesh in the islands of the Far East had circulated in Europe since the times of Ptolemy. The sources of these stories tended to be native chieftains

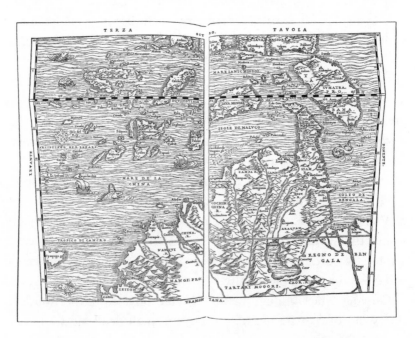

Map of southern China and the Indo-Pacific Ocean by Giacomo Gastaldi, first published by Ramusio in 1550 in *Navigationi et Viaggi,* Book One

who lived along the coast and came into contact with foreign travelers. Whether they were speaking of actual customs or were simply trying to impress and perhaps scare visitors off is unclear. There is no record of European travelers witnessing cannibalistic rituals, and apparently Marco was no exception. It is possible that he included these stories in *Travels* for their dramatic effect.

Trade was his overriding interest, but the island of Samara was not especially rich in spices. The fish, instead, was tasty and the coconuts were sweet and fleshy: "The milk has the transparency of fresh, clear water and tastes better than the most delicate wine." Marco was served his favorite dish while visiting the Kingdom of Fansur, where the dried berries of a local tree were crushed to produce an aromatic flour, which was then mixed with water to make pasta that tasted like oat bread.

"They made a pretty good lasagna with it," he reported.

THE JOURNEY HOME

After Marco's return from his latest mission abroad, an opportunity arose to start planning the journey back to Venice. For some time his father and uncle had been expressing their wish to go home, especially as they were getting old. So was the Great Khan, and there was no telling what would happen to the Polos once he was no longer emperor.

The Great Khan, however, had no desire to see them leave. So the Venetians were trapped. They were respected and protected and made a very good living, but they knew it was impossible to plan and finance a complicated journey back to Europe without the consent and support of their imperial host.

One day, seeing that the Great Khan was in good spirits, Marco's father threw himself at his feet and implored him to let them leave. The Great Khan was surprised and offended. Why would they even contemplate so perilous a journey? They wouldn't survive. The answer was no.

Around this time three Persian ambassadors arrived at the imperial court. They had been sent by King Arghun, the young Mongol king who ruled Persia. Arghun, a grandnephew of the Great Khan, had married Bulughan, a Mongol princess of the Yuan Dynasty. Bulughan had fallen very ill and, on her deathbed, had asked her husband to take a young princess from her own family as his new bride. And so a brokenhearted King Arghun had sent his emissaries to China.

The Great Khan selected Kokachin, a beautiful seventeen-year-old Yuan princess. Kokachin headed for Persia with the three ambassadors; but ongoing wars in Central Asia made the overland journey impossible, and after eight months they were back.

Meanwhile, Marco had returned from his mission to Southeast Asia, and the three ambassadors, upon hearing that he had traveled safely down the South China Sea, asked the Great Khan permission to return to Persia by sea.

The Polos seized their chance, arguing that their presence would ensure the princess would reach her destination, and the Emperor finally granted his consent. Fourteen ships were built for the journey, some of them large enough to have a crew of 250. Provisions for two years were loaded on board.

The Great Khan gave the Polos rubies and other precious stones for their loyal service during the previous seventeen years. And the Polos added to that treasure by selling all their merchandise and purchasing gems to travel home more lightly.

The sea journey back to Venice took roughly three years. Starting in late 1291 or early 1292, the Polos sailed south to Sumatra, then headed west, passing the Andaman Islands, until they reached Sri Lanka, "where the most beautiful and valuable rubies in the world are found," then up the western coast of India to the Gulf of Oman and the Strait of Hormuz, at the southern tip of Persia, which they reached in early 1294.

King Arghun, meanwhile, had died—possibly poisoned. So Kokachin, the Yuan princess, was presented to his son Ghazan, who now reigned in Persia and took her as his bride.

The Polos traveled in Persia for nine months, tending to their business. Marco gave no details on the last leg of the journey home, but Ramusio surmised they eventually made their way to Trebizond, a trading center on the Black Sea, and from there to Constantinople, where the Venetians had a strong commercial presence and where it was easy to find passage on a ship headed to the Adriatic Sea.

Nobody recognized the Polos when they finally arrived in Venice. "What happened to Ulysses, happened to them," Ramusio observed. "They had been away so long that their faces had taken on Tartar features, and in their heavy woolen clothes, they had a hard time convincing their own family who they were."

Two and a half centuries after the journey to China, the colorful story of the Polos' return to Venice was still being passed on from one generation to the next. Ramusio himself had heard it many times, especially from old Senator Gasparo Malipiero, who lived next to the house where the Polos had lived in the neighborhood of San Giovanni Grisostomo.

The Polos, so the story went, invited their relatives to a sumptuous dinner. When all the guests had arrived, Niccolò, Maffio and Marco walked into the dining hall clad in long satin robes. After washing their hands ceremoniously, they took their robes off, cut them into pieces and offered the precious swatches of cloth to the servants.

The three men withdrew, then came back wearing beautiful robes made of crimson damask, and everyone sat for dinner. After a while, they left the room to change again, into velvet robes, while the damask ones were also cut into pieces and given to the servants. More dishes were served and then the same was done to the velvet robes. After this bizarre ritual, the three appeared wearing traditional Venetian evening gowns. According to Ramusio, "Everyone in the room was awed by the magnificence of the clothes they had seen and the quality of the fabrics."

Later, the dining table was cleared, the servants were sent away and Marco went to fetch the three rough woolen coats they had worn on their journey home. He cut the inside lining with a small penknife and released the precious stones carefully sewn inside. The stitching had been done with such artistry that no one would have suspected the coats were loaded with rubies, sapphires, diamonds and emeralds that were now spread out for all the guests to see: the sparkling treasure they had accumulated over the years.

"No one doubted anymore that they truly were who they claimed to be," Ramusio wrote. "Word of their riches quickly spread and soon everyone came to visit, noblemen as well as humble Venetians. And every day children gathered around Marco to hear his stories about China and the Great Khan."

The Polos settled into the large compound near San Giovanni Grisostomo (it was later destroyed in a fire, but a small part survived and traces of it are still visible today). Marco's uncle Maffio, being the eldest of the family, was given a government position—possibly an initial step toward the ennoblement of the Polos.

Marco, now forty, resumed his trading activity, taking advantage of the respect he now commanded on the Rialto, as well as his experience and the connections he had established in the Mediterranean and the Near East. But he was soon off again, for reasons that are not entirely clear.

One view holds that he went to war against the Genoese, the traditional enemies of Venice. In the summer of 1296, the Republic sent a fleet of ninety galleys to meet the Genoese ships near the island of Curzola, off the Dalmatian coast. It is possible that the Polos financed one of the Venetian galleys and that it sailed under Marco's command.

The Battle of Curzola was fought on September 9, 1298. It turned into a crushing defeat for the Venetians. In one day they lost their entire fleet and more than seven thousand men. At least another seven thousand were taken prisoner, including Polo, according to this story.

Another view holds that Polo sailed to the Black Sea, possibly to attend to unfinished family business there, and was captured by Genoese pirates in the Gulf of Alexandretta in the eastern Mediterranean.

In both versions, Polo was taken to Genoa and imprisoned. His rank ensured he was treated relatively well during his detention, and he was released three years later, after Venice and Genoa reached a peace agreement.

During his detention, Polo befriended another inmate, Rustichello da Pisa, a jack-of-all-trades who made a living in part by writing Arthurian potboilers in medieval French, which was the most common vernacular language among readers in southern Europe. The two had time to spare and decided to collaborate on a book about Polo's travels in Asia.

Today most scholars believe Rustichello worked from an earlier manuscript Polo had written in a language that was a mixture of Venetian and French and was commonly used in Constantinople. Polo had probably intended this early version as a practical guide for traveling merchants, compiling it in a dry and factual style: place-name, dominant religion, weather, local staples, commercial possibilities and so on.

Rustichello, together with Polo, rewrote the text in medieval French and may have juiced up the story to broaden the appeal. The original guide-like structure remained, but some of the more colorful digressions about peculiar sexual mores, unsavory cannibalistic practices or exotic culinary recipes sometimes feel as if they were wedged into the narrative mostly to excite the attention of the general reader.

Still, Rustichello's formula worked. The book, initially titled *Divisament dou monde,* was very successful—so successful, in fact, that it was translated, copied, edited and embellished, to the point that the original version by Polo and Rustichello was soon lost. As Ramusio wrote two and a half centuries later, "The demand was so great, so many had waited so long to read this story, that in just a few months all of Italy was flooded with different versions of it."

Which, of course, was the principal problem Ramusio now faced. How to reach into the past to the earliest, most authentic version of the book? As we have seen, the more established version at the time, and the only one in print, was the one Francesco Pipino, the Benedictine monk, had translated into Latin in the early fourteenth century, and of which Ramusio owned a copy. But how reliable was that version? Pipino vouched for the trustworthiness of the manuscript he had translated, saying that Polo was "a wise and honest and highly respected man, and his father Niccolò had confirmed the account, and his uncle Maffio, on point of death, had told his confessor that everything in the book was true."

But for Ramusio, a scholar trained in Aldus's workshop, this was hardly sufficient. While the word of the Polos was important in establishing the overall veracity of the tale, it was no guarantee of the correctness of the details. It was unclear how much of the book was the work of Marco and how much of it had been rewritten by Rustichello; or, for that matter, how much had been changed or deleted by Pipino himself.

The Ghisi manuscript discovered in the house of his friend provided an exciting new prospect, for what Ramusio now had in his hands looked like a Latin translation of the earliest version of all—the one Marco himself had allegedly composed in Franco-Venetian (and which remains to this day the lost Holy Grail of Polo scholars).

Ramusio carefully collated the two manuscripts, making verifications and edits and changes along the way. He even added elements to the narrative here and there when he felt he was on firm ground, inevitably opening up the possibility that he too would contribute his own mistakes. Although Ramusio had a reverential respect for the Ghisi manuscript, he turned out to be a more invasive editor than Aldus would have allowed in his workshop.

Once the laborious editing process was over, Ramusio translated the text from Latin into Italian vernacular. Ramusio's version of Polo's travels—the first to be printed in a modern language—became hugely influential. Published in 1559, it was continuously reprinted and translated in all the major European languages. Thus the myth that the Polos' voyages were nothing but "a fabulous tale" gradually dissolved.

Ramusio came away from his labors with a powerful new sense of the importance of Polo's achievement. And of the stature of the man behind it—a true Venetian hero whom the Republic had never rightfully celebrated.

Although an admirer of Columbus, Ramusio was now convinced that, as travelers and explorers went, the Polos had been superior to him. "I have asked myself many times who had completed the greatest voyage," he wrote. "If the affection I feel for my country does not deceive me, I can now safely say that the journey by land must take the prize over the journey by sea. Columbus carried with him all he needed on his ships, and with a good wind he reached his destination in thirty to forty days; think instead of the desperately long distance our Venetian gentlemen had to cover, the harshness of the journey, the great deserts they crossed, the rushing rivers they waded; not to mention the extreme difficulty of finding enough supplies along the road for themselves and their beasts of burden to last not days but months."

If further proof were needed, it was enough to remember "that after [the Polos] no other European has had the courage to make a similar journey whereas no sooner had Columbus discovered the West Indies than a great number of ships followed suit, and now they leave daily for those shores."*

Ramusio lamented the fact that the memory of Marco Polo's voyage had been allowed to fade. In Venice, there was not a single statue dedicated to the man, not a painting, not even a plaque of some kind to remember him by. In fact, very little was known about the Polos. So Ramusio went rooting around for old documents and deeds to find out what had happened to the family. Marco, he discovered, had settled down after his return from Genoa. In 1300 he'd married Donata Badoer, who belonged to one of Venice's oldest families. They had three daughters—Fantina, Bellela and Moretta. When his father, Niccolò, died, Marco arranged for his burial in the Church of San Lorenzo, and Ramusio found the grave "near the entrance on the right-hand side." Above it was a faded family crest—a crossbar with three ravens, "which in Venetian dialect are called *pole*."

---

* This is incorrect. Odorico da Pordenone, a Franciscan friar, traveled from Venice to India and China in the 1320s and was the first known European to reach Lhasa, the capital of Tibet.

Polo died in 1324, leaving no male heirs. He had wished to be buried near his father, with whom he had shared so much during his life; but Ramusio was unable to locate the tomb. The Polo family name became extinct a century later, in 1417, when the last of Marco's male nephews died without issue.

At the time of Marco's death, an inventory of his belongings was drawn up in order to divide them between his three daughters. The items were listed randomly, so that next to sheets, blankets, pots and pans and other mundane domestic implements, there were entries that mentioned precious fabrics, small flasks of musk oil, envelopes with dried rhubarb and other exotic vestiges of his great journey to China. They included "a small satchel stuffed with the silky hairs" of the yak Marco had seen so many years before in the province of Tangut.

CHAPTER ELEVEN

STEALING
TIME FROM TIME

B Y THE TIME HE REACHED SIXTY, IN 1545, RAMUSIO HAD QUIETLY PUT TOGETHER A VAST PRIVATE COLLECTION that included official documents, top-secret reports, private letters and a vast array of travel narratives both in manuscript and in printed form.

Impressed by the range of his network, Fracastoro teasingly told Ramusio he expected one of his many informers "to reach out to you from the Antarctic Pole to tell you how things are in that part of the world."

Now that Ramusio was getting close to retirement, the question was what to do with the invaluable material he had collected over the years. Away from the Senate, he would soon be free to live between his house in Padua and his villa in the country, and to spend more time with Paolino, still a young teenager.

The easy thing would have been to put his massive collection in order and turn it over to Venice's library, with which he had been so closely associated. Instead, Ramusio gave himself a monumental task: to get everything out in print. He was going to sort out, edit, translate and assemble the wealth of geographical information he had accumulated, and publish it as a single collection.

Ramusio felt thoroughly at home in Venice's printing culture. He was a skilled and versatile editor—he had prepared manuscripts for publication since his early days in Aldus's shop. But no one had ever attempted anything remotely on the scale he had in mind: he was looking at a project of about two million words!

As a high-ranking public official, Ramusio understood more than others the importance of reliable information. But he also saw the benefit to society of making it available to the broadest public possible—not just princes and noblemen but scholars, merchants, professionals and fellow public servants, not to mention cartographers. After a life spent in the secretive chambers of the Republic, he was now planning a massive release of documents, many of which were either still classified or had never been published before.

Ramusio decided to print everything in one language, Italian; this would give uniformity to the project and, more important, would make the material accessible to a wider audience. Latin was still the language of scientific discourse, but Ramusio was a strenuous supporter of modern Italian. In a way, he was quietly paying tribute to his old friend Cardinal Bembo, who had recently died in Rome after devoting a lifetime to shaping a common Italian language.

The political climate was not ideal, however. The relative freedom in which the publishing industry had thrived in Venice had come increasingly under attack by the Counter-Reformation. At first the Republic had resisted the Inquisition's pressure, but by the end of the 1540s it had capitulated, agreeing to promulgate an Index of banned books broadly aimed at any publication perceived as anti-Catholic.

The definition was so vague, the Venetians argued in their defense, that the measure could be enforced very blandly. But the opposite was also true: any book that was not militantly Catholic could become a possible target of the Inquisitors.

Ramusio, long used to gauging the shifting tensions between Rome and Venice from inside the government, suspected that things were not likely to get any better in the near future. On the surface, travel narratives did not seem particularly at risk. But censorship had its own fickle, inscrutable ways. Who knew how the Inquisition would react to the benevolent description of Muslim life in Africa by al-Wazzan, who was himself suspected of never having abjured his faith? Or Navagero's palpable nostalgia for the lost Islamic world in Andalusia? Or Marco Polo's appreciation of religious tolerance under Kublai Khan?

The project acquired a sense of urgency from the start. If the growing climate of intolerance was a factor, so was Ramusio's age. Would he have the energy or indeed the time to complete the work?

It was Fracastoro who swept away any lingering doubts. "He was the one who encouraged me and comforted me with his wise reasoning," Ramusio readily admitted, "and in the end convinced me that this enterprise would benefit mankind."

The task then was to find a publisher who would agree to take on such a sprawling, time-consuming and expensive undertaking, especially in a time of uncertainty for the industry. A project of this proposed size could easily bring down a publishing house.

Ramusio turned to Tommaso Giunti, owner of the eponymous publishing house founded by his father, Luca Antonio Giunti, a Florentine who had migrated to Venice as young man. Tommaso was responsible for the editorial side of the business, while his younger brother Giovan Maria oversaw the administrative one. The house published schoolbooks, liturgical pamphlets and professional textbooks. But Giunti also financed big projects in which he had a personal interest. He published the complete works of Aristotle, for example, as well as a multivolume edition of the works of Galen, the Greek physician and philosopher of science. And in 1546 he put out *De Contagionibus e contagiosis morbis et eorum curatione,* Fracastoro's landmark treatise on infectious maladies.

Giunti was two years younger than Ramusio; like him, he belonged to the generation shaped by the great discoveries. He too had a keen interest in geography, and had frequently tapped into his own Europe-wide network of correspondents to find books or manuscripts Ramusio was looking for. He was the ideal partner for the project; and he was willing to take on the financial risk.

"TO SEE WITH OUR OWN EYES"

Ramusio began to organize the material, taking into account the geopolitical shifts of the late fifteenth and early sixteenth centuries. In the first volume of the planned trilogy that was to be called *Navigationi et Viaggi* (Journeys and Navigations), he concentrated on the vast southern swath of the globe, now controlled by the Portuguese, that stretched from Brazil to Africa and over to India and the Spice Islands in the Far East.

The volume was truly a product of its time. Vasco da Gama's rounding of the Cape of Good Hope in 1498 had done away with the old Ptolemaic idea that Africa and Asia were joined in their southern part. The Atlantic Ocean and the Indian Ocean were now connected, and the Portuguese had led the way in establishing a European presence where Arab and Persian merchants had traded with their Indian counterparts for centuries.

After building a system of fortifications along the coasts of Africa and the Indian subcontinent, the Portuguese had come to dominate the region within a matter of a few years, choking off the traffic through the Red Sea, where spices and fabrics from the East had traditionally transited in their journey to the Mediterranean. By 1505, up to three-quarters of goods imported from the Orient to Europe passed through Lisbon.

Ramusio included reports on the three great sea journeys that had framed the perimeter of the new Portuguese sphere of influence: Vasco da Gama's first trip to India, Amerigo Vespucci's exploration of the coast of Brazil and Ferdinand Magellan's circumnavigation of the globe as narrated by Pigafetta.

There was a rich section on Africa, based primarily on al-Wazzan's majestic narrative, which was being published for the first time; Alvise da Mosto's account of his journeys down the coast of West Africa; and Francisco Álvares's journey across Ethiopia, which finally brought some clarity to the legend of Prester John.

And there was new, illuminating material on India and the Spice

Islands. In the half century since Vasco da Gama had sailed around the Cape of Good Hope, the Portuguese had allowed very little information to trickle out. The officially sponsored *História do descobrimento e conquista da India pelos portugueses* by Fernão Lopes de Castanheda and João de Barros's *Décadas da Ásia* had yet to come out. But Ramusio was able to fill that void with his own collection of papers, notably his translation of Varthema's *Itinerario* and Barbosa's manuscript about his years in India.

A useful complement to these two works was the *Suma oriental,* the first attempt to provide a more systematic description of India and the Far East. The author, whose identity was long held secret by the Portuguese, was Tomé Pires, an apothecary at the court of King Manuel. Pires was sent out to India to purchase and catalogue medicinal herbs, roots and spices. He also traveled to the Far East and China, where he died in captivity. He left behind a fascinating work of geography and natural history that the Portuguese government kept under lock. Ramusio was able to obtain a copy of the original manuscript from a contact in Lisbon who has remained anonymous.

By 1550, the first volume of the trilogy was ready to print. Gastaldi, the cartographer, produced up-to-date maps of Africa, the Indian subcontinent and Southeast Asia. Giunti, meanwhile, sold subscriptions to cover his considerable costs.

The preparatory work had been exhausting. Ramusio himself, usually so self-effacing, confessed that it had nearly broken him: "I won't even begin to tell you," he told his readers, "the complexity— the difficulty of translating from different languages. Not to mention the fact that so many of the manuscripts were in terrible shape and invariably filled with all sorts of mistakes."

Ramusio used as many sources as were available to him to cross-reference the text he was working on. But weeding out "mistakes" was very tricky, for he operated in a gray area filled with uncertainty. Geography was still a humanistic field based on the written word rather than on scientific data. It was not a matter of simple fact-checking; for the most part, there were no facts to check against. In this he was not unlike a scholar collating old manuscripts of classical texts in the hope of coming as close to the original as possible.

It was an arduous and very taxing process, but necessary to achieve Ramusio's declared goal, which was nothing less than to consign to history the age-old Ptolemaic model of the world inherited from antiquity. As a trained humanist, he was never comfortable drawing attention to the limits of the Ancients. But having labored all his life with the great geographers of antiquity—Aristotle, Pliny, Strabo and most of all Ptolemy—peering over his shoulders, he now felt confident to break free. "The reason I have willingly put so much effort in this task is that we know so much more than they did," he told his readers. "Ptolemy's tables on Africa and India in his *Geographia* appear very imperfect relative to the knowledge we have today of those regions. I felt it was important—and useful for the world—to bring together the narratives of the writers of our time who have been to those regions and have written about them extensively."

Still, he refused to have his name on the book. Giunti, his publisher, was disappointed, but he accepted the decision as quintessentially Ramusian—always thriving backstage.

The volume came out in November 1550. Three more editions were printed in the following years—an achievement for such a massive volume. But then the book was so much more than a trove of geographical information. In assembling and editing his dazzling collection, Ramusio had made it possible for readers to make their own journey of discovery in the company of al-Wazzan, Pigafetta, Álvares and Varthema, to name a few—great travelers who had turned out to be great writers as well.

The volume was user-friendly. Each narrative was preceded by an introduction in which Ramusio presented the material, underscored its importance and, where necessary, clarified particular aspects that might otherwise have appeared too obscure. Sometimes he revealed how he had obtained a particular manuscript. He also added pertinent anecdotes—always with the intent of engaging the reader. And his writing is still very accessible today. Ramusio's voice runs through every page of the volume.

"I have read and reread it," wrote one enthusiastic reviewer, Giovan Battista Sassetti, a Florentine merchant. Sassetti was also grateful for the pleasure of reading the material "in our mother tongue," in spite of those who claimed that "one can only write about learned things in Greek and Latin." Not only was it so much easier to understand what one was reading: "We are able to touch it with our hands and to see it with our own eyes."

In fact, Sassetti was so enthralled by the experience that he wrote a summary of the volume and produced a handy booklet for his ten-year-old son, Filippo.

Inspired by that childhood reading, Filippo Sassetti went on to read the real thing as soon as he was old enough. The impact was so powerful that he sailed to India hoping to make his fortune there as a merchant.

It didn't work out for him. The Portuguese presence was in decline by the time he got there, and European traders were being squeezed out. He struggled for a few years and eventually died in Goa in 1588, leaving a young wife and a child named Ventura—the Florentine word for adventure.

CABOT REDUX

The preparation of the second volume, which was centered on continental Asia, slowed down dramatically in 1553 when Ramusio, now sixty-eight, was suddenly and quite unexpectedly (given his age) appointed secretary general of the Council of Ten, the secretive executive body that effectively governed the Republic.

It was the crowning achievement in his long career as a trusted and highly competent public servant. But the practical result was that he was now even more involved in the daily grind of government. His salary was raised to the princely sum of 250 gold ducats a year, but time, at this crucial juncture, was increasingly more valuable to him than money.

Among the urgent dossiers to land on his desk, oddly enough, was one with which he had an old familiarity. Thirty years after

Sebastian Cabot had first reached out to the Venetian government offering to lead an expedition in search of a northwest passage to China—a plan Cabot himself had abandoned—he was at it again. Only now he was proposing to find a northeast passage to China by navigating the freezing seas between Siberia and the Arctic.

After serving for nearly three decades as Charles V's pilot major, Cabot had left Spain and had settled in London to plan this new expedition under the auspices of King Edward VI. His idea had quickly gained traction and he was now president of a consortium of English investors, the Muscovy Company, set up to open this potentially lucrative new route.

Cabot contacted the Venetian ambassador in London, Giacomo Soranzo, and once again secretly offered his services to the Republic, asking to be invited to Venice to discuss the proposal. Remembering their dealings thirty years earlier, he specifically requested that Ramusio be entrusted with the matter.

It remains unclear why Cabot would want to involve the Venetians at this late date, betraying the trust of the British Crown. Ramusio, perhaps naively, was convinced that Cabot had always conceived his plan "for the benefit and use of his fatherland." Still, there was a certain poignancy in this belated reprise between Ramusio and Cabot—two old Venetians still nursing the hope that Venice might break out of the Mediterranean and find its own passage to Asia, to stay in the game with the other great European naval powers.

It was not to be. The English ambassador in Venice, the wily Peter Vannes, got wind of Cabot's secret dealings with Ramusio and scuttled the talks even before they had started in earnest. With no great loss for Venice: Cabot's expedition never found the northeastern passage to China. Two ships were stranded on the Kola Peninsula in winter and all the men froze to death; a third one reached the White Sea but did not go farther and returned to London.

While Ramusio was absorbed by his new job, Giunti, the publisher, was distracted by problems of his own. The Inquisition summoned him, once about his dealings with a foreign publisher and another time about a book by a Protestant writer that had been smuggled into Venice. Fortunately, nothing serious came of these early intimidations. But in 1553, Giunti was forced to declare bankruptcy when one of his creditors suddenly called in loans of up to 100,000 ducats. He absorbed the shock and soon reopened the house, but it took him years to pay back his debt.

There was more bad news that summer. In August, Fracastoro died of a heart attack at his villa near Verona. Ramusio lost the closest companion of his later years and the staunchest supporter of his project—the one man he could always turn to for advice on controversial points of geographical interest, from the causes of the yearly floods of the Nile to the idea of digging a canal across the Panama isthmus to reach the Spice Islands.

Work on the second volume was piling up fast. Ramusio brought in his son Paolino, whom he had trained as a geographer, to supervise the project and take over secretarial work: no editing for the moment but a full-time job putting papers in order, sending out requests to his father's far-flung correspondents, responding to numerous queries from cartographers all over Europe.

Nevertheless, in 1554 the second volume was still a work in progress and publication had to be delayed. To fill the gap, Giunti and Ramusio brought forward publication of the third volume, on the New World, which was nearly complete.[*]

Peter Martyr's *Decades* and Oviedo's *Historia,* the two extensive works Navagero had brought back from Spain and which Ramusio had helped to edit, translate and publish in the 1530s, provided the basic framework for a wide-ranging narrative about the New World, starting with an in-depth account of Spain's gradual colonization of the Caribbean.

A large section was taken up by Hernán Cortés's report on the conquest of Mexico and Central America. Cortés had written five

[*] In lieu of *"Nuovo Mondo"* (New World), Ramusio sometimes used the more poetic *"Mondo Ritrovato"*—the world found anew.

"letters" to Charles V chronicling the establishment of New Spain. The first of these letters was lost, and Ramusio assured his readers that he had "searched for it diligently" using his channels in Europe and the New World, but had been unable to find it (it only resurfaced in 1842).

Word that Ramusio was looking for that letter had spread among antiquarians. Shortly before he went to press, he received a letter from someone who claimed to have a copy and was wondering how much Ramusio was willing to pay for it. Paolino deftly handled the matter, saying his father was sure the manuscript was *"cosa bella"*—a good piece—but didn't know how much the Giunti brothers were willing to pay for it, as they didn't know how long the manuscript was and in what shape.

A handwritten copy of Cortés's fifth letter had also gone missing—it too was not found until the nineteenth century. So Ramusio was only able to publish letters two, three and four. The word "letter" is perhaps misleading: the combined word count of the three he published ran to about 120,000 words.

To the Cortés letters, Ramusio added a scoop of his own—a report on New Spain by an anonymous gentleman in Cortés's entourage. The narrative was less about the history of the conquest and more about the landscape of the region. "New Spain is not unlike Spain," it began, "as the countryside, the mountains, the valleys are similar to those at home . . ." The author wrote about the local flora and the wildlife. He described mining prospects—not just gold and silver but also iron, copper and tin. He included the first detailed description of Tenochtitlán—its temples, its neat brick-paved streets, its well-organized market squares. He dwelt on the social customs of the country, such as weddings, burials and sacrifices; on the colorful tribal clothes; on the main dishes of the local cuisine. And he raved about hot cocoa: "It's very healthy and energetic; one cup and you will need to eat nothing else the rest of the day no matter how far you need to walk."

This was Ramusio's favorite type of narrative—detailed yet not dutiful, and richly evocative. Because he never revealed the source

An anonymous source gave Ramusio the first detailed
description of the Aztec capital Tenochtitlán, also known as Mexico,
with its temples, brick-paved streets and market squares. This city plan was
published by Ramusio in 1556 in *Navigationi et Viaggi,* Book Three.

of this document, it was later suspected of being a fake. Today we
are no closer to knowing who the author was, but nothing has come
up to suggest that the document was not authentic. And from all we
know about Ramusio's character, his diligence, his sheer tenacity in
the pursuit of reliable facts, it seems unlikely that he would know-
ingly use a forged document, let alone make one himself.

The section Ramusio devoted to Francisco Pizarro's conquest of
Peru was largely based on the work he had done back in the mid-
1530s, when the first reports by Cristóbal de Mena and Francisco
Xerez had reached him in Venice. Ramusio complemented that

material with another exclusive: a letter to Charles V by Pedro Sancho de la Hoz, Pizarro's last secretary. (The original letter was lost and all subsequent editions of the letter were based on the version published by Ramusio.)

De la Hoz described the Spanish takeover of the capital city of Cuzco and the rapid, brutal conquest of the Inca Empire, from Quito to northern Chile, as more Spanish captains answered Pizarro's call to colonize what was now being called New Castile.

In a cautionary introduction, Ramusio reminded his readers that many of those associated with the capture of Atahualpa—Pizarro included—suffered "a bad end." Although some argued this was the result of a curse related to a particular astral alignment, he wrote, "The more prudent observers have ascribed it to malice and greed."

Indeed, the aftermath of the Spanish conquest of Peru turned into a bloody mafia-type war between enemy factions.

In 1534, Diego de Almagro, a sometimes ally, sometimes rival of Pizarro who had pulled out of the first expedition to Peru, obtained from the Spanish Crown "rights" over all the land south of Cuzco and promptly launched his own expedition down into Chile (1535–1537).

Almagro's title of *adelantado* made him a subordinate of Pizarro. But he was soon operating as his own man, and the two inevitably clashed. Pizarro had Almagro arrested and decapitated in Cuzco's public square in 1538.

Almagro never married but had lived in Panama *more uxorio* with a native woman. Their son, Diego de Almagro el Mozo (*el mozo* means "the young one"), swore he would avenge his father. As Ramusio explained, Pizarro was warned of this many times by the people of his own clan, "but he chose not to believe them until the conspirators were upon him and killed him with their swords."

The murder took place in the new capital of Peru, Ciudad de Los Reyes, the future Lima, on June 24, 1541. A year later, the governor, Cristóbal Vaca de Castro, under pressure from Pizarro's people, had young Almagro decapitated.

Two of Pizarro's younger brothers also suffered violent deaths.

Juan died after he was hit on the head by a rock during a clash with rebel Incas. Gonzalo, who proclaimed himself King of Cuzco, was arrested by forces loyal to the Emperor and decapitated in 1548.

And the list of casualties continued, Ramusio wrote, "so that those interested in looking back and tracking the record are likely to find more than a hundred and fifty men of arms or government officials killed by the natives or by their own."

Ramusio got his hands on a trove of additional classified material. This included a copy of da Nizza's report to Charles V on his mission to the Pueblo Indians; Coronado's report on his exploration of the American southwest; and a report on Ulloa's journey up the Pacific coast, written by Francisco Preciado, the ship's scribe. Ramusio was the first to publish each of these documents.

The source of the leaks is not certain, but there is a prime suspect: Diego Hurtado de Mendoza, Spanish ambassador to Venice and brother of the Viceroy of New Spain.

Diego was a diplomat and a humanist. Peter Martyr had been his Latin tutor when he was a young boy. He later studied Greek, Arabic and Hebrew in Salamanca. After university he served in the imperial army and distinguished himself in the Battle of Pavia (1525), where Charles V's forces crushed the French army and took Francis I hostage. Afterward, Diego elected to stay in Italy, where he pursued his humanistic education in Padua, Bologna and Rome.

After Charles V made him ambassador to Venice in 1539, Diego settled into luxurious apartments on the Grand Canal, where he assembled a collection of coins, paintings, marble inscriptions and a library of rare Greek and Latin manuscripts—the typical décor of the house of a wealthy humanist. But Venetian visitors to his home were also able to admire a fabulous collection of artifacts from the New World, including a series of Mexican idols made of malachite and gold that he presumably received from his brother the Viceroy.

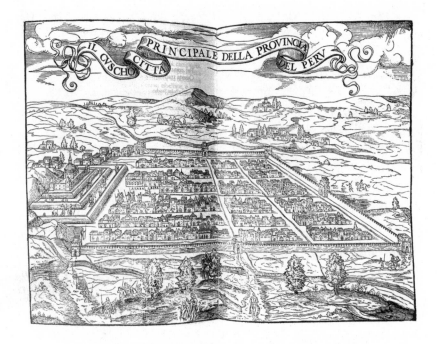

"Malice and greed," Ramusio wrote, were at the root
of the bloody conquest of the Inca Empire. This city plan of Cuzco,
the capital, was published in Book Three of *Navigationi et Viaggi*.

Diego made his way easily into Ramusio's circle of friends during his time in Venice, and although scholars have found no clear evidence, he is generally thought of as having been the source of the documents coming out of Mexico.

Cartier's voyages were the last tassels to fill the third volume. Ramusio played an important role in publicizing the French explorer's achievement outside of France. The report on his second journey was published in Paris in 1545. But the report on his first trip was a Ramusio exclusive, leaked to him by those anonymous "literary gentlemen" in France. Ramusio published both documents, plus the first map of the Gulf of Saint Lawrence and the surrounding area, which the French were now calling New France.

The third volume went to press in 1556. Readers had good reason to be satisfied: it was by far the most comprehensive and up-to-date

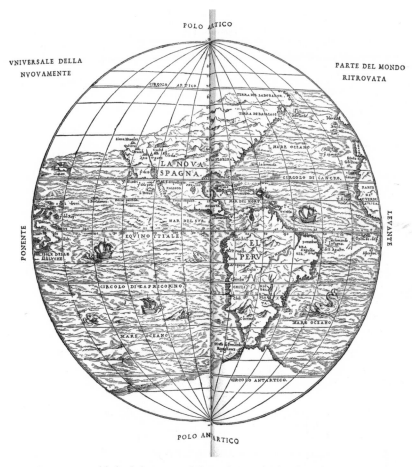

Ramusio published this map of the Americas by his friend Giacomo
Gastaldi in Book Three of *Navigationi et Viaggi*.

description of the American continent, with a number of private
reports and documents never printed before—and which had never
been intended for publication! Giunti printed between four hundred and five hundred copies, a considerable number for such a large
and expensive volume (the equivalent of several thousand dollars in
today's currency), and a clear indication that the subscription campaign had been a success. Copies sold across Europe, and it is a testa-
ment to the influence the volume had in giving shape to this part of
the world in the public mind that demand for the book remained

strong for many years. The house of Giunti was still publishing the book as late as 1606, a full half century after the first edition was printed.

LIMPETS AND MOLLUSKS

Despite the pressing demands of his day job, Ramusio gave no sign of slowing down as he turned his attention to the final, unfinished second volume, on Asia. At seventy-one, he was still editing late into the night and sleeping very little. As Giunti observed, in awe of his friend's dedication and stamina, he was "stealing time from Time itself."

The second volume covered an immense part of the world that stretched from the Lofoten archipelago in the North Sea all the way to the Moluccan Islands in the Pacific Ocean.

Marco Polo's travels formed the basis of this last collection. To provide more background to Polo's narrative, Ramusio included a history of the Mongolian Empire written by Hethum the Armenian, a Premonstratensian monk who had been a contemporary of the Venetian traveler. "It adheres well to Marco's narrative," he explained, adding that readers shouldn't fret if places and names were sometimes spelled differently; or if events were not always narrated in the same order. "Men don't tell a story the same way but according to their specific intellect."

Persia, too, loomed large in Ramusio's Asia, for geopolitical as well as geographic reasons. After the Portuguese had rounded the Cape of Good Hope and the Ottomans had conquered Egypt, gaining control over the Red Sea, Persia had acquired a new strategic relevance for Venice: it was the only route to India and the Spice Islands open to Venetian merchants.

Ramusio did not have far to look for material. There was more information on Persia in Venice than anywhere else in Europe. In the 1470s, a couple of generations before Ramusio's time, Venice had formed a close relationship with Uzun Hasan, the powerful

Turkic ruler of Persia, in order to contain the rise of the Ottoman Empire. A succession of Venetian ambassadors had traveled extensively in the region and had delivered detailed reports to the Senate once they had returned from their mission, which Ramusio was now in a position to publish. "Together," he assured his readers, "they form an account of Persia which, though somewhat disconnected, is written well enough to give the reader satisfaction."

The vast region that lay north of the Black Sea, on the other hand, was so uncharted in Ramusio's time that he was forced to rely on the Ancients. In his *Treaty on Airs, Waters and Places,* Hippocrates (fifth century B.C.) had written about the Scythes and about the Sarmatians, who lived farther east. Another source from antiquity was a letter on the Caucasus that Flavius Arrianus, a diplomat and former student of Epictetus, addressed to his friend Emperor Hadrian around the year A.D. 132 after being stationed in Cappadocia. Ramusio included both texts in his collection.

The only relatively recent account he had on the region was by Giorgio Interiano, a Genoese humanist who had traveled to the Orient at the end of the fifteenth century and had written a short narrative on the Circassian people (the Sarmatians of old), who lived beyond the river Don, in constant friction with the Mongols.

Interiano had later come through Venice and had paid a visit to Aldus, who was delighted with the book and had it printed in 1502, when Ramusio was at best an errand boy at the shop. "Pliny and Strabo mentioned these people"—that is, the Circassians—Aldus pointed out in the dedication, suggesting that the reference by two great geographers of antiquity gave Interiano's booklet more credibility.

Muscovy, farther north, long a terra incognita, was only beginning to come into focus. After the disintegration of the Rus kingdom, founded by Slavs who had descended from Scandinavia, the region had slid into decline. For several centuries there had been little or no trade with Europe and communications had broken down.

Russia's embrace of the Orthodox Church had further reduced the residual contacts with Rome.

Now Ivan IV, the self-proclaimed Czar of Muscovy, was unifying and expanding his kingdom, and opening up to the West after centuries of isolation.

The first to shed light on the territories of the new Russia was Sigmund von Herberstein, an Austrian diplomat who traveled to Poland and Muscovy in the service of Emperor Maximilian I. His *Commentaries,* written in Latin, were translated into Italian and first published in Venice in 1550, in time for Ramusio to include them in his collection and for Gastaldi to produce a map of Muscovy.

Scandinavia, to the north of Muscovy, was also emerging with greater clarity, thanks to Olaus Magnus, a Swedish prelate who had settled in Rome after the Reformation. Olaus had traveled to remote areas of Scandinavia as a young papal legate, observing up close the life of native communities. Years later, in Venice, he used his notes to produce a wood engraving of a large map of Scandinavia (70 by 50 inches). Ramusio met Olaus during his Venetian sojourn and studied the map closely. He was also familiar with *Historia de Gentibus Septentrionalibus* (A History of the People of the North), which Olaus published in 1555. The multivolume book described the landscape of Scandinavia, the social organization, the customs and the commercial activities.

Ramusio could not include Olaus's work in *Navigationi et Viaggi* for reasons of copyright, let alone production scheduling. Instead, he published two separate Venetian manuscripts that dealt with the topic of Scandinavia. Both documents told the same gripping story about a Venetian shipwreck at the northern tip of Norway. And they revealed that life at those extreme latitudes was not only possible but also very civilized. Indeed, often more so than in violent, warring Europe.

This extraordinary story of survival and resilience bookended the second volume. It is still very popular in Venice today and worth sketching out for the reader.

In 1431 a Venetian merchant, Pietro Querini, sailed to Flanders at the helm of the *Querina,* a sturdy cog carrying malmsey, spices, beeswax and other goods from Crete. The ship was blown off course during a storm in the Channel and drifted for six weeks at the mercy of strong winds and rough seas, until it had to be abandoned. Forty-seven men, including Querini, crammed into the lifeboat. Only sixteen were still barely alive a few weeks later when they crashed onto the tiny island of Sandøya, at the tip of the Lofoten archipelago, a hundred miles north of the Arctic Circle. They clambered onto the shore, stuffing snow into their mouths in their thirst; to ease their hunger pangs, they scraped limpets and other mollusks off the rocks.

Fishermen from the nearby island of Røst found them and brought them to their hamlet. Querini and the other survivors spent the rest of the winter there—101 days in all. They were fed and housed and treated kindly. It was, Querini later wrote, as if they had spent "a season in paradise compared to the chaos and confusion back home." The natives were "pure souls and very handsome." They lived simply and happily—the men were capable craftsmen and skilled fishermen; the women took care of the household and the children. All were devout and harbored no ill feelings. Most notable was "the absence of greed." If they closed their homes, it was only to keep wild animals away. Their ease and natural spontaneity were beguiling—especially in the women, "who thought nothing of undressing and bathing naked in front of us." At night, the natives and the survivors slept together "like little children."

Querini and his men lived through the long winter on a diet of fish, acid milk and an occasional cup of rye beer. Cod was the main staple and source of income on the island. The natives did not salt the fish but hung it to dry in the wind until it was "hard as wood" and easily transportable. Every spring, the fishermen loaded piles of *stokfisk* (stockfish) and sailed to Bergen, a thousand miles down the coast, where they sold it to merchants from Germany, England, Scotland and Prussia.

In May, when the time came for the fishermen's yearly trip to Bergen, Querini and ten other surviving members of his original crew sailed south with them as far as Trondheim and then continued overland. They walked for fifty-five days until they reached Lödöse, a major harbor on the river Göta (near present-day Göteborg). Three men found passage on a ship sailing to the German port of Rostock, while the other eight, including Querini, sailed to the coast of England, continued by riverboat to Cambridge and from there to London. They were feted by the Venetian ambassador and the large community of Venetian merchants as if they had returned from the dead.

Once back in Venice, Querini wrote a report for the Senate describing the circumstances of the shipwreck, the winter they spent in Lofoten and the long journey home. A second report was written by the men who returned via Germany. Given his position in government, Ramusio had access to both manuscripts, and was eager to finally get them into print, side by side.

Querini's prolonged stay in Lofoten led to an unexpected consequence: *stoccafisso* became a staple of Venetian cuisine. And it has remained so ever since: today 90 percent of Lofoten's stockfish is exported to Italy, mostly to Venice and the Veneto region, where it is used for dishes like the popular cod spread *baccalà mantecato* or the more elaborate milk-stewed *baccalà alla vicentina*.

In early 1557 Ramusio delivered "several more manuscripts to print" and Giunti felt confident they would go to press that same year or the next one at the latest. But with the first summer heat, Ramusio's health suddenly failed him.

After the prodigious physical and mental energies he expended to complete his life's work, the end came very swiftly. He died in his house in via del Patriarcato, in Padua, on July 10.

Ramusio chose to be buried in Venice, in the Chiesa della Madonna dell'Orto, a Late Gothic church on the northern side of the city. On the right, by the entrance, was a magnificent altarpiece by Cima da Conegliano, the Renaissance master of the Veneto landscape. The painting is still there. It depicts John the Baptist (Giovambattista) flanked by Peter, Mark, Paul and Jerome. It is a stirring coincidence: Ramusio's patron saint standing sentinel at his resting place.*

Paolino, the sole heir to the family holdings, was utterly bereft. Ramusio had been a loving father and an assiduous teacher. He'd always had his eye out for his only son, including him in his activities and looking for editing and translating jobs that might help him on his way. Only recently he had obtained for him a government contract to translate and print in Italian, French and Latin a special edition of Geoffroy de Villehardouin's narrative on the conquest of Constantinople during the Fourth Crusade, which marked the beginning of Venice's empire in the Mediterranean. The job came with an annual stipend of 150 ducats, enough to make sure that Paolino would be well provided for in the future.† He had grown to depend on his father—just as Ramusio had depended on Paolino in his later years.

Giunti and Ramusio had been friends for more than twenty years, sharing a passion for geography and books. They had become even closer working together on the publication of *Navigationi et Viaggi*. "It is such a bitter loss for me," the publisher confided to his readers. "Those who know the great love we had developed for one another over these many years can easily imagine how painful this is."

Giunti decided to go ahead and publish the second volume posthumously. It was practically finished, and he and Paolino worked on the last details. Then, on November 4, as they were about to go to press, the Giunti print shop went up in flames. And with it went

---

* Today visitors from all over the world come to see the church, which is also known as "Tintoretto's Church" because the great Renaissance painter was buried there, in 1594, thirty-seven years after Ramusio. Several large works by him adorn the interior. Tintoretto's tomb is in the center of a small apsidal chapel to the right of the main altar. The exact location of Ramusio's tomb in the church is unknown; it is possible that it was damaged or destroyed during one of the numerous renovations.

† Paolino never got around to finishing the task, which was completed by his son Girolamo.

much of the material about to be printed—manuscripts as well as maps.

Coming only four months after Ramusio's death, this new blow was a calamity. What to do? With Paolino's blessing and collaboration, Giunti forged on and spent the next year painstakingly reassembling the salvaged material. The result was a much reduced volume: it included Marco Polo's travels, the material on Persia, the two narratives on the Querini shipwreck and little else. Giunti decided to publish anyway, hoping his readers would understand why it was not "as full and rich as the other two." The book came out in 1559. This time Ramusio's name was on it. Giunti explained to his readers that the previous volumes had been printed without it "because of the typical modesty he showed in everything he did. But I loved him more than anyone else in this world and will love him in death as long as I live. Now I will do all I can to contribute to his fame. So I must not, I cannot withhold his name any longer."

POSTSCRIPT

O N A SUNNY DAY IN THE WINTER OF 2022, SOON AFTER COVID RESTRICTIONS WERE RELAXED, I DROVE UP THE Valsugana, the old Roman road that runs north from Padua toward the mountains. Ten miles out of the city, I reached a crossroad and took a right turn onto via Ramusio, and suddenly there it was, at the end of a straight alley: Villa Ramusia, a graying late fifteenth-century villa, stranded in the flat farmland of the Veneto.

The house today belongs to Francesco Vallerani, a university professor, and to his wife, Maria Grazia, a retired schoolteacher. Vallerani, a reserved, soft-spoken academic, purchased the building in the 1980s. He had been looking for a cheap property to use mostly as storage space. The house was very run-down, he told me. Several farm laborers and their families had lived there in the decades after the Second World War—as many as sixty people at a time—and then had gradually abandoned the place. Neighbors referred to the crumbling building as *"La Ramusa,"* but no one seemed to know where the name came from.

Professor Vallerani—strange and delightful coincidence—happens to be a geographer. He did not make the connection between the house and Ramusio immediately; but after exploring the premises and having several more conversations with local residents, it occurred to him that the sprawling ruin he had just purchased might be the house that had once belonged to the author of *Navigationi et Viaggi*. A trip to the local archives confirmed his hypothesis.

"Serendipity," he said with a grin, using the English word.

The two-story building—now well cared for by the professor and his wife—has a square floor plan typical of a Renaissance country house in the Veneto. The *androne* (entrance hall) is flanked on each side by two rooms (in Ramusio's time, an office for the farm manager, a kitchen and two cellars). A staircase leads to the living quarters on the first floor, or *piano nobile,* and continues to the second floor—the *granaio,* where threshed wheat was stored to dry. Back in the day, the carts, laden with grain and drawn by a couple of oxen, entered the building through the front porch and stopped in front of the staircase; once the sacks were unloaded and taken upstairs, the empty carts exited through the back porch and returned to the fields.

In the back of the house is the traditional *brolo,* an enclosed garden that today is mostly lawn and laurels but back then would have included a small orchard (apricot, peach, cherry and apple trees), a vegetable patch, and rosebushes or other decorative plants. According to Vallerani, it is where Ramusio planted corn, tomatoes and potatoes from seeds sent to him by Oviedo, his pen pal in the Spanish colonies overseas.

The full restoration of Villa Ramusia has become Vallerani's life's work—and a considerable drain on his savings. But he has never regretted embarking on this project. He showed me around his house with understandable pride, drawing my attention to the original parts that he was able to save: a marble sink where Ramusio probably washed his hands, old larch beams, certain Latin inscriptions. Vallerani indicated one in particular, carved over a window that looked out on the *brolo:* it read MORTALI SATIS, which he loosely translated as "enough to fill a man's life."

Rumor that Vallerani had settled into Ramusio's house spread quickly in the international community of geographers. Colleagues from Great Britain, the United States and other countries soon came to visit. Villa Ramusia became, as it had once been, a convivial gathering place of like-minded intellectuals and academics. Vallerani, an avid outdoorsman who has studied and explored the old waterways of the Veneto, organized nature hikes and canoe trips down the nearby Brenta River for his guests.

The geography professor has made it easy to imagine Ramusio at work in his villa. There are old maps on the walls, geographical instruments scattered around the house, and stacks of books about distant and exotic places. Together we leafed through an edition of Peter Martyr's *De Orbe Novo,* translated and edited by Ramusio and printed by Giunti in 1565.

Pride of place in the library, however, belongs to a modern six-volume edition of *Navigazioni e viaggi* (with a slightly different spelling), published by Einaudi in the 1970s and expertly edited by Marica Milanesi, a professor of geography at the University of Padua and the foremost Ramusio specialist.

The original edition of *Navigationi et Viaggi* that Giunti put out in the 1550s was one of the great publishing feats of the sixteenth century. It played a vital role in the final emancipation from a vision of the world still anchored to antiquity and became an indispensable source for the great cartographers of the second half of the sixteenth century. Gerhard Mercator, the Flemish mathematician who gave us the first modern map of the world (1569), owned and consulted all three volumes of the Ramusio trilogy. His friend and rival Abraham Ortelius made ample use of it for large sections of his own maps.

The trilogy was also popular with the general reader—as Ramusio had wanted. Book One, with maps of Africa, the eastern coast of Brazil, India and Southeast Asia, was continuously in print, with new editions in 1554, 1563, 1588, 1606 and 1613. Book Three, entirely devoted to the Americas and first published in 1556, saw new editions in 1565 and in 1606. The slim Book Two, which had overcome so many obstacles before seeing the light in 1559, was published again in 1574, 1583 and 1606, with much of the missing material restored.

"It was the *National Geographic* of the time," Professor Vallerani observed.

It appears that Ramusio had in mind a Book Four. In the introduction to the posthumous edition of Book Two, Giunti writes: "If that portion of the world that lies to the south, toward the Antarctic Pole, had been discovered and fully explored during his lifetime, Ramusio would have worked himself to exhaustion in order to obtain all the reports and travel narratives necessary to publish a fourth volume." At which point Giunti concludes, "It would have been no longer necessary to read anything by Ptolemy, Strabo or Pliny or any of the authors of antiquity who wrote about geography."

Fracastoro's earlier remark that Ramusio would soon have informers sending dispatches from the South Pole was perhaps not so casual after all. Antarctica was clearly in Ramusio's thoughts. But in what form? Ptolemy and other geographers from antiquity had posited the existence of a vast continent at the southern pole to counterbalance the heavy landmasses in the Northern Hemisphere. But in Ramusio's time no European, as far as we know, had yet sailed far south enough to glimpse this mythical continent—it was first sighted by a Russian expedition in 1820. It is not impossible that Ramusio had heard or read information about the South Pole that we have since lost; but it is more likely that, despite his lifelong effort to surpass the Ancients, he was, if only in the case of Antarctica, guided by a Ptolemaic assumption.

Still, Ramusio's three volumes were more than "enough to fill a man's life."

BIBLIOGRAPHICAL NOTE

This note is not meant to be an exhaustive bibliography; it is a personal guide to the books, essays and articles that helped me write This Earthly Globe.

The original editions of Ramusio's *Navigationi et Viaggi* (Venice: Giunti, 1550–1559) that I consulted are in the Biblioteca Marciana in Venice, and I am grateful to the staff of that beloved institution for their help and patience in lugging the heavy volumes down from the stacks so many times.

Marica Milanesi's six-volume edition of *Navigazioni e viaggi,* published by Einaudi (1978–1988), is the most complete contemporary edition of Giovambattista Ramusio's magnum opus; Ms. Milanesi's vision and scholarship sustained me throughout this project. A useful complement was the three-volume facsimile edition of the Italian original, *Navigationi et Viaggi,* published in Amsterdam by Theatrum Orbis Terrarum (1967–1970), with an introduction by R. A. Skelton and an analysis by George B. Parks.

The initial spark for this book came from Massimo Donattini's engaging essay "Giovanni Battista Ramusio e le sue 'Navigazioni': Appunti per una biografia" in *Critica storica* 17 (1980), pp. 55–100. Donattini's exhaustive entry on Ramusio in the *Dizionario biografico degli italiani* served as an indispensable reference point.

There are few surviving letters by Ramusio. Limited samples of his correspondence with his friends Pietro Bembo, Andrea Navagero and Girolamo Fracastoro are in *Lettere di XIII huomini illustri,* published in Venice in 1560, and in *Inscrizioni veneziane,* edited by Emmanuele Cicogna and published between 1824 and 1853 (see vol. 2, pp. 311–330). Forty-five letters by Ramusio to Bembo, edited by Andrea Del Ben, are in *Giovanni Battista Ramusio cancelliere e umanista* (Trieste: Edizioni Goliardiche, 2012 [2004]). I also made ample use of *Lettere di Pietro Bembo,* edited by Ernesto Travi (Bologna: Commissione per i testi di lingua, 1987–1993).

An indispensable tool for anyone writing about Venice in the first half of the sixteenth century is the *Diarii* of Marin Sanudo, a unique collection of daily entries by a Venetian senator spanning more than half a century. The diaries were edited by Rinaldo Fulin (Venice: 1879–1902). They are available for consultation in the reading room of the Biblioteca Marciana and online at onlinebooks.library.upenn.edu.

The following is an additional list of articles and essays on Ramusio that offered insights and new perspectives on his life and career:

Barbieri, Alvaro. "Un'antologia di viaggio del Cinquecento: Sul laboratorio editoriale di G. B. Ramusio." *Textual Cultures* 3 (2008), pp. 113–121.

Donattini, Massimo. "Ombre imperiali. Le *Navigationi et Viaggi* di G. B. Ramusio e l'immagine di Venezia." In *L'Europa divisa e i nuovi mondi. Per Adriano Prosperi,* vol. 2, eds. Massimo Donattini, Giuseppe Marcocci and Stefania Pastore (Pisa: Edizioni della Normale, 2011), pp. 33–44.

Milanesi, Marica. "Giovanni Battista Ramusio e le *Navigazioni e viaggi* (1550–1559)." In *L'epopea delle scoperte,* ed. Renzo Zorzi (Venice: Leo S. Olschki, 1994), pp. 75–101.

Parks, George B. "Ramusio's Literary History." *Studies in Philology* 52 (1955), pp. 127–148.

Stegagno Picchio, Luciana. "*Navigationi et Viaggi* di Giovanni Battista Ramusio." In *Letteratura italiana. Le Opere II. Dal Cinquecento al Settecento,* ed. Alberto Asor Rosa (Turin: Einaudi, 1993), pp. 479–515.

Veneri, Toni. "Giovanni Battista Ramusio, molto più di uno spettatore. Le quinte delle *Navigationi et Viaggi.*" *Italica* 89, no. 2 (2012), pp. 162–201.

Among the general histories of Venice in English, I recommend two classics— Frederic Lane's *Venice: A Maritime Republic* (1973) and John Julius Norwich's *A History of Venice* (1977–1982)—and the more recent *Venice: A New History* by Thomas Madden (New York: Viking, 2012). For an interesting analysis of Ramusio's Venice, see Margaret King's *Venetian Humanism in an Age of Patrician Dominance* (Princeton: Princeton University Press, 1986) and my personal favorite, *Venice and the Renaissance,* by Manfredo Tafuri, translated by Jessica Levine (Cambridge, Mass.: MIT Press, 1990).

CHAPTER ONE
The Education of a Geographer

The main source on the Ramusio family is the *Cronaca Ramusia,* an eighteenth-century manuscript account written by a descendant of Giovambattista, now in the Biblioteca Marciana (ms. It. VII. 325, 8839). On the same topic, see Massimo Donattini's "Una famiglia riminese nella società e cultura veneziane: I Ramusio" in *Ravenna in età veneziana,* ed. Dante Bolognesi (Ravenna: Interventi classensi, 1986), pp. 279–294, and Donattini's exhaustive entry for Ramusio in the *Dizionario biografico degli italiani.*

Details on Alvise Mocenigo's mission to France were gleaned from Sanudo's diaries. The quotes by Emperor Maximilian come from the same source.

On Pietro Bembo, see Carlo Dionisotti's introduction in the classic edition of *Prose della volgar lingua* (Turin: UTET, 1931). By Bembo, see *Gli Asolani* (Turin: UTET, 1932); *De Aetna,* translated from the Latin by Vittorio Enzo Alfieri (Palermo: Sellerio, 1981); for an English translation of the latter, see Ross Kilpatrick's version in "The *De Aetna* of Pietro Bembo: A Translation," *Studies in Philology* 83, no. 3 (Summer 1986), pp. 331–358. The only biography of Bembo in English is Carol Kidwell's *Pietro Bembo: Lover, Linguist, Cardinal* (Montreal: McGill-Queen's University Press, 2004).

On Aldus Manutius, see Martin Lowry's *The World of Aldus Manutius* (Ithaca: Cornell University Press, 1979) and Carlo Dionisotti's *Aldo Manuzio, umanista e editore* (Milan: Il Polifilo, 1995), as well as Dionisotti's fine entry for Aldus in the *Dizionario biografico degli italiani.* Alessandro Marzo Magno's more recent *L'inventore di libri. Aldo Manuzio, Venezia e il suo tempo* (Bari: Laterza, 2020) is a useful and very readable account of Aldus's life and milieu. The quotes by Aldus are mostly from *Lettere prefatorie a edizioni greche,* edited by Claudio Bevegni (Milan: Adelphi, 2017). On Erasmus and Aldus, see the little volume edited by Lodovica Braida, *Opulentia sordida e altri scritti attorno ad Aldo Manuzio* (Venice: Marsilio, 2015).

CHAPTER TWO
Pigafetta's Diary

The best and most complete edition of Pigafetta's diary in Italian, in my view, is *Il primo viaggio intorno al mondo,* edited and annotated by Mario Pozzi (Vicenza: Neri Pozza, 1994), which includes a facsimile of the original manuscript. Another useful critical edition of Pigafetta's *Relazione del primo viaggio attorno al mondo* was edited by Andrea Canova (Padua: Antenore, 1999). *Magellan's Voyage: A Narrative Account of the First Navigation Around the World,* based on a copy of Pigafetta's narrative held at the Beinecke Library, has an excellent introduction by R. A. Skelton (London: Folio Society, 1975). See also *The First Voyage Around the World, 1519–1522: An Account of Magellan's Expedition,* edited by Theodore Cachey Jr. (Toronto: Toronto University Press, 2007). Two narrative works on Magellan's journey stand out: Stefan Zweig's masterly *Magellan* (1938), translated from the German by Cedar Paul (London: Pushkin Press, 2011), and the more recent *Over the Edge of the World* by Laurence Bergreen (New York: Morrow, 2003).

A good starting point for any research on Pigafetta is Daria Perocco's excellent entry in the *Dizionario biografico degli italiani.*

Chiericati's description of Pigafetta is in a letter to Isabella d'Este in the Archivio di Stato di Mantova, dated January 10, 1523. "The Knight Errant of

Vicenza" quip is by Marin Sanudo, the diarist, and so is the description of the audience listening in "rapt attention." Ramusio's opinion that the Ancients would have erected a monument to Pigafetta is in Milanesi's edition of *Navigazioni e viaggi* (vol. 2, p. 838).

CHAPTER THREE
Cadamosto

The main source for this chapter is Cadamosto's own report on his two journeys to Africa. I consulted two separate manuscript copies dating from the fifteenth century at the Biblioteca Marciana. The scholar Fracanzio da Montalboddo edited and published the first edition of Cadamosto's manuscript in Vicenza in 1507 as part of an anthology of travel narratives. I used Ramusio's later and more complete edition of 1550. The two best contemporary editions are *Le navigazioni atlantiche del veneziano Alvise da Mosto* by Tullia Gasparini Leporace (Rome: Istituto poligrafico dello Stato, 1966), and Marica Milanesi's own well-annotated edition in *Navigazioni e viaggi* (vol. 1, pp. 461–542).

Ugo Tucci's entry on Cadamosto in the *Dizionario biografico degli italiani* provided much valuable background. A notable contribution on the influence of classical sources with regard to Africa is Marica Milanesi's essay " 'Come dicono gl'istorici antichi . . .': Nearco come fonte nelle *Navigazioni* di Giovanni Battista Ramusio (1550–1559)" in *Geographia Antiqua* 22 (2013), pp. 69–76.

Peter Russell's *Prince Henry "the Navigator": A Life* (New Haven: Yale University Press, 2001) was most helpful in illustrating the Portuguese context in which Cadamosto operated.

CHAPTER FOUR
An African Masterpiece

The manuscript of al-Wazzan's *Libro de la Cosmogrophia* [sic] *et Geographia de Affrica* [sic] is in the Biblioteca Nazionale Centrale in Rome (Vitt. Eman. 953). Ramusio's heavily edited version, published in 1550, doesn't capture the flavor and language of the original. Still, Marica Milanesi's annotated edition of the Ramusio text in *Navigazioni e viaggi* was a precious guide. See also the recent edition by Gabriele Amadori, *La cosmographia de l'Affrica* (Rome: Aracne, 2014).

Anyone delving into the enigma represented by al-Wazzan is indebted to Angela Codazzi, one of the greatest experts on the topic, even though her output was relatively small. A good starting point is her entry on al-Wazzan ("Leone Africano") in the *Enciclopedia italiana di scienze, lettere ed arti*, vol. 20, p. 899, now also available on Treccani.it. See also her two essays "Il 'Trattato dell'arte metrica' di Giovanni Leone Africano" in *Studi orientalistici in onore di Giorgio Levi della Vida* (Rome: Istituto per l'Oriente, 1956), vol. 1, pp. 180–198, and "Dell'unico manoscritto della 'Cosmografia dell'Africa' di Giovanni Leone l'Africano" in *Comptes rendus du Congrès international de Géographie. Lisbonne, 1949* (Lisbon, 1952), vol. 4, pp. 225–226.

For a recent summary of the scholarship on al-Wazzan, see Fabio Romanini's "Note sul testo della *Cosmographia et Geographia de Affrica* di Giovanni Leone Africano" in *Tilelli: Scritti in onore di Vermondo Brugnatelli,* eds. Giorgio Francesco Arcodia et al. (Cesena/Rome: Caissa Italia, 2013), pp. 153–163. Dietrich Rauchenberger and Wolfgang Schweickard have recently concentrated on the philological aspects of al-Wazzan's work.

The best and most complete account in English of al-Wazzan's life and achievements is Natalie Zemon Davis's *Trickster Travels* (New York: Hill and Wang, 2006).

Two essays by Giorgio Levi della Vida—*Elenco dei manoscritti arabi islamici della Biblioteca Vaticana* (1935) and *Ricerche sulla formazione del più antico fondo dei manoscritti orientali della Biblioteca Vaticana* (1939), both published by the Biblioteca Apostolica Vaticana—were useful to understand al-Wazzan's activity in the papal library during his captivity.

Other notable contributions to the study of al-Wazzan are in *La Géographie de la Renaissance, 1420–1620* by Numa Broc (Paris: CTHS, 2019 [1980]); "L'Africa nella cultura europea tra Medioevo e Rinascimento," by Francesco Surdich, in *Relazioni di viaggio e conoscenza fra Medioevo e Umanesimo,* ed. Stefano Pittaluga (Genoa: AMUL/Università di Genova, 1993), pp. 165–240; "Leone l'Africano e l'immaginazione narrativa," by Toni Veneri, in *Studi culturali* 7, no. 2 (2010), pp. 301–318.

Oumelbanine Zhiri also stands out for her significant contribution to al-Wazzan studies with her two books *L'Afrique au miroir de l'Europe: Fortunes de Jean-Léon l'Africain à la Renaissance* (Geneva: Droz, 1991) and *Les sillages de Jean-Léon l'Africain, du XVIe au XXe siècle* (Casablanca: La Croisée des Chemins, 2009 [1995]). I was especially intrigued by her article "Leo Africanus, Translated and Betrayed" in *The Politics of Translation in the Middle Ages and the Renaissance,* eds. Renate Blumenfeld-Kosinski, Luise von Flotow and Daniel Russell (Ottawa: University of Ottawa Press, 2001), pp. 161–174.

The details on the news of al-Wazzan's arrival in Rome and the related quotes from Ambassador Minio to Venice are gleaned from the diaries of Marin Sanudo.

For an engaging fictional account of al-Wazzan's life, see *Léon l'Africain* by the Lebanese novelist Amin Maalouf (Paris: France Loisirs, 1986).

CHAPTER FIVE
Meeting Prester John

Francisco Álvares's account of his journey to Ethiopia is the main source for this chapter. I used Ramusio's edition of 1550, which, as he told his readers, was based on a Portuguese edition of 1540 and a manuscript given to him by the Portuguese humanist Damião de Góis. "Both were very different in many parts," he explained, "so that I had to shape my own version from two mutilated and imperfect ones . . . A confusing and at times rough writing style, full of asperities, seems to be their natural way of writing. I hope it will not be too tedious for those readers who will have the patience to read it from start to finish. In the end they will know enough about Ethiopia." I made ample use, as usual, of Milanesi's notes and comments to her own edition of the Ramusio text (*Navigazioni e viaggi,* vol. 2, pp. 75–385). Ramusio's final considerations about the commercial opportunities offered by establishing good relations with Prester John are from his introduction to the text (see Milanesi's edition of *Navigazioni e viaggi,* vol. 2, p. 80).

The Prester John of the Indies, edited by C. F. Beckingham and G. W. B. Huntingford (Cambridge: Cambridge University Press for the Hakluyt Society, 1961; reprint, 2017) gives a good overview of the Prester John legend. I found Alastair Lamb's "Prester John" in *History Today* (vol. 7, no. 5, May 1957, pp. 313–321) very useful; in fact, it was republished online as "The Search for Prester John" in February 2018 (www.historytoday.com).

Enrico Cerulli's entry for Prester John ("Prete Gianni," 1935) in the *Enciclopedia italiana* is a good initial source. It is also available on Treccani.it. Carlo Conti Rossini's classic *Storia d'Etiopia* (Bergamo: Istituto italiano d'arti grafiche, 1928) offers background on the history of Ethiopia at the time of the Prester John legend. On the early Christian churches of Ethiopia, see *Lalibelà: Le chiese ipogee e monolitiche e gli altri monumenti medievali del Lasta* by Alessandro Augusto Monti della Corte (Rome: Istituto italiano d'arti grafiche, 1940).

For an overview of Ethiopian history in English, I recommend Harold Marcus's *A History of Ethiopia* (Berkeley: University of California Press, 1994; updated, 2002).

CHAPTER SIX
Indian Journeys

Ramusio's 1550 edition of Ludovico di Varthema's *Itinerario* was a translation of a Spanish edition, which was in turn based on a Latin translation of the original. I have used Ramusio's version, as published by Marica Milanesi (*Navigazioni e viaggi,* vol. 1, pp. 763–892). Other important editions of the *Itinerario* include the one published by Paolo Giudici (Milan: Alpes, 1928) and the more recent one by Enrico Musacchio (Bologna: Fusconi, 1991).

The best editions in English are *The Itinerary of Ludovico di Varthema,* edited by Richard Carnac Temple and translated by John Winter Jones (London: Argonaut Press, 1928), and *Travelers in Disguise: Narratives of Eastern Travels by Poggio Bracciolini and Ludovico de Varthema,* edited by Lincoln Davis Hammond and translated by John Winter Jones (Cambridge, Mass.: Harvard University, 1963).

More recently, Carla Forti has published "Sull'itinerario di Ludovico di Var-thema," in *L'Europa divisa e i nuovi mondi. Per Adriano Prosperi,* vol. 2, eds. Massimo Donattini, Giuseppe Marcocci and Stefania Pastore (Pisa: Edizioni della Normale, 2011), pp. 21–31. Carla Forti also wrote the entry on Varthema in the *Dizionario biografico degli italiani.*

On Varthema's visit to Venice, the reactions of the public to his talk and the fee he was paid, see the diaries of Marin Sanudo. The Contarini-Cabot affair and the relevant quotations were also gleaned from the Sanudo diaries.

For the parts on Duarte Barbosa, I used the Ramusio edition published in 1550 and reprinted by Milanesi in *Navigazioni e viaggi* (vol. 2, pp. 541–709). Ramusio had received from Spain, possibly around 1529, a Spanish translation of the original Portuguese manuscript, which in turn he translated into Italian. On the tension between the Portuguese and Hindu rulers at the time of Varthema's journey to India, see Chapter Twelve in Peter Frankopan's masterly *The Silk Roads* (London: Bloomsbury, 2015).

CHAPTER SEVEN
Navagero's Embassy

This chapter is built around five extensive letters from Andrea Navagero to Ramusio, written during his tenure as ambassador to Spain. The letters were first published in *Lettere di XIII huomini illustri* (Venice, 1560) and later included in the complete works of Andrea Navagero, *Opera Omnia Naugerii Andreae,* edited by Giovanni Antonio Volpi and Gaetano Volpi (Padua, 1718, and Venice, 1754). The only complete modern edition of the letters is in Spanish: *Viaje por España,* translated from the Italian and edited by Antonio María Fabié (Madrid: Turner, 1983). The translation from Navagero's letters into English is my own.

Useful secondary sources on Navagero's trip to Spain are: *Andrea Navagero alla corte di Spagna,* edited by Giovanni Maria Malvezzi (Pinerolo, 1871); "Andrea Navagero e l'*Itinerario* in Spagna (1524–1528)," by Claudio Griggio, in *Miscellanea di studi in onore di Marco Pecoraro,* vol. 1, eds. Bianca Maria Da Rif and Claudio Griggio (Florence: Olschki, 1991), pp. 153–178; "Un diplomatico naturalista del Rinascimento: Andrea Navagero," by Mario Cermenati, in *Nuovo Archivio Veneto* 24 (1912), pp. 164–205; "Andrea Navagero e il mito dell'Alhambra," by Bruno Basile, in *Filologia e critica* 21, no. 2 (1996), pp. 255–263; "Per l'edizione dell' 'Itinerario in Spagna' di Andrea Navagero," by Roberto Norbedo, in *Lettere italiane* 52, no. 1 (2000), pp. 58–73.

Navagero's diplomatic reports covering the same period are in *Relazioni di ambasciatori veneti al Senato,* edited by Luigi Firpo (Turin: Bottega d'Erasmo, 1965).

Navagero and Ramusio played a key role in publicizing Peter Martyr's *De Orbe Novo.* The first Italian edition, which they translated and edited, was published in 1534. Ramusio reorganized the material, dividing it into chapters for the 1556 edition, published in Book Three of his *Navigationi et Viaggi*. I have relied on that version, as published by Marica Milanesi in *Navigazioni e viaggi* (vol. 5, pp. 25–205). Gonzalo de Oviedo's *Sumario de la natural historia de las Indias* was published in Italian in 1534 and reprinted in 1556 in Book Three of *Navigationi et Viaggi*. Again, I used the Milanesi edition from *Navigazioni e viaggi* (vol. 5, pp. 211–339). Oviedo published *Primera parte de la Historia general y natural de las Indias, islas y tierra firme del mar oceano* in Seville in 1535. Ramusio translated the first twenty books into Italian and published them in 1556 in Book Three of *Navigationi et Viaggi*. That version is in Milanesi's *Navigazioni e viaggi* (vol. 5, pp. 345–956).

The quotes about the Spanish making "bombastic" claims about what they had found overseas, the descriptions of the cities in Mexico, and the complaints about Navagero's negligence as official historian of the Republic are in Sanudo's diaries.

Bembo's letter of congratulation to Navagero on his appointment as ambassador to Spain and his letter to Ramusio expressing relief that Navagero survived the crossing to Barcelona are in the collection of his letters edited by Ernesto Travi, *Lettere di Pietro Bembo* (Bologna: Commissione per i testi di lingua, 1987–1993). The details of the excursion to Tivoli are in a letter by Bembo to Cardinal Bernardo Bibbiena, in the same collection.

For general background, I recommend Hugh Thomas's *Rivers of Gold: The Rise of the Spanish Empire* (London: Weidenfeld & Nicolson, 2003) and *The Golden Age: The Spanish Empire of Charles V* (London: Allen Lane, 2010). And despite the passing of time, I found Samuel Eliot Morison's classic *The European Discovery of America* (Oxford: Oxford University Press, 1971) to be a trusty companion throughout the writing of this chapter. Finally, Antonello Gerbi's *La natura delle Indie nuove* (Milan: Ricciardi, 1975) and Rosario Romeo's *Le scoperte americane nella coscienza italiana nel Cinquecento* (Bari: Laterza, 1989) offer insightful overviews of the impact in Europe of the discoveries overseas.

CHAPTER EIGHT
In the Land of Biru

Ramusio's official report on the Reuveni affair ("Summario delle cose de David judeo, fiol de Re Salomon de Tabor et fratello del Re Joseph venuto novamente in Venezia") is in the *Diarii* of Marin Sanudo. The most exhaustive treatment of the affair is by Toni Veneri (see his PhD thesis, "Geografia di Stato: Il viaggio rinascimentale da Venezia a Costantinopoli fra letteratura e cartografia," Trieste University, 2010). See also "The Man Who Wanted to Be the Mashiach: The Fantastic Tale of David Reuveni," by Isaac Cohen, in *Niv Hamidrashia* 24/25 (1993), pp. 67–77, and "Nota sul secondo soggiorno veneziano di David Reuveni," by Gianfranco Di Segni, *Rassegna mensile di Israel* 45, no. 6–7 (1979), pp. 266–268.

Early reactions in the Senate to the news of Pizarro's advances are in Sanudo's *Diarii*. An anonymous narrative (usually ascribed to Cristóbal de Mena, a
disgruntled officer who had been one of Pizarro's first captains in Peru) titled *La
conquista del Peru. Llamada la Nueva Castilla* was published in Seville in April 1534.
Ramusio published his own Italian translation in Book Three of *Navigationi et
Viaggi* (1556) together with *La Verdadera Relacion,* the more official version of
events by Francisco Xerez, Pizarro's secretary. For both of these texts, I used
Milanesi's edition in *Navigazioni e viaggi* (vol. 6, pp. 674–791).

The reports by Cabeza de Vaca, Marco da Nizza and Hernando de Soto are
also in vol. 6 of Milanesi's edition.

CHAPTER NINE
Sailing to Hochelaga

Verrazzano's report to the King of France is in Milanesi (vol. 6, pp. 891–906).
For a complete account of Verrazzano's journeys, the best work in English
remains Lawrence C. Wroth's *The Voyages of Giovanni da Verrazzano, 1524–1528*
(New Haven: Yale University Press, 1970).

The reference to the "literary gentlemen" who provided the Cartier manuscripts is in Ramusio's introduction to Book Three of *Navigationi et Viaggi,*
and in Milanesi's edition (vol. 5, p. 16). Cartier's reports are in Milanesi (vol. 6,
pp. 931–1003). For more on the texts, see the introduction and notes by Henry
P. Biggar in *The Voyages of Jacques Cartier,* vol. 11 (Ottawa: Public Archives of
Canada, 1924), and Bernard G. Hoffman *Cabot to Cartier* (Toronto: University
of Toronto Press, 1961). In French, see *Le monde de Jacques Cartier: L'aventure au
XVIe siècle,* edited by Fernand Braudel and Michel Mollat du Jourdin (Paris:
Berger-Levrault, 1984).

CHAPTER TEN
The Return of Marco Polo

The original manuscript of Marco Polo's travels, in a literary language described
as Franco-Venetian, is lost. Ramusio based his own version of the book on the
Latin translation of an early Venetian text by the Dominican friar Francesco
Pipino, published in 1532, and on several earlier manuscripts, including the
so-called Ghisi manuscript. Ramusio's final version, published posthumously
(1559) in Book Two of *Navigationi et Viaggi,* is reprinted in Milanesi's *Navigazioni e viaggi* (vol. 3, pp. 9–297), with the editor's very useful notes and comments.
The Travels of Marco Polo, edited by Milton Rugoff (New York: New American
Library, 1961), is the English-language version that I used.

A number of classic studies framed the discourse on Marco Polo in the twen-
tieth century and are still relevant today. Among them: *The Book of Ser Marco*

Polo the Venetian, edited by Henry Yule and Henri Cordier (London: Murray, 1903, 2 vols.); *Il libro di Messer Marco Polo, cittadino di Venezia detto Milione,* edited by Luigi Foscolo Benedetto (Milan: Treves-Treccani-Tumminelli, 1932); *Notes on Marco Polo,* by Paul Pelliot (Paris, 1959–1963, 3 vols.).

Among contemporary scholars I am indebted to Toni Veneri for "Il riscatto geografico di Marco Polo," *Quaderni veneti* 1, no. 2 (2012); Eugenio Burgio for *Giovanni Battista Ramusio: "Editor" del* Milione: *Trattamento del testo e manipolazione dei modelli* (Rome/Padua: Antenore, 2011); Philippe Ménard for "Le problème de la version originale du *Devisement du monde*" in *De Marco Polo à Savinio: Écrivains italiens en langue française,* ed. François Livi (Paris: Presses de l'Université Paris-Sorbonne, 2003); Christine Gadrat-Ouerfelli for *Lire Marco Polo au Moyen Age* (Paris: Brepols, 2015). Among recent books in English, see *Marco Polo's Book* by John Critchley (Aldershot, UK: Ashgate Variorum, 1992).

I am especially grateful to Tiziana Plebani for the excellent *Il testamento di Marco Polo* (Milan: Unicopli, 2019). The book is dedicated to Alvise Zorzi, who edited *Marco Polo: Venezia e l'Oriente* (Milan: Electa, 1981), a thorough introduction to Marco Polo and his time. See also the biography by Zorzi, *Vita di Marco Polo Veneziano* (Milan: Bompiani, 2000). An engaging English-language narrative of Polo's travels is Laurence Bergreen's *Marco Polo: From Venice to Xanadu* (New York: Knopf, 2007). For a more controversial approach to Polo's memoirs, see *Did Marco Polo Go to China?* by Frances Wood (London: Secker and Warburg, 1995). For a new assessment of the rise of the Mongolian Empire and its impact on Europe during the Middle Ages, see Peter Frankopan's *The Silk Roads* (London: Bloomsbury, 2015).

Finally and most important: in 2011, Eugenio Burgio, Marina Buzzoni and Antonella Ghersetti of Università Ca' Foscari in Venice launched a digital edition of Ramusio's *Dei viaggi di Messer Marco Polo* as it was published in Book Two of *Navigationi et Viaggi* (1559). It is currently accessible at http://virgo.unive.it /ecf-workflow/books/Ramusio/main/index.html. The project is ongoing and continues to be enriched by comments and additions by Polo scholars. It proved an invaluable resource in the writing of this chapter.

CHAPTER ELEVEN
Stealing Time from Time

The quote by Fracastoro on Ramusio's informers in Antarctica is in *Lettere di XIII huomini illustri* (Venice, 1560), and in Donattini's "Giovanni Battista Ramusio e le sue 'Navigazioni': Appunti per una biografia" in *Critica storica* 17 (1980), p. 89. Ramusio's quote about Fracastoro's role in convincing him to embark on the publishing is in Milanesi (vol. 1, p. 3).

For a thorough account of Ramusio as editor, see Fabio Romanini's *"Se fussero più ordinate, e meglio scritte . . .": Giovanni Battista Ramusio correttore ed editore delle Navigationi et Viaggi* (Rome: Viella, 2007).

The narratives by Vasco da Gama and Amerigo Vespucci are in Milanesi (vol. 1).

The quotes by Ramusio on the frustrations and sheer exhaustion of assembling the book are in Milanesi (vol. 1, p. 5).

Giovan Battista Sassetti's book review is in Milanesi (vol. 1, p. xxxiii). For details on the story of Filippo Sassetti, see *Lettere dall'India (1583–1588)*, edited by Adele Dai (Rome: Salerno Editrice, 1995), and *Filippo Sassetti* by Marica Milanesi (Florence: La Nuova Italia, 1973); Francesco Surdich has written a thorough entry for Filippo Sassetti in the *Dizionario biografico degli italiani*.

On Sebastian Cabot's last attempt to lead a Venetian expedition, see Donattini, "Giovanni Battista Ramusio" (p. 79), and Sanudo's *Diarii*, both cited above.

The Cortés letters, translated and edited by Ramusio, are in Milanesi (vol. 4, pp. 15–303).

Ramusio's comments on the "malice and greed" of the invading Spaniards are in Milanesi (vol. 6, pp. 669–670). For his take on Hayton the Armenian, see his introduction to the text in Milanesi (vol. 3, pp. 303–309).

The manuscript account by Pietro Querini of his shipwreck in the Lofoten archipelago is in the Vatican Library (Vat. Lat. 5256); the second report, by Cristoforo Fioravanti and Nicolò di Michiel, is in the Biblioteca Marciana in Venice (Ms. It. cl. VII, 368). Both versions were published side by side at the end of the posthumous first edition of Ramusio's Book Two. Both are reprinted in Milanesi (vol. 4, pp. 51–98).

The quotes by Giunti on revealing Ramusio's name, on Ramusio stealing "time from Time" and on his plans to write Book Four are all from Giunti's letter to the readers, which introduced the posthumous Book Two, and are in Milanesi (vol. 1, pp. 7–8).

INDEX

(Page references in *italics* refer to illustrations.)

Afghanistan, 98
  Polos' journey through, 171,
    174–5
Africa, 3, 47–95
  Ancients' explorations of, 47–8, 60
  Cadamosto's travels in, 47, 48–60,
    210
  fierce tribes in, 54–6
  Land of the Black People in, 49,
    50, 62, 66, 71
  Leo Africanus's book on, 65–72,
    73–7, 210
  maps of, published by Ramusio,
    56, 74–5, 211, 231
  Portuguese domination of trade
    with, 49, 50, 210
  in Ptolemaic view of world, 5–6,
    6, 210, 212
  publishing of Ramusio's volumes
    on, 209, 210
  see also Ethiopia
Agnadello, Venetian defeat at (1508),
    23–4, 115, 166
Alberto Pio, Prince of Carpi, 17, 31,
    64–5
Albo, Francisco, 40, 41, 45
Aldus Manutius, 11, 15–22, 24–5,
    27–30, 43, 46, 64, 65, 111, 115,
    146, 204, 208, 223
  Aldine press established by, 17,
    17–19
Bembo's *Gli Asolani* and, 20–1
book formats and typefaces
    innovated by, 20
Codex Parisinus published by, 16
death and burial of, 29–30, 31
Greek and Roman authors
    published by, 18–19, 21, 25, 28
Ramusio's assistance in print shop
    of, 15–16, 28–9, 169, 208
Strabo's *Geography* and, 31–2
Aleandro, Girolamo, 21
Alexander III, Pope, 79
Alexander VI, Pope, 15n, 20
Alexander the Great, 175, 176
Alfonso VI, King, 213
Alhambra, Granada, Navagero's
    letter to Ramusio about, 141–2
Almagro, Diego de, 218
Almeida, Lourenço de, 101
Álvares, Father Francisco, 82–95, 86,
    95, 133, 210, 212
  travels in Ethiopia chronicled by,
    93–5
Alviano, Bartolomeo d', 23–4, 28–9,
    115–16, 117
Alvise da Mosto. *See* Cadamosto
al-Wazzan, al-Hasan ibn
    Muhammad. *See* Leo Africanus
American southwest, explorations of,
    157, 219
Americas, Gastaldi's map of, 221

Anatolia, Polos' journey through, 171–2
Antarctica, 232
Arabic translations of Latin texts, 68
Arctic Circle, 214
    Querini's prolonged stay in, 224–6
Arghun, King, 200
Aristotle, 18–19, 65, 209, 232
Arrianus, Flavius, 223
Asia:
    in Ptolemaic view of world, 5–6, 6, 210
    publishing of Ramusio's volumes on, 210–11, 213, 222–3
    See also China; India; specific places
Atahualpa, 153–4, 218
Atlantic Ocean, 210
    ancients' exploration of, 47–8
    Columbus's journeys across, 4, 112, 125–7, 205
    Magellan expedition's crossings of, 37, 40
    Portuguese explorations of, 47–51. See also Cadamosto
    Spanish shipping operations in, 139–40
    Venetian vessels cut off from, 108
    Verrazzano's crossings of, 159
Atlas Mountains, 67–8, 70
Axum, Portuguese caravan at, 84–5
Ayllón, Lucas Vázquez de, 128
Aztecs, 114, 217

Badakhshan, Kingdom of, 175–6
Badoer, Donata, 205
Balboa, Vasco Núñez de, 4, 113, 127, 130, 131, 153
Balkh, Polos' stop in, 174–5
Barbarigo, Pierfrancesco, 18
Barbosa, Duarte, 104–5, 211
Barros, João de, 211
Battimansa, 58, 59
Beazzano, Agostino, 116, 117

Behaim, Martin, 34, 35, 36
Bembo, Bernardo, 19, 21
Bembo, Pietro, 28, 111, 115, 116, 118, 120, 146, 148, 149, 152, 165, 166–7, 208
    Gli Asolani by, 20–1
    Lascaris's old Greek grammar and, 19
    Leo Africanus's manuscript and, 65, 76
    modern Italian language and, 19, 20, 28, 166
Berbers, 50, 68, 71
Bessarion, Cardinal, library of, 116–18, 119, 167
Blyth, Edward, 177
Bobadilla, Don Pedro, 61, 63
Borgia, Lucretia, 20–1
Borneo, 99, 197
Bourbon, Charles de, 72
Brazil, 4, 37, 114, 210, 231
Bucignolo, Girolamo, 107
Buddhism, 175, 178, 179, 180–1, 188

Cabeza de Vaca, Álvar Núñez, 156, 157
Cabot, John, 4, 107
Cabot, Sebastian, 107–9, 112, 118, 214
Cabo Verde archipelago, 40, 46n, 47, 57
Cabral, Pedro Álvares, 104
Cadamosto (Alvise da Mosto), 36, 47, 48–60, 210
    Cabo Verde reached by, 46n, 47, 57
    in Gambia region, 55–6, 57, 58–9
    printed edition of writings of, 60
Calixtus II, Pope, 78
Calvus, Minutius, 45
Campion (Zhangye), Polos' stop in, 180–2
Canada, Cartier's journeys to, 160–4
cannibalism, 55, 99–100, 135, 159, 198–9, 203

canoes, in New Indies, *134*

Cape of Good Hope, 4, 40, 66, 81, 96, 210, 211, 222

Cape Verde Peninsula, 54, 57–8

Caribbean region, 112–13, 129–36, 152, 215–16
  mapping of, 113, *113*, 114
  See also New Indies

Cartier, Jacques, 4, *160*, 160–4, *161*, 220

Casa de Contratación de las Indias, 139, 140

Castanheda, Fernão Lopes de, 211

Castiglione, Baldassare, 144
  The Courtier by, 116, 122, 146
  Navagero's friendship with, 116, 122, 145, 146

Cayor, Cadamosto's stay with Budomei, King of, 51–3

Cazazionor, 98–100

Charles V, Emperor (Charles I, King of Spain), 72, 107, 108, 124, 130, 140–1, 151, 214
  administration of Spanish-controlled territories overseas and, 114, 125, 153, 156–7, 216, 218, 219
  Magellan's voyage and, 33, 34, 36–7, 40–1, 42, 45
  Navagero as ambassador to court of, 114–15, 118–23, 136–7, 144–6, 148
  in war against France, 120, 122, 136–7, 140, 144, 145, 149, 219
  wedding of Isabella of Portugal and, 137, 140, 141

Chicora, Francisco de, 128

Chiericati, Francesco, 36, 42, 43

Chiesa della Madonna dell'Orto, Venice, 226–7

China, 34, 79, 113, 167–200, 211
  Cabot's proposals to find passage to, 107–9, 214

Gastaldi's map of, *258*

Maffio and Niccolò Polo's first journey to, 169–70

Marco Polo's sixteen-year stay in, 187–200. *See also* Polo, Marco

Marco Polo's three-year-long journey to, with his father and uncle, 167, 171–87

paper money in, 187–8, 190, 191

Prester John's legendary kingdom in, 183–4

restrictions on travel to, in Ramusio's time, 182

transportation system, 188

yaks, musk deer, and white camels in, 183

See also Kublai Khan

Christianity, 188
  Ethiopian Church and, 82
  Kublai Khan's interest in, 170, 171
  proselytizing campaigns and, 39, 50, 63–4, 155
  struggles between Islam and, 61, 63, 64, 78, 80–2, 91, 92–3, 99, 125, 141, 143, 150

Church of Our Savior, Lalibela, *86*, 86–8

Church of Saint Mary of Zion, Axum, 84–5

Ci Lapu Lapu, 39

Cima da Conegliano, 226–7

Circassian people, 223

Clement IV, Pope, 170–1

Clement VII, Pope, 44–5, 72, 93, 122, 144, 145, 151

cloves, 33–4, 39–40, 92, 190–1, 197

Codex Parisinus, 16

Colón, Bartolomeo, 130

Colón, Diego, 112, 121–2, 128, 130, 137, 148

Colón, Luis, 137

Columbus, Christopher, 4, 6, 34, 36, 95, 111, 112, 121, 130, 137
  Martyr's assessment of, 125–7
  Polo-inspired fantasy of, 126, 168, 197
  Polos deemed superior to, by Ramusio, 205
Commynes, Philippe de, 12
Condulmer, Antonio, 14–15
Contarini, Gasparo, 34, 107–9, 118, 122
corn (maize), 111, 139
Coronado, Francisco Vázquez de, 157, 219
Cortés, Hernán, 4, 114, 127, 153, 156–7, 215–16
Council of Ten, 21, 24, 25, 43, 45, 106, 107–8, 151, 213
Council of the Indies, 121–2, 125, 137, 148
Counter-Reformation, 208
Covilhã, Pedro da, 81, 89, 91
Crates of Mallus, 34
Crete, 44, 48, 166, 225
crocodiles, 133, 192
Crusades, 78–80, 170, 227
Cunha, Tristão da, 101
Cuzco, city plan of, 220

Dali, Polo's time in, 191–2
Darién:
  Dávila's cruel regime in, 130, 131, 132, 136
  establishment of Spanish colony in, 113, 127
  Oviedo's years in, 129, 130–6. See also Oviedo y Valdés, Gonzalo Fernández de
  See also New Indies
Dávila, Pedro Arias, 127, 130, 131, 132, 136
Dias, Dinis, 51
Donnacona, Chief, 162, 163, 164

Edward VI, King of England, 214
Egidio da Viterbo, 64, 65, 73, 76
Egrigaia (Ningxia), white camels in, 183
Egypt, 61, 62, 94, 151, 222
Elcano, Juan Sebastián, 33, 34, 40, 41, 45, 124
elephants, 58–9, 104
Epistula Presbyterius Johannis, 79
Erasmus, 21–2
  Adagia by, 21
Erginul (Qinghai), Polos' journey in, 182
Essen Temur, 191
Ethiopia, 77, 80–95, 94
  Álvares's manuscript on, 93–5, 210
  Portuguese search for Prester John in, 81–92
  remains of great city of Axum in, 84–5
Eugenius III, Pope, 79
Euripides, 19, 21

Federico II, Duke of Mantua, 42, 45
Ferdinand, King of Spain, 13, 22, 124, 125, 129, 130
Fez, Leo Africanus's description of, 69–70
Fracastoro, Girolamo, 111, 152, 166, 207, 209, 215, 232
France:
  in coalition of Venetians' enemies, 11–15, 22–7
  exploration of North America and, 158–64. See also New France
  Ramusio as aide in diplomatic mission to, 11–15, 16
Francis I, King of France, 42, 64, 158
  Cartier's expeditions and, 161, 163
  Verrazzano's expeditions and, 158–60
  in war against Spain, 119–20, 122, 136–7, 140, 144–5, 149, 219

Gaetani, Pier Antonio, 5
Galvão, Odoardo, 81–2, 92
Gama, Vasco da, 4, 36, 49, 66, 81, 96, 97, 100, 105–6, 210, 211
Gambia region, Cadamosto's exploration of, 55–6, 57, 58–9
García de Loaysa, Juan, 148
Gastaldi, Giacomo, 166, 211, 224
  full map of Africa by, 74–5
  map of Hispaniola by, 113
  map of Indian subcontinent by, 102–3
  map of Nile basin by, 94
  map of southern China and the Indo-Pacific Ocean by, 198
  map of the Americas by, 221
Gattinara, Mercurino, 34, 122
Genesis, 51
Genghis Khan, 80, 169, 170, 174, 185
Ghazi, Sultan Ahmad al-, 85, 93
Ghisi manuscript of Polo's Travels, 168–9, 204
Giova, Bernardino, 106
Giovanmaria, 100–1
Giovio, Paolo, 65, 76
Giunti, house of (publisher), 3
Giunti, Tommaso, 4, 209, 211, 212, 221–2, 226, 227–8, 231, 232
  Inquisition's intimidations of, 214–15
Giunti brothers, 216
globe, world first represented as, 34–5, 35
Gobi Desert, Polos' crossing of, 178–9
Góis, Damião de, 81, 93–5
gold, 97
  in Africa, 49, 50, 55, 58, 71, 84, 85, 90, 92
  in the Americas, 125, 130, 154, 155, 163
Gómez, Esteban, 38, 148
Gonzales, Antonio, 49

Gordillo, Francisco, 128
Granada, Navagero's letter to Ramusio about, 141–4
Greek language and literature, 18–20
Gregory X, Pope (Tebaldo da Piacenza), 170, 171
Griffo, Francesco, 18, 19
Gritti, Andrea, 23, 26, 112, 119
Gulf of Saint Lawrence, 160, 161, 220

Hadrian, Emperor, 116, 223
hammocks, in New Indies, 132
Hangzhou, 192, 195–6
Hanno the Navigator, 47
Henry, Prince of Portugal, 48–50, 51, 54, 57, 59
Henry VII, King of England, 107
Herberstein, Sigmund von, 224
Hethum the Armenian, 222
Hexi Corridor, Polos' passage through, 179, 180–2
Hindu kingdoms, 97, 99, 101–4
Hindu Kush, Polos' journey through, 171–7
Hippocrates, Treaty on Airs, Waters and Places by, 223
Hirtzhorn, Eucharius, 45
Hispaniola, 112, 113, 121–2, 128, 137
Hochelaga, 161, 162–3
Holy Sepulchre, Jerusalem:
  Polos' mission for Kublai Khan at, 170, 171, 186
  Prester John and, 79–80
Honorius III, Pope, 80
Horace, 19
  Odes by, 25
Hormuz, Polos' stop in, 173–4
Huascar, 153–4
Hurtado de Mendoza, Antonio, 156–7, 219
Hurtado de Mendoza, Diego, 219–20
huts, built by natives in New Indies, 131

iguanas, *129*

Inca Empire, 4, 153–4, *220*

India, 3, 82, 92, 95, 96, 172, 210–11
  Barbosa's manuscript about his
    years in, 104–5, 211
  da Gama's route around Cape of
    Good Hope to, 96, 97
  Portugal's aggressive policies in,
    99, 100–1
  Prester John legend and, 79, 80
  Ramusio's collection of travel
    narratives about, 104, 211
  Varthema's travels in, 96, 98–101
  Varthema's vivid depiction of, in
    Itinerario, 101–4, 211
  Venice's spice trade with, 96–7,
    222

Indian Ocean, 40, 96, 106, 108, 210

Indian subcontinent, Gastaldi's map
  of, *102–3*

Indonesia, 3, 40
  Venice's spice trade with, 96–7

infectious diseases, 101, 111, 209

Inquisition, 104, 143, 151, 208–9,
  214–15

Interiano, Giorgio, 223

Isabella, Queen of Spain, 13, 124, 125,
  129

Isabella d'Este, 42–4, 45, 46

Isabella of Portugal, 137, 140, 141,
  144

Islamic world, 49, 50, 53, 178, 209
  Asia and, 172, 178, 179, 188, 198
  of Grenada, Navagero's letter to
    Ramusio about, 141–4
  Leo Africanus as source of
    information on, 61, 63, 209
  rule over Spain and, 123, 125
  struggles between Christianity
    and, 61, 63, 64, 78, 80–2, 91,
    92–3, 99, 125, 141, 143, 150

Italian vernacular, 19, 20, 28, 166, 213

Ivan IV, Czar of Muscovy, 224

João II, King of Portugal, 81

João III, King of Portugal, 42, 45, 92,
  93–5, 151

John, Patriarch, 78

John Leo. *See* Leo Africanus

Juan, Don, 129

Julius II, Pope, 12, 23, 25, 26–7, 101

Kharcan River, 178

Khotan, Kingdom of, 178

Kokachin, 200

Kublai Khan, 178, 183, 184, 193, 195,
  202, 209
  Cianganor hunting estate of, 184
  conquests of, 190, 191–2, 197
  Maffio and Niccolò Polo's mission
    for, 170, 171, 186
  Marco Polo's admiration for
    policies of, 187–9
  Marco Polo's first meeting with,
    186, 187
  Marco Polo's official missions for,
    187, 189–95, 197–9
  Polos' departure and, 199–200
  Xanadu residence of, 184–6

Labrador, 160, *160*, 162

Lalibela, search for Prester John in,
  85–7

Lascaris, Constantin, 19, 28

las Casas, Father Bartolomé de, 135

League of Cambrai, 22–7, 115, 117

League of Cognac, 144, 145

Leo X, Pope, 28, 36, 61–2, 63–4, 116,
  118

Leo Africanus (al-Hasan ibn
  Muhammad al-Wazzan, or John
  Leo), 61–77, 133, 209, 210, 212
  capture of, 61, 62, 63
  conversion of, to Christianity,
    63–4
  Descrizione dell'Africa by, 65–72,
    73–7

Italian prose of, 66
life of, before capture, 61–3
lyrical inclinations of, 67–8, 76
presented to Leo X as gift, 61–2
Ramusio's interest in, 62, 64, 65,
    66, 72, 73–7, 210, 212
return to North Africa, 73
Sack of Rome and, 72, 73
travels in Italy of, 65
Leonardo da Vinci, 130
Lima, Rodrigo de, 82, 83, 84, 88,
    89, 91
López de Mendoza, Íñigo, 124–5, 145
Loredan, Doge, 26, 118
Louis IX, King of France, 80
Louis XII, King of France, 11–14, 22,
    23, 158
Louise of Savoy, 42

Madrignani, Arcangelo, 104
Magellan, Ferdinand, 4, 33–46, 105,
    106, 109, 113
Charles V's backing of, 36–7
death of, 39, 41
failed mutiny against, 38, 105
first published accounts of voyage
    of, 45
Pacific crossed by, 38–9
Pigafetta's diary of expedition of,
    35–6, 37, 40–6, 210, 212
Ramusio's desire to publish
    account of, 45–6
route to and around South
    America taken by, 37–8
Victoria's return and, 33–5, 37,
    39–40, 45
maize (corn), 111, 139
Malatesta, Pandolfo, 15n
Malipiero, Gasparo, 201
Mamluks, 61, 93, 97, 106
Mandeville, John, Travels by, 167
Mantegna, Andrea, 130
Mantino, Jacob, 65

Manuel I, King of Portugal, 36, 41,
    81, 100, 105, 140, 211
Martyr, Peter (Pietro Martire
    d'Anghiera), 124–9
Columbus's journeys as viewed by,
    125–7
death of, 144
Decades, De Orbe Novo, 41, 124,
    125, 127–8, 148, 152, 153, 155,
    215, 231
Magellan's crew members
    debriefed by, 41, 124
military career of, 124–5
Navagero's relationship with, 124,
    125, 127, 128–9
as Official Historian of the Spanish
    Possessions Overseas, 132, 133,
    144
Matthew, Father, 81, 83, 84
Maximilian I, Emperor, 11, 12, 13, 14,
    22, 24, 25, 26, 224
Mazzucchelli, Giovanni Maria, 4
Mecca, Varthema's impressions
    of, 98
Medici, Lorenzo de', 18
Medici court, 5, 64
Memet, Chaggi, 180, 182
Mena, Cristóbal de, 154–5, 217
Mercator, Gerhard, 231
Mesopotamia, 170
    See also Persia
Mexico, 4, 153, 217
Cortés's conquest of, 4, 114, 127,
    215–16
Mi'kmaq people, 161–2
Minio, Marco, 61, 62, 64
Mocenigo, Alvise, 11, 12–14, 16, 97,
    158, 210
Moghuls, 104
Moluccan Islands, 33, 99, 156, 222
Mongolian Empire, 167, 169, 172,
    182, 187, 222
    See also China; Kublai Khan

Mongol tribes, 79, 80, 178, 223
Mosto, Alvise da. *See* Cadamosto
Muhammad al-Burtughali, Sultan of
    Fez, 62, 67
Muscovy, 31, 223–4
Muscovy Company, 214
Museum Mazzuchellianum, 4, 5
Muslims. *See* Islamic world
Musuro, Marco, 18

Narváez, Pánfilo de, 148, 156
Navagero, Andrea, 104n, 114–24,
    136–49, 150, 152, 166–7, 209,
    215
  in Aldus's circle, 28–9, 111, 115
  as ambassador to court of
      Charles V, 114–15, 118–23,
      136–7, 144–6, 148
  as ambassador to France, 149
  Bessarion library managed by, 116,
      117–18, 119
  death of, 149
  Granada described to Ramusio by,
      141–4
  Martyr's relationship with, 124,
      125, 127, 128–9
  Murano garden of, 119, 142, 148,
      149
  named Official Historian of the
      Republic, 116, 148
  Raphael's portrait of, 116–17
  returned to Venice via Paris,
      146–8
  Riformatori dello Studio di
      Padova job sought by, 148–9
  Seville described to Ramusio by,
      138–41
  as soldier, 28–9, 115–16
  as source of information for
      Ramusio, 114, 119, 121, 124,
      128–9, 136, 148, 149, 152
Navagero, Franceschina (Ramusio's
    wife), 110, 152, 165

Navigationi et Viaggi (Journeys and
    Navigations), 3, 207–28
  anonymous and classified material
      in, 211, 216–17, 219–20
  first volume of, 56, 74–5, 94, 102–3,
      198, 210–13, 231
  Inquisition and political climate as
      concerns for, 208–9
  publisher selected for, 209. *See also*
      Giunti, Tommaso
  Ramusio's overall concept for,
      207–9
  Ramusio's refusal to have his name
      on, 212
  Sassetti's enthusiastic reponse to,
      213
  second volume of, 213, 215, 222–6,
      227–8, 231, 232
  third volume of, 129, 131, 132, 134,
      135, 139, 160, 161, 215–22, 217,
      220, 221, 231
  written in Italian vernacular, 208,
      213
  See also specific topics
Negro, Giovanni, 120
Negus, 81, 83, 84, 87, 90, 91
New Brunswick, 161, 162
Newfoundland, 4, 107, 160–1
New France, 163, 220
  Cartier's explorations and, 4, 160,
      160–4, 161, 220
  Verrazzano's expedition and,
      158–60
New Indies, 42, 129–36, 137, 139,
    144
  Columbus's journeys to, 4, 112,
      125–7, 205
  fruits and other foods native to,
      111, 133–4, 135, 139
  lives of natives in, 114, 131, 132, 134,
      134–6
  mapping of, 113, 113, 114, 139,
      156

Martyr's official chronicle of
  Spanish expansion in, 124,
  125–7
Oviedo's opus on geography,
  fauna, and flora of (*Historia* and
  Sumario), 129, 131–6, 148, 153,
  215
Oviedo's wood engravings of,
  republished by Ramusio, *129,
  131, 132, 134, 135, 139*
Ramusio and Oviedo's business
  venture in, 152
seeds from, grown at Villa
  Ramusia, 111, 230
shipping operations between
  Seville and, 139–40
New Spain, 163
  anonymous and classified material
    on, acquired by Ramusio,
    216–17, 219–20
  bloody aftermath of conquests in,
    218–19
  Cortés's conquests in Mexico and
    Central America and, 4, 114,
    127, 156–7, 215–16
  Pizarro's conquest of Peru and, 4,
    153–5, 217–18
  Ramusio's gathering of
    information about, 114, 152
  Ramusio's third volume and,
    215–22, *217, 220*
  Spanish expansion northward and
    southward of, 153–7
"New World," first use of term, 114
Nile basin, Gastaldi's map of, *94*
Nizza, Marco da, 157, 219
Numidia, 66, 70–1

Odorico da Pordenone, 205n
Olaus Magnus, 224
Order of the Knights of Rhodes, 44
Ottomans, 25, 61–2, 63, 82, 98, 108,
  166, 222, 223

Oviedo, Catalina de Ribafrecha
  (third wife), 132
Oviedo, Isabel de Aguilar (second
  wife), 130, 131
Oviedo, Margarita de Vergara (first
  wife), 130
Oviedo y Valdés, Gonzalo Fernández
  de, 129–36, 137
  Dávila's cruel regime denounced
    by, 130, 131, 132, 136
  Martyr's job as Official Historian
    of the Spanish Possessions
    Overseas sought by, 132, 133,
    144
  Navagero's interest in publishing
    work of, 136, 148–9, 152, 215
  opus on geography, fauna, and
    flora of New Indies written by
    (*Historia, Sumario*), 129, 131–6,
    148, 153, 155, 215
  Ramusio's business venture with,
    152
  Ramusio's work on texts written
    by, 136, 152, 153, 155, 215
  seeds sent to Ramusio by, 230
  wood engravings by, republished
    by Ramusio, *129, 131, 132, 134,
    135, 139*

Pacific Ocean, 156, 169
  explorations and travels along
    coasts of, 157, 194–5, 219
  first Europeans to see, 4, 37n,
    38–40, 113, 127, 130, 153
  Gastaldi's map of Indo-Pacific
    Ocean, *198*
  search for passage from Atlantic
    to, 159
Padua:
  Ramusio's home in, 10, 15, 110,
    165
  Venice's loss and recapture of, 22,
    23, 24, 25–6, 112

Pamir plateau, Polos' journey across, 171, 179

Paris, Navagero's letter to Ramusio about, 147

Paul III, Pope, 166

Persia, 98, 99, 199–201, 228
  Polos' travels in, 170, 171, 172–3, 201
  Ramusio's access to information on, 222–3

Peru, 217–19
  Pizarro's conquest of, 153–5, 217–18

Pietrantonio, 100–1

Pigafetta, Antonio, 35–6, 37, 40–6, 105, 124, 210, 212

Pindar, 28, 115

Pipino, Francesco, 168, 169, 203–4

Pires, Tomé, 211

Pitigliano, Nicolò Orsini da, 23, 24

Pizarro, Francisco, 4, 153–5, 156, 157, 217–18

Pizarro, Hernando, 154

plague, 92, 119, 120, 145, 147, 166

plantains, 134, 135

Pliny the Elder, 131, 212, 223, 232

Pliny the Younger, 16

Polo, Maffio (brother), 170

Polo, Maffio (uncle), 169–86, 204
  first journey to China, 169–70
  Kublai Khan's meetings with, 170, 186
  return to Venice, 199–202
  second journey to China, 171–86

Polo, Marco, 49, 165–206, 209
  account of journey and travels in China written by (Travels), 167–9, 171–2, 180–3, 185, 186–7, 199, 203–5
  after his return to Venice, 202–3, 205–6
  Columbus inspired by, 126, 168, 197

death of, 206
father's first meeting with, 170
greatest source of factual information about Asia, 186–7
guest at Kublai Khan's Xanadu residence, 184–6
Kublai Khan's first meeting with, 186, 187
Kublai Khan's policies admired by, 187–9
memory of, allowed to fade in Venice, 205–6
official missions of, for Kublai Khan, 187, 189–95, 197–9
Prester John legend and, 80, 183–4
Ramusio's publishing of material on, 203–4, 222, 228
return to Venice, 199–202
sheep of Pamir named after, 177
three-year-long journey to China with his father and uncle, 171–84

Polo, Marco, the Elder (uncle), 160, 169

Polo, Niccolò (father), 169–86, 204, 206
  death and burial of, 205, 206
  first journey to China, 169–70
  Kublai Khan's meetings with, 170, 186
  on mission for Kublai Khan, 170–1
  return to Venice, 199–202
  second journey to China, 171–86

Polybius, 48

Pomponazzi, Pietro, 65

Ponce de León, Juan, 113

portolan charts, 5, 57, 127

Portugal:
  aggressive policies of, in India, 99, 100–1
  Magellan's expedition and, 36–7, 40, 41, 42

Prester John and, 81–93. *See also*
    Prester John
Ramusio's first volume
    concentrated on swath of globe
    controlled by, 210–13
spice trade of, 81, 96, 105–6, 112
Prester John (Lebda Dengel, or King
    David), 78–95, 126
alliance with Portugal sought by,
    91, 92–3
Álvares's manuscript on Ethiopia
    and, 93–5, 210
defeat and death of, 93
origins of legend of, 78–80
Polo's interest in empire of, 80,
    183–4
Portuguese delegation's audience
    with, 90–1
Portuguese mission in search of,
    81–92
Priuli, Antonio, 152
Priuli, Lorenzo, 119, 120, 121, 122
Ptolemy, 32, 35, 48, 198, 232
    Geographia by, 5–6, 6, 7, 212
Pueblo Indians, 157, 219

Querini, Pietro, 224–6, 228
Quexos, Pedro de, 128
Quintilianus, 28, 29

Ramusio, Franceschina Navagero
    (wife), 110, 152, 165
Ramusio, Giovambattista, 3
Álvares's manuscript on Ethiopia
    and, 93–5
assisting in Aldus's print shop,
    15–16, 28–9, 169, 208
Bessarion library and, 118, 119, 148,
    166–7
birth of, 10
Cabot's proposals and, 107–9, 214
death and burial of, 226
education of, 10–11

family background of, 9–10
as father, 152–3, 165–6
homes of, 10, 15, 110–11, 229–31
language skills of, 30, 158
Leo Africanus's writings on Africa
    and, 62, 64, 65, 66, 72, 73–7,
    212. *See also* Leo Africanus
marriage of, 110, 152, 165
Navagero as source of information
    for, 114, 119, 121, 124, 128–9,
    136, 148, 149, 152
new geography envisioned by,
    31–2, 76
Oviedo's business venture with, 152
Oviedo's *Historia* and *Sumario* and,
    136, 152, 153, 155, 215
Pigafetta's manuscript on Magellan
    and, 45–6, 210, 212
Polo's *Travels* and, 167–9, 179–80,
    186–7, 203–5
portraits of, 3–4, 5
positions held by, in Venetian
    Republic, 7, 9, 11, 15, 30–1, 62,
    111–12, 158, 207, 213
Reuveni affair and, 150–2
two accounts printed side by side
    by, 155
various spellings of surname of, 3
Varthema's *Itinerario* and, 104, 211
see also Navigationi et Viaggi; *specific
    topics*
Ramusio, Girolamo (uncle), 10
Ramusio, Paolo (father), 10, 11, 14, 15
Ramusio, Paolo (son), 31, 152–3,
    165–6, 207, 215, 227–8
Ramusio, Tomyris Macachiò
    (mother), 10, 14
Rangoni, Guido, 150
Raphael, 116–17
Rapicio, Giovita, 166
Reconquista (1492), 125, 143
Red Sea, 82, 91–2, 93, 106, 108, 151,
    210, 222

Regius, Raphael, 29
Reuveni, David, 150–2
rhubarb, 179–80, *180*, 182, 206
Riformatori dello Studio di Padova,
    148–9
Rome, Sack of (1527), 72–3, 76, 145
Russia, 223–4, 232
Rustichello da Pisa, 203, 204

Sachion (Dunhuang), 178–9
Sack of Rome (1527), 72–3, 76, 145
Saint Lawrence River, 4, 158, *160*,
    161, 162, 163
Sancho de la Hoz, Pedro, 218
Sansovino, Francesco, 117
Sassetti, Giovan Battista, 213
Scandinavia, 223, 224–6
Schöner Map of 1515, 32
Scipio, 47–8
scurvy, 38, 163
Seljuks, 79
Sereri tribes, 54–5
Seville, Navagero's letter to Ramusio
    about, 138–41
Sichuan, Polo's mission to, 189,
    190–1
Sintra, Pedro da, 59
slave trade, 49, 50, 53–4, 71, 125, 128
Soranzo, Giacomo, 214
Soto, Hernando de, 154, 157
Southeast Asia:
    Gastaldi's map of, *198*
    Polo's mission to, 197–8, 200
Southern Cross, 56–7
South Pole, 232
Spain:
    French war against, 120, 122,
        136–7, 140, 144, 145, 149, 219
    territories overseas controlled by,
        112–14, 129–36. *See also* New
        Indies; New Spain
    See also Charles V, Emperor
        (Charles I, King of Spain)

Spice Islands, 81, 96, 113, 127, 168,
    190, 210–11, 215
    Cabot's proposals to search for
        Venetian route to, 107–9, 112,
        214
    Magellan's search for western
        route to, 33–42, 45, 105, 106,
        109
    Portuguese route to, opened by da
        Gama, 81, 96, 105–6
    in sphere of influence of Spain vs.
        Portugal, 37
    Venetian quest for its own route
        to, 105–9, 222
Stewart, Alexander, 21
stoccafisso (stockfish), 225, 226
Strabo, 212, 223, 232
    Geography by, 31–2
Succuir (Jiuquan), rhubarb market
    in, 179–80
Suleiman the Magnificent, 44, 166
Suma oriental (Pires), 211
Sumatra (Samara), 197–8
Sung Dynasty, 192, 195
syphilis, 101, 111, 136

Taklamakan Desert, 177
Tebaldo da Piacenza (Gregory X),
    170, 171
Teldi, Francesco, 106
Tenduc (Hohhot), Prester John
    legend and, 183–4
Tenochtitlán, city plan of, *217*
Tibetan plateau, 190, 205n
    Polos' route along, 177–9, 205n
Tintoretto, 112, 117n, 227n
Tirreno, Benedetto, 31
Torresano, Andrea, 18, 31
Torresano, Maria, 20, 30
Trajan, Emperor, 16
Transylvanus, Maximilian, 41
    De Moluccis Insulis by, 45
Tristão, Nuno, 50, 54

Ulloa, Francisco de, 156, 219
Usodimare, Antoniotto, 54, 57
Uzun Hasan, 222–3

Vallerani, Francesco, 229–32
Vallerini, Maria Grazia, 229
Vannes, Peter, 214
Varthema, Ludovico di, 96, 97–104,
    105, 155, 211, 212
  audience at Doge's Palace
    addressed by, 96, 97, 101
  Itinerario written by, 101–4, 211
  in land of Mamluks and in India,
    97–101
Venetian Republic:
  canal project and, 106
  Chancery of, 9, 11, 20, 30, 47, 106,
    107, 108, 152
  expansion of, into northern Italy,
    met with coalition of enemies,
    11–15, 22–7, 115, 117
  flourishing of arts in, 112
  Persia's strategic relevance for,
    222–3
  publishing industry in, 17–19, 112,
    208. See also Aldus Manutius
  Ramusio family's status in, 9–10
  Ramusio's official positions in, 7,
    9, 11, 15, 30–1, 62, 111–12, 158,
    207, 213
  Reuveni affair and, 150–1
  Senate of, 30–1, 213
  spice trade of, 96–7, 105–6, 112,
    222
  struggling to hold onto
    commercial empire after
    opening of competing oceanic
    routes, 105–6, 112

Varthema's audience at Doge's
  Place and, 96, 97, 101
Veronese, Paolo, 3
Verrazzano, Giovanni da, 158–60
Vespucci, Amerigo, 4, 36, 114, 210
Viart, Pierre, 45
Victoria, 33–5, 37, 39–40, 45, 105, 107
Vietnam, 191, 197
Villa Ramusia (near Cittadella), 15,
    110–11, 229–31
  seeds from New Indies grown at,
    111, 230
Villehardouin, Geoffroy de, 227
Villiers de l'Isle-Adam, Philippe de,
    44, 46

Waldseemüller Map of 1507,
    32, *32*
Wazzan, al-, al-Hasan ibn
    Muhammad. See Leo Africanus
Widmanstadt, Johann, 73
William of Rubruck, 80
Wolof Empire, 51–4

Xanadu, Polos as guests at Kublai
    Khan's residence at, 184–6
Xerez, Francisco, 155, 217

yak hair, 183, 206
Yangtze River, 183, 190, 191, 194
Yangui (Yangzhou), Polo's official
    mission to, 187, 192–5
Yellow River, 80, 183, 192, 193
Yunnan, Polo's mission to, 187, 189,
    191

Zagazabo, Father, 91, 92
Zamorin, 97, 100

5 Etching of Giovanni Battista Ramusio. Museum Mazzuchellianum. By concession of the Ministry of Culture—Biblioteca Nazionale Marciana. No reproduction allowed. Photo Andrea di Robilant.

6 Ptolemy Map of Europe, Africa and Asia, 1545. Granger—Historical Picture Archive/Alamy Foto Stock.

17 Logo of the Aldine Press. By concession of the Ministry of Culture— Biblioteca Nazionale Marciana. No reproduction allowed. Photo Andrea di Robilant.

32 Martin Waldseemüller World Map, 1507. Library of Congress.

35 Martin Behaim's Planisphere of 1492. Universal History Archive via Getty Images.

56 Coast of West Africa. *Navigationi et Viaggi*, vol. 1, 1550. By concession of the Ministry of Culture—Biblioteca Nazionale Marciana. No reproduction allowed. Photo Clementina di Robilant.

74–75 Map of Africa by Giacomo Gastaldi. *Navigationi et Viaggi*, vol. 1, 1550. By concession of the Ministry of Culture—Biblioteca Nazionale Marciana. No reproduction allowed. Photo Andrea di Robilant.

86 Floor plan of the Church of Our Savior. *Navigationi et Viaggi*, vol. 1, 1550. By concession of the Ministry of Culture—Biblioteca Nazionale Marciana. No reproduction allowed. Photo Andrea di Robilant.

94 Map of Egypt and the Sudan by Giacomo Gastaldi. *Navigationi et Viaggi*, vol. 1, 1550. By concession of the Ministry of Culture— Biblioteca Nazionale Marciana. No reproduction allowed. Photo Clementina di Robilant.

102–103 Map of the Indian Sub-Continent by Giacomo Gastaldi. *Navigationi et Viaggi*, vol. 1, 1550. By concession of the Ministry of Culture— Biblioteca Nazionale Marciana. Reproduction not allowed. Photo Andrea di Robilant.

113 Map of Hispaniola. *Navigationi et Viaggi*, vol. 3, 1556. By concession of the Ministry of Culture—Biblioteca Nazionale Marciana. Reproduction not allowed. Photo Andrea di Robilant.

129 Wood engraving of an iguana. *Navigationi et Viaggi*, vol. 3, 1556. By concession of the Ministry of Culture—Biblioteca Nazionale Marciana. Reproduction not allowed. Photo Clementina di Robilant.

131 Wood engraving of a native's hut in Central America. *Navigationi et Viaggi,* vol. 3, 1556. By concession of the Ministry of Culture—Biblioteca Nazionale Marciana. Reproduction not allowed. Photo Clementina di Robilant.

132 Wood engraving of a hammock. *Navigationi et Viaggi,* vol. 3, 1556. By concession of the Ministry of Culture—Biblioteca Nazionale Marciana. Reproduction not allowed. Photo Clementina di Robilant.

134 Wood engraving of a canoe. *Navigationi et Viaggi,* vol. 3, 1556. By concession of the Ministry of Culture—Biblioteca Nazionale Marciana. Reproduction not allowed. Photo Clementina di Robilant.

135 Wood engraving of a plantain leaf. *Navigationi et Viaggi,* vol. 3, 1556. By concession of the Ministry of Culture—Biblioteca Nazionale Marciana. Reproduction not allowed. Photo Clementina di Robilant.

139 Wood engraving of a husk of maize. *Navigationi et Viaggi,* vol. 3, 1556. By concession of the Ministry of Culture—Biblioteca Nazionale Marciana. Reproduction not allowed. Photo Clementina di Robilant.

160 Map of Labrador. *Navigationi et Viaggi,* vol. 3, 1556. By concession of the Ministry of Culture—Biblioteca Nazionale Marciana. Reproduction not allowed. Photo Clementina di Robilant.

161 Map of Hochelaga. *Navigationi et Viaggi,* vol. 3, 1556. By concession of the Ministry of Culture—Biblioteca Nazionale Marciana. Reproduction not allowed. Photo Clementina di Robilant.

180 Wood engraving of a rhubarb. *Navigationi et Viaggi,* vol. 2, 1559. By concession of the Ministry of Culture—Biblioteca Nazionale Marciana. No reproduction allowed. Photo Andrea di Robilant.

198 Map of Southern China and South East Asia by Giacomo Gastaldi. *Navigationi et Viaggi,* vol. 1, 1550. By concession of the Ministry of Culture—Biblioteca Nazionale Marciana. No reproduction allowed. Photo Andrea di Robilant.

217 Map of Mexico. *Navigationi et Viaggi,* vol. 3, 1556. By concession of the Ministry of Culture—Biblioteca Nazionale Marciana. No reproduction allowed. Photo Clementina di Robilant.

220 Map of Cuzco. *Navigationi et Viaggi,* vol. 3, 1556. By concession of the Ministry of Culture—Biblioteca Nazionale Marciana. No reproduction allowed. Photo Clementina di Robilant.

221 Map of the Americas by Giacomo Gastaldi. *Navigationi et Viaggi,* vol. 3, 1556. By concession of the Ministry of Culture—Biblioteca Nazionale Marciana. No reproduction allowed. Photo Andrea di Robilant.

A NOTE ABOUT THE AUTHOR

Andrea di Robilant was born in Italy and educated in the United States at Columbia University, where he specialized in international affairs. He is the author of *A Venetian Affair, Lucia: A Venetian Life in the Age of Napoleon, Irresistible North: From Venice to Greenland on the Trail of the Zen Brothers, Chasing the Rose* and *Autumn in Venice: Ernest Hemingway and His Last Muse*. He lives in Rome.

A NOTE ON THE TYPE

This book was set in a version of the well-known Monotype face Bembo. This letter was cut for the celebrated Venetian printer Aldus Manutius by Francesco Griffo, and first used in Pietro Cardinal Bembo's *De Aetna* of 1495.

COMPOSED BY NORTH MARKET STREET GRAPHICS,
LANCASTER, PENNSYLVANIA

PRINTED AND BOUND BY BERRYVILLE GRAPHICS,
BERRYVILLE, VIRGINIA

DESIGNED BY MAGGIE HINDERS